Listening to the Lomax Archive

Listening to the Lomax Archive

The Sonic Rhetorics of African American Folksong in the 1930s

JONATHAN W. STONE

UNIVERSITY OF MICHIGAN PRESS
ANN ARBOR

Published in the United States of America by the University of Michigan Press
Manufactured in the United States of America
Printed on acid-free paper
First published November 2021

A CIP catalog record for this book is available from the British Library.

Library of Congress Cataloging-in-Publication data has been applied for.

https://doi.org/10.3998/mpub.9871097

ISBN 978-0-472-03855-8 (paper: alk. paper)
ISBN 978-0-472-90244-6 (OA e-book)

J. Willard Marriott Library
THE UNIVERSITY OF UTAH

The University of Utah's Department of Writing & Rhetoric Studies and J. Willard Marriott Library provided financial support toward the production of and free access to this book.

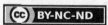

For Seth, Maryn, Jonas, and Asher—

the best sounding quartet I know

Contents

Throughout *Listening to the Lomax Archive*, there are a number of audio resources for readers to listen to, including songs, oral histories, and radio program excerpts. Each resource is marked with a ♫ in the text. These digital materials can be found on the Fulcrum platform via the following citable URL: https://doi.org/10.3998/mpub.9871097

Acknowledgments

This book probably began in the aisles of Zia Record Exchange in Tucson, Arizona. There, as a teenager in the mid-1990s, I first experienced the excitement and anticipation of finding and listening to music, old and new. Members of my ragtag high school rock band, Only Anything, attempted to glean and re-present what sonic knowledge we could from the records we collected and admired. John Heidenreich, Jon Thwaits, Mat and Joe Richins, and I spent summers and holiday breaks in a house we called "Sauna Studios" down the road from Saguaro National Park, playing music by The Cure and Nirvana and eventually writing songs with such titles as "Footsteps to a Castle," "Starmaster," and "Danger Boy." As those original songs became album projects, I learned something about collaboration, creativity, and seeing a project through to its end—experience that has served me well. Against all odds and over 25 years later, I still love to get together with those friends and jam.

Listening to the Lomax Archive had its official genesis as a dissertation in the Center for Writing Studies at the University of Illinois at Urbana-Champaign. Peter Mortensen, Spencer Schaffner, Cara Finnegan, and Ned O'Gorman guided me and the draft through its earliest iterations. The host of others who shepherded and mentored me toward some semblance of scholarly acumen include Gail Hawisher, Paul Prior, Catherine Prendergast, Debra Hawhee, Kelly Ritter, Thomas Conley, and Thomas Turino, as well as fellow grad students Christa Olson, Michael Burns, Patrick Berry, and Amber Buck. Others I met at U of I (many from CWS) remain treasured friends and mentors, none more so than Maggie Shelledy, Pamela Saunders, Kaia Simon, and Tom McNamara.

Along the way, this project was encouraged by academic pals with similar interests, among them Kyle Stedman, Steph Ceraso, Harley Ferris, Steven Hammer, Eric Detweiler, Joel Overall, Jared Colton, Abraham Romney, and Kati Fargo Ahern. Colleagues who led Rhetoric Society of America seminars and workshops—especially Greg Goodale, Joshua Gunn, Byron Hawk, and Jonathan Alexander—helped me realize that "sonic rhetorics" was not a new subdiscipline, but a reverberant tradition. Other associates, such as Susan Jarratt, Diane Davis, Vanessa Beasley, Jim Brown, and Casey Boyle, helped me chart and navigate a broader disciplinary trajectory between historiography, nonrational rhetorics, sensation, and digital rhetorics. *Enculturation: A Journal of Rhetoric, Writing, and Culture* published an earlier version of chapter 2 in 2015.

Upon arrival in the Department of Writing and Rhetoric Studies at the University of Utah, I was again blessed with incredible colleagues. Jay Jordan, Jenny Andrus, Maureen Mathison, Joy Pierce, Natalie Stillman-Webb, David Hawkins, Pauline Light, Lisa Shaw, and Kelli Bowerman supported me and this project in unique ways. José Cortez, Romeo García, LuMing Mao, and Christie Toth read drafts and offered feedback. Other friends, especially Bryan Hall, Brian Jackson, and Steven Hopkins, have been listening to me talk about this project for the better part of decade. Those conversations always made it and me better.

The anonymous reviewers for the University of Michigan Press took extraordinary care in the feedback they offered for this work's improvement. At the press, former editorial director, Mary Francis offered initial interest and careful guidance as I prepared my first book proposal, and Sara Cohen, Anna Pohlod, and Mary K. Hashman have been crucial to the book's completion. Fulcrum, the University of Michigan's publishing platform, has brought this book's content onto the internet.

This project is especially indebted to the Library of Congress and the American Folklife Center. A generous grant from the U of I Graduate College sponsored an initial trip to Washington, DC, in 2013, and I have been back numerous times. Todd Harvey, curator of the AFC's Alan Lomax Collection, guided me through John and Alan Lomax's papers and recordings with enthusiasm and skill. I am sure he treats all of the center's patrons that way, but the time, access, and insight he gave me during my visits and in dozens of emails between trips made me and my project feel singular and important. He has continued to be a friend and counselor to this project over its many years of development. Much of the audio content utilized herein is presented with the gracious permission of the Library of Congress and the AFC. Other people and entities who granted permission to use their audio content include the estate of Huddie "Lead Belly" Ledbetter, the Newport Folk Festival, NPR, Tinya Seeger, and Dakota Waddell. Special thanks also to Brett Affrunti whose illustration of Jelly Roll Morton in conversation with Alan Lomax in the Coolidge Auditorium at the Library of Congress provided the perfect art for the book's cover. Thanks also to my sister, Michelle Ross, for the piano performance included in chapter 2. Michelle is my longest and most cherished collaborator.

My work for this book was supported by a National Endowment for the Humanities fellowship, including an additional NEH grant to support its intended digital, open-source iteration. At the University of Utah, I received a faculty fellowship from the University Research Committee and a semester of pre-tenure leave. Both were crucial to the book's development and completion. Additional financial support from the university's College of Humanities, Department of Writing and Rhetoric Studies, and J. Willard Marriot Library offset production costs and enabled free digital access to the book. For that aid, I thank Stuart Culver, Jakob Jenson, Allyson Mower, and LuMing Mao.

Tina, my spouse and partner, is the key to this whole scholarly endeavor. Her companionship, expediency, and love ground and scaffold the work herein and, really, my whole life. As the late John Prine put it, "She is my everything." It has taken nearly the length of my childrens' childhoods to complete this study. It would be a different book without their influence and without my hope for their future. They are strong, smart, faithful, and brave, each in their own unique and powerful ways. My parents, Jean and Walter Stone, and my parents-in-law, Patricia and David Bertoglio, have supported me at each step as well.

For Pete's Sake: Audio Preface

(Dakota Waddell's clawhammer banjo performance of "Home on the Range" plays in the background.)

♫ JONATHAN STONE: *Listening to the Lomax Archive: The Sonic Rhetorics of African American Folksong in the 1930s*, by Jonathan W. Stone, "For Pete's Sake: Audio Preface" (read by the author).

When Pete Seeger passed away on January 27, 2014, at the age of 94, his death prompted hundreds of articles, memorials, and remembrances. The *National Post* published one such remembrance by Geoffrey Clarfield, former director of research and development for the Alan Lomax Archive housed with the Association for Cultural Equity (or ACE for short) in New York City. In the piece, Clarfield relates some of the details of his first and only visit with the aging folksinger and activist in the fall of 2012. They spoke about the various ongoing projects at the Alan Lomax Archive, and, as he writes,

> After lunch, we retired to the living room. Pete took down his banjo from the wall, and [. . .] spontaneously sang a tongue-in-cheek version of the Texan cowboy song Home on the Range. Just as we were all finishing the most popular verse, Pete said, "There's another verse, did you ever hear this one?" And then he sang, "How often at night, when the heavens are bright, by the light of the glittering stars. I stood there amazed, and I ask as I age, does their glory exceed that of ours?"

In his evocation of this vivid but often overlooked verse, Seeger acknowledges, perhaps, his own pondering of the unknown cosmos. But also, Pete's rendering offered a lyrical update to the third verse of the well-known folksong: "I ask as I *gaze*" is how the verse typically ends. Pete's playfully profound change in reference to his own aging body juxtaposed against the cosmic eternities was also an example of what he often called the "folk process"—the notion that folksongs are not static entities but are in constant flux. They change to suit the needs of the singer, the moment, the audience, the cause.

> (*Jonathan Stone's guitar performance of "Home on the Range," with whistling, plays in the background.*)

Much has been written about this profoundly political nature of folksong, but they are political because they are first rhetorical. And they are rhetorical because of their power to evoke a response in the listener—be it reflection, reaffirmation, or even revaluation. People are moved by song, and folksongs move people in particular ways.

After his impromptu revision of "Home on the Range," Seeger related a story about the song's origins. Said Pete,

> The man who wrote it, oh, that goes back over a hundred years to about 1875. He was a man from New England, who split up with his wife and went from Connecticut out west to Kansas. But he liked to write poems and he wrote the words down, and a friend of his, a young man who worked in a local drug store said, "Would you mind if I try and put a tune to those words?" And the man who wrote the words said, "Sure, if you want to." And with his girlfriend and his girlfriend's brother, the three of them made up this tune. And a few people sang it here and there.
>
> John Lomax who was in Texas, heard that there was a cook in a cowboy camp and he knew this song and sang it. Lomax wrote it down and put it in his book and then it became famous . . . but the man who wrote the words was dead and he never knew how famous the song had become.

In addition to their rhetorical nature, then, folksongs are also historical. With Seeger's update to "Home on the Range," he teaches about the historiographical nature of folklore collection and, implicitly, the ways that the mystery of song origins often motivates that study. It is that mystery—that unknowing—that compels the search: for identity, for belonging, for truth, whatever shape that truth may take. This is a book in part about that unknowing and the search it inspires.

This is not, however, a book about Pete Seeger. But Pete's work, life, and legacy is, in many ways, its inspiration. Pete was a folksinger, though he was always quick to complicate what and whom the "folk" were. He was a rhapsodist: he foraged for songs and song fragments wherever he could—from friends and archives, roadside bars, and hollers—and then he stitched them back together with help from a banjo emblazoned with the motto "This machine surrounds hate and forces it to surrender." He was an activist, a teacher, a family man, and an advocate for marginalized voices. It was in Seeger's musical advocacy for unions and labor rights in the 1940s, for race equality and civil rights in the '50s and the '60s, as well as his sustained environmental work cleaning up the Hudson River in New York, that I began to see and hear how music and folk traditions intricately tie everyday lived values with civic experience.

In Pete Seeger, we also get a sense for what activism looks like from a place of racial and economic privilege. Pete's advocacy for the marginalized was frequently astounding, but it was also imperfect. For all of the good that he did, there were also missteps and blind spots. The following work acknowledges the persistence of what might be termed the "never perfect (and often problematic) work of the well-meaning progressive white scholar/activist." This paradox will be a reoccurring theme in my analysis of John and Alan Lomax and their archive, but I am also not immune from the possibility of missteps and miscalculations inherent to my various privileges. I have worked to avoid such hazards, but I also request the reader's grace as I proceed. It might help to keep this quote from Seeger in mind: "When you play the 12-string guitar, you spend half your life tuning the instrument and the other half playing it out of tune."

(*A clip from NPR's coverage of Pete Seeger's set at the 2009 Newport Folk Festival begins.*)

In 2009, I made a pilgrimage to Rhode Island to see Pete perform at the 50th anniversary of the Newport Folk Festival, an event he had appeared at frequently since its founding in 1959. He and his grandson Tao Rodríguez-Seeger were the final performers on Saturday afternoon. And though Pete, who turned 90 that year, sang with a voice somewhat diminished from what it had once been, he was as tenacious as ever. As the sun set into Newport Harbor, he led us in song.

SEEGER: Friends, I don't have much voice left, but I can accompany you. I'll—I'll give you a tune I think you all know, and I'll give you the words as we go along so you can sing the verses as well as the chorus. "To everything there is a season." Let me hear you sing it.
CROWD: To everything (turn, turn, turn). There is a season (turn, turn, turn).
SEEGER: "And a time!"
CROWD: And a time for every purpose under heaven.

(*Singing continues underneath narration.*)

STONE: We were a motley and sunburned choir, but our voices rose together, strong and clear even as tears rolled down our cheeks. We had become, for a moment, Pete's voice, resonant, unified, and determined: "And a time to every purpose, under heaven."

"A time to build up, a time to break down," the refrain from Pete's take on Ecclesiastes continues—"A time to dance, a time to mourn [. . .] A time to rend, a time to sew [. . .] A time you may embrace, a time to refrain from embracing." Time then was to stand together and sing in celebration of the moment. But times and seasons are always turning. This is a book borne of my deep love and admiration of folk traditions and folk heroes, but turned—as must we all—toward a necessary critique of those traditions. Turning in this way is a legacy I think Pete Seeger would be proud of.

SEEGER: "A time to build up; a time to break down!"
CROWD: A time to build up [. . .]

(*Singing continues underneath narration.*)

STONE: To "turn" is to respect tradition, yes, but there is also a responsibility to disabuse tradition of its outdated orthodoxies. "Turning" takes tradition off the pedestal and examines the cracks, shakes it, holds it up to the ear, finds new and surprising uses for it, and when necessary, changes some of its words. Turn, turn, turn!—but don't turn away. Keep revolving. Revolution is evoked in acts of revision, resounding, and reformation. Learning to turn in this way has led me to the materials I use to build from in this book, materials I am using to build my own home on the range—a range of rhetoric, rhythm, and reverence for both tradition and progression.

CROWD WITH RODRIQUEZ-SEEGER: And a time for every purpose under heaven.

(*Singing continues underneath narration.*)

STONE: *Listening to the Lomax Archive* is a historical project, but with an asterisk. It is set, more or less, within the temporal parameters of the 1930s in the United States, which puts it in the same historical epoch as the Great Depression—but it is not a history of the Great Depression. Instead, it is about stories of American lives, historically marginalized but made more audible through the crucible of the Depression, and, in turn, about how advancing technologies—in this case, audio recording and radio—were changing America's understanding of itself. The reemergence of musical folklore collecting as a viable scholarly, historiographical, and rhetorical practice was made possible within and through Depression-era historical events and was a response to them but also was part of a larger set of practices that made the upheavals of the interwar period manageable and coherent for many during that time and, it follows, part of what makes the 1930s discernible to us now. The book, then, is an analysis of what it means to try to hear history when boiling it down to its mythopoetic bones. It is a study of the many ways the collection of folk music contributed to the composition of a usable past and of this music's movement from mere artifacts to rich rhetorics.

SEEGER AND RODRIQUEZ-SEEGER: A time of love, a time of hate—
SEEGER: "Peace!"
CROWD: A time of peace; I swear it's not too late.

Introduction

Finding Folkness in the Rhetorical Tradition (Turn, Turn, Turn)

> A beautiful melody will leap language barriers or religious barriers or political barriers. Yes, a beautiful melody will help tie this world together and sometimes extraordinary words will. I didn't realize when I improvised a melody to a short poem in the Old Testament that these few words would be some of the most important words I ever would latch onto.
>
> —Pete Seeger Discusses "Turn! Turn! Turn!" with Smithsonian Folkways

> If you could strip from all poetry its music, rhythm, and meter, the residue would be nothing else but rhetoric.
>
> —Plato, *Gorgias* 502c[1]

Forgetting History: Folk Symbols, Folk Seasons, and Root Systems

When compared with the many songs that come to be called "traditional," it is remarkable that the folksong "Home on the Range" (mentioned in the preface to this book) has a recorded author or origin at all. As a byline, "traditional" usually designates authorial indeterminacy, and the mystery and the myth such forgetting enables is an important component of folk ethos. Stephen Wade, a contemporary folk historian, musician, and author of *The Beautiful Music All Around Us* (2012), taught about the excitement but rarity of discovering folksong origins—a kind of holy grail for many folklorists.[2] Wade's own discovery came during research for the song "Rock Island Line," a popular regional song in the South that was also "discovered" by John A. Lomax and a travel companion, Huddie "Lead Belly" Ledbetter, in an Arkansas African American penitentiary in 1934 (Wade 56). The disembodied voice of Kelly Pace leading seven other incarcerated men in the song is retained on acetate in the archives of the Library of Congress.

♫ KELLY PACE: I said the Rock Island Line is
CHORUS OF MEN: a mighty good road
PACE: I said the Rock Island Line
MEN: is the road to ride
PACE: I said the Rock Island Line
MEN: is a mighty good road
ALL: If you want to ride, you got to ride it like you find
Buy your ticket at the station on the Rock Island Line
(*whistle blows*)
PACE: Well, Jesus died to save me f'm all of my sins
ALL: A-well-a glory to God we're going to meet him again
PACE: I said the Rock Island Line
MEN: is a mighty good road
PACE: I said the Rock Island Line
MEN: is the road to ride
PACE: I said the Rock Island Line
MEN: is a mighty good road
ALL: If you want to ride, you got to ride it like you find
Buy your ticket at the station on the Rock Island Line
(*whistle blows, recording fades*)

In careful analysis of that and other recordings, Wade deduced that "Rock Island Line" was originally arranged as "a quartet song—unaccompanied, social, church based, arranged for singing, and staged for listening" (48) and that Pace's rendering maintains that form, despite Lomax's tendency to associate the song with the various labors of outdoor work (Wade 47). The transformation from a staged quartet arrangement to a work song may have occurred at the hand of Lead Belly, who brought the sonic imagery of ax chopping into his recorded renditions of the tune three years later (Wade 63). From those insights and with a couple of lucky leads, Wade was able to trace the song back to a booster campaign initiated to draw attention to the Chicago, Rock Island and Pacific Railroad, which was, in the years preceding the Great Depression, experiencing declining patronage.

Among the campaign documents, Wade found the lyrics to a booster song titled "Buy Your Ticket Over Rock Island Lines," composed by Clarence Wilson for his vocal quartet and published in the internal railroad union newsletter *Rock Island Magazine*. The lyrics printed in tiny letters in the railroad magazine differ in some ways from the idiomatic "Rock Island Line," but there were enough similarities between them that Wade knew he had found the source (47). In a strange but satisfying flip of the typical folksong narrative, "Rock Island Line" began as a commercial entity, rather than ending up there. Those details, however obscure, contribute to a small corner of the history of the Chicago, Rock Island and Pacific Railroad, which was in operation for over 100 years (1852–1970). Wade's discovery of Wilson's composition, a discovery made some 50 years after the song's heyday, is remarkable but perhaps inconsequential. The song did just fine without widespread knowledge of its origin. The memory of the Rock Island line resonates the longest and with the widest audience, perhaps, when the historical details are obscured or even forgotten. Like other railway songs, such as "Midnight Special" or "Wabash Cannonball," "Rock Island Line" best memorializes a bygone epoch of North American commerce, the ideals of the Progressive Era, and their relationship to African American identity through folk mythos. In other words, a song like "Rock Island Line" best circulates and informs as folklore, not as history (in the formal sense). For "Rock Island Line" to become culturally useful—for it to become a powerful sonic rhetoric—its origin had to be forgotten and replaced by something more mythic.

As a historian of folksong, Wade understands that necessity.

> [T]he song, like a trunk line whose branches radiate across the countryside, soon moved beyond this work site making new stops, shifting its contents, and streamlining its load. It migrated from a gospel quartet that the Arkansas prisoners performed to a rhythmic fable that Huddie Ledbetter created as he traveled with John Lomax as chauffer, auto mechanic, and musical demonstrator. Eventually, the song reached an incalculable number of players, singers, and listeners via skiffle, rock and roll, country, pop, and the folksong revival. Yet for all these crossings and couplings, "Rock Island Line" hung onto its proud message, emblazoned in boxcar letters of a train fleeting past, to become the poetry by which a proud railroad is still remembered. (48)

Forgetting, it would seem, is as important to the folk process as remembering. Indeed, a strategic kind of "turning," forgetting history is a condition of possibility for folk processes. In this case, history forgotten turns into useful lore. Wade's arresting passage above draws on an elaborate metaphor of forgetting embedded within natural phenomenon: the trunk lines, roots, and branches of a tree with sapling days too far gone to remember. The material reality of the complex root and branch systems of aged trees stand in as symbols of memory, forgetting, and the passage of time—symbols to aid our understanding of how traditions through music "radiate across the countryside." These natural metaphors also evoke a kind of seasonal, revolving temporality in the circulation of public memory (and public forgetting) in and through musical material culture—memories with bright and pungent springtime blooms and cross-pollinations, summer abundance and fruit, autumn migrations and golden decay, all punctuated by periods of desolate winter. This dynamic ecology—reliant, for the survival of its root system, on a continuum of blossom and decline, remembering and forgetting, progression and regression—sets a framework for understanding and articulating the natural drama of folk musical traditions as sonic rhetorical culture and evokes Pete Seeger's ecclesiastical refrain "turn, turn, turn."

Overture

Listening to the Lomax Archive: The Sonic Rhetorics of African American Folksong in the 1930s is a work of sonic rhetorical history centered on the careers and field recordings of folklorists John A. Lomax and his son, Alan Lomax. It is an examination of the ways that the Lomax archive contributed to the United States' understanding of itself and of its history during the interwar period of the 1930s. As such, it is an investigation of sound's and music's rhetorical role in building and maintaining personal, cultural, and political myth and, in turn, of the relationship of mythos to history-making. The book investigates the various sonic rhetorics of folksong—from the music itself to the ways it was recorded and distributed—and how folksong was constitutive of national identity, history, and race during that era. *Listening to the Lomax Archive* brings to rhetoric a study of sound and music that amplifies what is known about rhythmic practice in the rhetorical tradition.

In my analysis of the Lomaxes' work during the uncertain and economically depressed 1930s (and early '40s), I argue that music was a powerful, if ambiguous, rhetoric that, depending on the situation, could render traditional and progressive values, often both at the same time. "If it was never new and never gets old, it's a folksong," quips the title character from the

Coen brothers' 2012 film *Inside Llewyn Davis*. A composite of journeyman folksingers in 1960s Greenwich Village, Davis sums up the appeal of folk music: it is both old and new simultaneously. Folk music had utility in the 1960s for the same reason that it did during the '30s. It could be a container of expression for current and emergent ideologies, packaged within the ethos of "tradition." The impact of such rhetoric is profound. As evidenced by the imagery of "Rock Island Line" and the railroad, folk ideals do not just hitch a ride on the historical locomotive but can be so influential as to determine the historical routes, junctures, and way stations on which we have come to rely.

Vernacular music traditions provide a kind of rail or road map for genealogical and ideological exploration or, to mix a different set of metaphors, a sonic keyhole to the past that can be traced and even incorporated as old folk traditions are adopted to meet contemporary exigencies. Recall, for example, Kurt Cobain's deft appropriation of Lead Belly's song "Where Did You Sleep Last Night" for Nirvana's 1994 live album *MTV Unplugged in New York*. Cobain was a fan of Lead Belly, and Cobain's cover of the folksong is a reminder of the deep connectivity between succeeding generations of "alternative" music—in this case, between Depression-era folk blues and 1990s grunge, both of which were (and continue to be) associated with a sense of raw primitivism and authenticity.

♫ LEAD BELLY: Black girl, black girl, don't lie to me
Tell me where did you sleep last night?
In the pines, in the pines, where the sun never shine
I shivered the whole night through.
Black girl, black girl, where will you go?
I'm going where the cold wind blows
In the pines, in the pines, where the sun never shine
I will shiver the whole night through.

The tune became Kurt Cobain's swan song—a final musical artifact before his suicide just five months after taping the *Unplugged* session. With that infamous series of events, "Where Did You Sleep Last Night," whose original author is unknown, took on new layers of signification. The song's roots stretch backward and forward, surfacing dramatically in the 1940s with Lead Belly's brilliant rendering and again in the '90s through the tortured genius of Cobain. That cycle will continue. "Where Did You Sleep Last Night" is a song that was never new and never gets old.

In what follows, I argue for the possibilities of folklore in rhetorical studies. Folklore is rendered in any number of modes: spoken, sung, written, painted, carved, crafted, and cooked, to name just a few.[3] My concern here oscillates between folklore as a broader category and folksong as a sonic phenomenon within it. Such a move is not meant to be exclusionary. I invite others with diverse folk interests to bring them to the table I set or to set new tables altogether. A study of folksong is one interesting way to interrogate sound's relationship to rhetorical history, and sonic archives are a compelling space for theorizing new methods of history-making, itself a rhetorical practice. Ironically, perhaps, folklore challenges traditional notions of rhetorical analysis, public memory, and rhetorical historiography. Folklore is deconstructive of each. Folklore's multivalence makes it a slippery subject for analysis, and its apparent timelessness within public memory is a result of forgetting as much as remembering. Folklore provides an opportunity to re-sound history—to parse various historiographical hegemonies, to interrogate and utilize memory and/as forgetting, and to intone history in a more multivalent key, one more inclusive, intersectional, and adept at representing history's many contradictory narratives.

Re-sound is a verb rendered not only as a sonic equivalent of *revise* (or *re-vision*) but also in the reverberant spirit of *resound*'s typical definition, "to fill a place with sound." Using distinctions offered by Byron Hawk (2018), "re-sounding" evokes this corrective or (better) transformative spirit and also resounds the unique temporal turning I describe above. For Hawk, re-sounding is a reorientation back to sound "after a long detour through print culture" and "forces a more substantial rethinking of our object of study—considering how sound work forces us to reconsider what composition proper might be" (5). In this sense, re-sounding is profoundly historiographical and also a broadening of the compositional wavelength and parameters in which "historiography" typically operates.

I re-sound folklore as a viable historiographical object, and I forward *folkness* as a term to describe its return. Folklore amplifies the paradoxes and tensions between history and memory and reintroduces mythos as an essential rhetoric of historiography, showing both its productive possibilities and its hazards. In short, folkness is a rhetorical oscillation—a turning from history and toward mythos (and then back)—that embodies and enacts the paradox of remembering an unrecoverable past. Folkness is both timeless and bound to time, as it turns on the present, especially when its vehicle is music. As a subgenre of folklore, folksong only intensifies these attributes, adding melody, rhythm, and pointed brevity to the discourse it names. The Lomaxes' archive of folksongs, then, is a rich resource for detailing how such rhetorics of folkness work.

Listening to the Lomax Archive's historical narrative begins in 1932, at the height of one of the United States' deepest crises, the Great Depression. In the wake of that crisis, folklorists John A. Lomax and his son, Alan, set out as emissaries for the Library of Congress to record the folksong of the "American Negro" in several Southern African American prisons. The music the Lomaxes recorded for the library's Archive of American Folk Song, during their initial trip and dozens more following, contributed to the assemblage of a new American mythology, collected in response to and for the potential succor of a people in financial, social, and identity crisis.[4] Photographers such as Dorothea Lange were engaged in similar work. Her 1936 portrait *Migrant Mother* is, perhaps, the most iconic image of the Great Depression era. The Lomaxes' efforts can be thought of in similar terms, except that they were interested in sound instead of image. During the 1930s, their iconographic, mythologizing efforts had the paradoxical effects I have mentioned: even as the songs could reify long-held conservative orthodoxies or petty prejudices, they also performed as agents for social change through the reconstitution of new histories, new traditions, and even new educational methodologies.

The recordings the Lomaxes made in the prisons were produced under the coercive auspices of white privilege yet also provided incarcerated African American men rhetorical agency they may not have had otherwise. For example, "Grey Goose," a work song sung by James "Iron Head" Baker and recorded in 1933, carried with it the tradition of both slave labor and slave resilience and escape—thinly veiled in the visage of a wily goose.

♫ BAKER: Well las' Monday morning
GROUP OF MEN: Lawd, Lawd, Lawd
BAKER: Well las' Monday morning
GROUP: Lawd, Lawd, Lawd
BAKER: My Daddy went a hunting
GROUP: Lawd, Lawd, Lawd
BAKER: My Daddy went a hunting
GROUP: Lawd, Lawd, Lawd
BAKER: Well he carried along his zooloo
GROUP: Lawd, Lawd, Lawd
BAKER: Well he carried along his zooloo
GROUP: Lawd, Lawd, Lawd

BAKER: Well along come a grey goose
GROUP: Lawd, Lawd, Lawd
BAKER: Well along come a grey goose
GROUP: Lawd, Lawd, Lawd
BAKER: Well he throwed it to his shoulder
GROUP: Lawd, Lawd, Lawd
BAKER: Well he throwed it to his shoulder
GROUP: Lawd, Lawd, Lawd
BAKER: Well he ride his hammer way back
GROUP: Lawd, Lawd, Lawd
BAKER: Well he ride his hammer way back
GROUP: Lawd, Lawd, Lawd
BAKER: Well he pulled on his trigger
GROUP: Lawd, Lawd, Lawd
BAKER: Well he pulled on his trigger
GROUP: Lawd, Lawd, Lawd
BAKER: Well a down he come winding
GROUP: Lawd, Lawd, Lawd
BAKER: Well a down he come winding
GROUP: Lawd, Lawd, Lawd
BAKER: He was six weeks a-fallin'
GROUP: Lawd, Lawd, Lawd
BAKER: He was six weeks a-fallin'
GROUP: Lawd, Lawd, Lawd
BAKER: We was six weeks a-findin'
GROUP: Lawd, Lawd, Lawd
BAKER: We was six weeks a-findin'
GROUP: Lawd, Lawd, Lawd

Baker and other incarcerated men sung the song to pass the long hours of prison work, likely relishing its audacious humor and wordplay. When it was sung by Baker for the Lomaxes and recorded for the Library of Congress's archive, however, the rhetorical situation shifted dramatically, and the song took on a number of new potential meanings and uses. In the moment, Baker's willingness to sing several songs for the Lomaxes' bulky recorder got him out of a few hours of work, but he also seemed to sense the potentials of the amplification taking place. Indeed, the recording gave James Baker a national audience.

Music like Baker's would have a profound impact on the Lomaxes—

one that they would communicate to the nation, with assistance from the Library of Congress, in both published and sonic material, books, radio, and LPs. For readers and especially listeners of the Lomax archival material, the preservation of an antebellum slave song such as "Grey Goose" in an African American work prison nearly 60 years after the Civil War carried an ethos of authenticity, a somber reminder of that conflict's lasting impact and tragedy. But Baker's resilience and tongue-in-cheek sophistication in the face of such dire and violent circumstances may have also been a boon to listeners when "Grey Goose" appeared on the radio in the early 1940s. In the twilight of the Great Depression, many listeners might have been all too aware of the pains of suffering under hopeless and desperate conditions. In ways both auspicious and perverse, "Grey Goose"—a slave song—became a song of hope.

Throughout this book, I argue that, for better and worse, John and Alan Lomax intuited the paradoxical power of the folksongs they collected and used it to advance national understanding of and agency for the subjects of their recordings, even as those same recordings advanced their own careers. Each chapter explores the implications of these paradoxes by re-sounding episodes from the Lomax archive, its stories and sources, and especially the Lomaxes work with African American musicians. The sounds of each archival holding—each song, oral history, and radio performance—can only be described as both wonderful and terrible. They insinuate national ideals and values, both condemning and expansive, and reverberate histories in conflict with each other. In each chapter, I argue how these seemingly contradictory dualities are crucial to understanding the rhetorical and historical impact of the sonic archive and, by extension, the ways that we now remember and write about the subjects of the Lomax archive and other repositories of historicized sound. While chapter 1 takes up the subject of historiography and the archive in detail, a through line of the book is that sound in general and folksongs in particular have a powerful historiographical multitonality that communicates complex historical experience in a seemingly simple package. Folksongs model a method for sonic rhetorical historiography, a way of hearing and then writing into our histories a dissonance that more accurately represents the various contradictions of everyday experience. My work here thus responds to rhetorical historians' recent urging away from an ideal of "completeness" or a sense of historical certainty and toward "theories [that] slip" and "conceptual frames that call tensions to the foreground" (Olson, "Places to Stand" 96).

There is precedent for this more fragmented approach to history in both ancient and contemporary rhetorical studies, and this book remixes earlier approaches with concepts and theories from a variety of disciplines: among them folklore, music, history, and critical race studies. *Listening to the Lomax Archive* also puts rhetoric in conversation with sound studies scholarship where interdisciplinarity is a given. Sound studies "reaches across registers, moments, and spaces, and it thinks across disciplines and traditions," amplifying work on sound within the disciplines where it has already flourished, but also bringing sound to disciplines where it has been conspicuously absent (Sterne, *Sound Studies Reader* 2). As a field interwoven with both communication and writing studies, rhetoric has, at various times, been used to investigate speaking and listening practices, historical and technological sound, and radio studies. *Listening to the Lomax Archive* expands on each investigation.

Finding Folkness

Beyond analysis and as a work of rhetorical criticism, this book brings a concern about language to other areas of inquiry and works to theorize several cross-disciplinary concepts for use in rhetorical studies more broadly. For example, from its inception as *folc* in Old English, the word *folk* has meant (more or less) "the common people." Yet, depending on the era and context, that somewhat innocuous descriptor has been taken up to describe those people through the perspectives of vastly different philosophies, from the working-class proletariat of Marxist political theory to the *volksgemeinschaft*, or "people's community," of fascist Nazi Germany. The designation "folk" and the phenomenology of "folkness" are malleable and can be politicized at either end of the political spectrum, a mutability that speaks to the conceptual and methodological power of folkness for rhetoric. *Folkness* is a term coined by Pete Seeger's father, Charles Seeger, a scholar who worked at the intersection of ethnomusicology and folklore studies for several decades in the early and middle parts of the 20th century, just as the Lomaxes' work with folk music was beginning to have a national impact. The elder Seeger describes folkness as

> a funded treasury of attitudes, beliefs, and feelings toward life and death, work and play, love, courtship and marriage, health and hearth, children and animals, prosperity and adversity—a veritable code of individual and collective behavior belonging to the people as a whole. (3)

In comparison, Jeffery Walker, scholar of ancient rhetoric, defines the Aristotelian notion of epideictic rhetoric as "that which shapes and cultivates the basic codes of value and belief by which a society or culture lives" (9). The term *epideictic rhetoric*, Walker argues, names a diverse array of rhetorical activity but especially rhetoric abounding in the ceremonial, rhythmic, and musical discourse of everyday life. In ways that defy simple conceptualization, the term *epideictic* describes affective, constitutive, and nonrational modes of rhetoric—the cultural fluency of the people. Here, "cultural fluency" is meant as a general descriptor for participation in the everyday discursive and nondiscursive activities of both public and private life. As I expand on below, *epideictic* is just one ancient civilization's name for knowing the songs, getting the jokes, and being susceptible to the particular ignominies of a given group of people. In Charles Seeger's rendering, *folkness* names the same, only in a different register and in language fashioned for a different era.[5]

The multidisciplinary, century-spanning definitional overlap in the terms *folkness* and *epideictic* is not coincidental. It indicates a kind of ahistorical commonplace found in any number of disciplines, where different names and epochs point to more or less the same thing: embedded (and often embodied) cultural fluency. Understood as a part of that broader family of signifiers, all discourse that works in and through the circulation of human traditions might be said to contain folkness; wherever you look and listen for tradition, folkness can be found and complicated. *Listening to the Lomax Archive* brings this theory of folkness, as well as several others with similar interdisciplinarity potential, to conversations about US musical traditions in the third decade of the 20th century. Folkness can be transformed into rhetorics that reinforce and reimagine traditional notions of race, nationalism, and even political, religious, or economic ideologies.

The balance of this introduction plays out in four brief sections that trace the parameters for such a study and parse a few of its complicating disciplinary factors. I call the sections "movements" to evoke the diverse, but coherent, parts of a symphony or concerto, which often feature a variation on a theme or (not incidentally) a folk melody. Here, the folk melody is rhetoric. The movements touch on the melody's origins, its underlying harmonic structures, and its potential relationships with other melodies, then work to deconstruct and recast the melody in a different key and voicing.

In the first movement, I describe the emerging field of sonic rhetorics, including its history and relationship to earlier movements and genres within rhetoric (visual studies, in particular) as well as its part in a larger expanding view of multimediated and sensory rhetorics. The second movement discusses some of the implications of this expanding view of rhetoric and parses the usefulness and shortcomings of both disciplinarity and multidisciplinarity in rhetorical studies. The third movement describes how disciplinary histories and terminology are important to sonic rhetorical projects, and the fourth demonstrates the need for new extradisciplinary terminology if rhetoric hopes to make a wider impact both in the academy and beyond.

Movement I: Sonic Rhetorics—Singing a Newer Song

Above, I introduced the notion of folkness as epideictic rhetoric and, as such, a marker of cultural fluency of the rhythms and traditions of everyday life. As I argue elsewhere, "Neither epideictic nor folkness is inherently sonic, but both have a close historical relationship with sounded and rhythmic expression which can also be found commonly at the vernacular level, particularly when paired with rhetorics of remembering" (Stone, "Rhetorical Folkness" 69). The connection between sound and how we remember the past (and, in turn, experience the present and imagine the future) is at the heart of my arguments about traditional music's various capacities as sonic rhetoric. But what exactly is "sonic rhetoric"? That designation has emerged in scholarship in recent years to describe rhetoric composed for the ear.[6] Designating some rhetorics as sonic might seem strange given rhetoric's origin as speech, an indisputably (if not completely) aural mode, but doing so responds to several notable movements within a more contemporary scholarly landscape that has been attentive to various multimediated discourses.[7]

An interest in sonic rhetorics can be understood, at least in part, as a response to the rise and prominence of visual rhetoric in rhetorical studies over the last several decades.[8] That movement is part of a much larger intellectual shift toward what some refer to as "ocularcentrism," which has prevailed since the rise of reproducible print in the 19th century and its continuance up to and including our contemporary electronic culture (Gunn et al. 486). Beginning in the mid-20th century and with help from such scholars as Marshall McLuhan and Walter J. Ong, a response to visuality's prominence began to gain intellectual steam. Noticing how the prominence of visual culture in scholarship contributed to a seeming neglect of theorizing oral and aural modes of communication, those media theorists worked to address that disparity. Regrettably, they also frequently perpetuated the same problematic binaries, associating sight with externality and scientific knowledge and associating sound with a more metaphysical truth. Such an approach idealized aurality "as manifesting a kind of pure interiority," elevating it above visuality, which is both defined and limited by its ability to "bathe us in the clear light of reason" (Sterne, *Audible Past* 15). That pitting of sound studies against visual studies is partly the stuff of disciplinary politics, but I mention it here because rhetorical historians have been among those to perpetuate sound's preeminence, sometimes with reprehensible implications about Western intellectual superiority.[9]

My use of the term *sonic rhetorics* acknowledges the ways that visuality has been understood as dominant (and occasionally oppressive). But it also works to complicate the binaries noted above, by forwarding a theoretical framework that takes advantage of developments in multimodal theory, which recognizes that neither experience nor material discourse occur in a single-sensory vacuum. My work is particularly indebted to Steph Ceraso and her notion of "multimodal listening," which builds on (among other precursors) Jodi Shipka's work on "multimodal soundness" (2006) and Cynthia Selfe's classic essay "The Movement of Air, the Breath of Meaning: Aurality and Multimodal Composing" (2009). Ceraso forwards multimodal listening as "the practice of attending to the sensory, contextual, and material aspects of a sonic event. Multimodal listening moves away from ear-centric approaches to sonic engagement and, instead, treats sonic experience as holistic and immersive" (6).[10] Ceraso's work explores that notion within writing studies pedagogy, but it also inspires a consideration of the ways that sound and listening offer opportunities for multisensory and, by extension, multivalent thinking that leads to similarly complex rhetorics and a more nuanced understanding of meaning-making. "What is compelling about sound," Byron Hawk argues in *Resounding the Rhetorical* (2018), "is the potential to develop newer rhetorical concepts and theoretical models grounded in affect, material engagement, and emergent methods" (2). A material engagement with sonic phenomena is, by necessity, a multimodal and therefore multisensory experience, but Hawk takes us even further: "Resounding suggests that the materiality of past conditions, embodiment in present listening practices, and the future impact on other bodies and ecologies is all a part of the same process" (15). In other words, sonic practices and phenomena resound and thus are born of and through a multivalent material world—one layered with and reverberant through ever-changing objects and circumstances.[11] Attending to the sound of things, then, is bound to lead to multivalent ways of knowing and being.

In related research, Jonathan Alexander's 2015 article "Glenn Gould and the Rhetorics of Sound" draws out the multivocal or polyphonic potentials of sound (more ways of naming "multivalence") and the ways in which sound's materiality "should bring to mind the multiplicity of realities we experience, understand, and articulate, and hear" (88). Gould (1932–1982) was a well-known pianist and composer who turned to experimental studio recording and mixing that included a practice he called "contrapuntal radio," where disparate radio voices were mixed overlapping each other "to create a 'fugal' set of voices that simultaneously resonated with and at times contradicted one another" (Alexander 83). In a fascinating analysis of Gould, Alexander explores polyphony and contrapuntality as material realities for sound and also as possibilities for listening.

My goal here is to explore those material realities and listening possibilities through some of the "newer" (Hawk 2) historical, theoretical, and methodological approaches to rhetoric that sound inspires. Sonic multivalence, as I hear it intoned by the composition scholars using those approaches, is one such space. Multivalence cuts across the wide spectrum of what might be considered sonic rhetoric, from soundscape design to the recording studio and from "Grey Goose" to the symphony orchestra. Each sounding on the spectrum is multimodal, multitonal, and often multitracked. Even basic soundings communicate multivalence: volume, pitch, duration, acoustic space or place, and any number of other factors determine the meaning, effect, and affect of the horn blast, human grunt, or cell phone beep. Sonic rhetorics call our attention to such materialities, reminding us that rhetoric is a concert even when it sounds like a solo.

Rhetorical studies tend to focus on the clearest communicative wavelength—the signal—and, with it, the Aristotelian doctrine of persuasion as the organizing ideal within the rhetorical tradition. But sound comes to us as both signal and noise, and sonic rhetorics call us to attend to both. In doing so, the concepts, histories, theories, and methods inspired by sound complicate the privileging of a clear signal as rhetoric's objective in any given situation. Reminding us of the rhetorical salience of noise was part of Jonathan Alexander's point in his study of Glenn Gould's various musical and sound experiments. Gould pushed his audiences to attend to the meaningful noise inherent to all sonic exchanges, by challenging listeners' typified expectations for "clarity" while listening to the symphony or radio programs. Gould's play with contrapuntal modes was about exploring the simultaneity of multiple voices, perspectives, places, and, by extension, noise. When the myth of the clear signal is diminished, so are its cronies: rightness, assurance, and dogmatic certainty. Sonic rhetorics make their impact in their ability to orient us toward the more common and noisy experiences of contradiction, ambivalence, and doubt. In these spaces of uncertainty, we might come to a better understanding of the patchworks of history, including its most beautiful and terrible fabrication: race.

Music—especially folk music—may not seem like a particularly noisy avenue in which to begin an exploration of what sonic phenomenon might have to contribute to our understanding of rhetoric. But as I will argue in various ways throughout this book, a folksong's power is best understood as a kind of sonic rhetorical distillation. It appears simple, when, in fact, its communicative capacity is broad and deep, often having been refined and concentrated over long periods of time. Music echoes and reverberates through its cultural and historical contexts and sometimes for years and years beyond. In his book *The Ballad Mongers: Rise of the Modern Folk Song* (1967), Oscar Brand references folksongs with the phrase "simple noise," which seems an apt description. But Brand fails to elaborate sufficiently, reducing folksongs, in a typical fashion, as "special sound" characterized by the "artless, unself-conscious quality in the music and lyrics which commends itself to [the] critical ear" (10). A folksong's "noise" is attributed to a maladroit lack of guile in an environment more attuned to the appreciation of musical sophistication.

Writing a few years later, Jacques Attali has a different take. He describes music—all music—as "inscribed between noise and silence, in the space of the social codification it reveals. Every code of music is rooted in the ideologies and technologies of its age, and at the same time produces them" (19). In his perspective, music is a symbiote with its noisy contexts, and "listening to music is listening to all noise, realizing that its appropriation and control is a reflection of power, that it is essentially political" (6). Attali's deft theory of music's noise economy provides a more robust sense of its rhetorical power and buoys my arguments about music's relationship to politics, power, ideology, and technology. Attali reminds us of music's capacity to broaden and complicate the rhetorical wavelength; he encourages us to listen carefully both to what is there but also to the noise that music organizes, obfuscates, and silences. Steven Hammer, a scholar who experiments with the relationship between sonic and rhetorical composition, comes to similar conclusions about noise. He invites us to use noise as a rhetorical strategy to disrupt the "myth of noiselessness" wherever it may be found, from slick audio production to closed and orthodox ideological systems ("Writing Dirt, Teaching Noise," 2018).

From the aforementioned ideas, a first tenet of sonic rhetorical theory emerges: sonic rhetorics are noisy. That noise resounds whenever there are multiple signals at play. That simultaneity—be it literal (actual sound waves in harmony and/or dissonance), ideological, or disciplinary—encourages analysis, understanding, or experience more resistant to binary, orthodox, and other calcified ways of thinking.

Two additional points need stating before I continue to the second movement of this introduction. The first point has to do with the size, scope, and potential of the emerging sonic rhetorical field. Sonic phenomena are, of course, utterly ubiquitous. Music, itself a broad conceptual and theoretical category, represents only a portion of possible sites of inquiry for the sonic rhetorician. Consider music's numerous cultural traditions, genres, instruments, styles, and performers, as well as their affects and effects on history, culture, and civic life (not to mention the academic and professional fields devoted to the study of music).[12] Now consider other sonic phenomena that might benefit from rhetorical study: to name just a few, soundscapes, sound effects, sound design and production (including recording techniques and technologies), and acoustics (bio-, archaeo-, electro-, psycho-, etc.). All of those phenomena have taxonomies just as complex as music's. The study of sound and sonic rhetoric is vast and emergent. Work at the intersection of sound studies and rhetorical studies addresses many of the above topics and more.[13]

This book brings a rhetorical perspective to a comparatively minute grouping of musical sounds (mostly) recorded in the 1930s for a particular archive funded by the US government. Given the vastness of the field, it is arguable that such a small sampling of music may not offer much of substance with which to theorize for the field—that there may be too much noise, not enough signal. The second point that bears stating here, then, is that music, particularly folksong, with its combination of poetic language, rhythm, and simple melody structures, is unique to other musical (and, by extension, sonic) rhetorics. The use of vernacular music as a rhythmic and poetic practice in the circulation of cultural traditions or mythos shares a direct genealogical line with another discursive practice: rhetoric. That those practices spring from the same roots is significant, especially for rhetoricians who are interested in sound's power to influence culture and history. Music does so profoundly. The movements ahead, then, are situated within that small but important niche, where music meets tradition meets rhetoric.

Movement II: Noisy Disciplinarity—Turning the Rhetorical Tradition Inside Out

Above, I compared Charles Seeger's notion of folkness with Jeffery Walker's definition of epideictic rhetoric. Both notions name rhetorical activity at the level of cultural production and maintenance, and music shares a relationship with both. While those notions hail from different disciplinary traditions, putting them in conversation and allowing them to resonate together increases our understanding of each and, in turn, deepens our understanding of rhetoric. To responsibly do the sonic rhetorical work I engage with in subsequent chapters, that cross-pollination (among concepts, disciplines, and cultural traditions) may be not only useful but required.

As I have been discussing, the work in the chapters ahead is multidisciplinary, often wildly so: I bring together, for example, rhetoric and the archive, folk music and Depression-era politics, race and radio, jazz and the American South. Each of those subjects fits squarely into one or even several disciplines, each with specialists, scholarship, and traditions of its own. Disciplinarity provides the focus, methods, expertise, and nomenclature needed to do robust intellectual work. Each of the subjects in this book benefits from attentive work done by in-discipline scholars. But strict disciplinarity can also create artificial borders, information silos, and counterproductive competition. We do our disciplines a disservice when our work leads to an overwrought sense of territory, certainty, or righteousness about a given topic.

Rhetorical studies is both typical and atypical as a discipline. Typically, its disciplinary grooves are deep and profoundly Western. Rhetoric hails from an ancient tradition and names the civic art of public speaking that developed alongside Athenian democracy in the fourth and fifth centuries BCE. The term *rhetoric* is, as George Kennedy writes, "derived from the Greek word *rhêkorikê*, the art or technique of a *rhêtôr*, or public speaker" (1). The word first shows up in Plato's dialogue *Gorgias*, written around 380 BCE. A few decades later, the rhetorical discipline would get a systematic treatment in Aristotle's *Rhetoric*, a series of lectures on the subject, compiled by his students. Much of contemporary rhetorical theory has its roots in that "classical" period in Greece, with a few innovations and neoclassical revivals along the way. But even "new" rhetoric, is usually steeped in the terms, turns, and trades of the tradition.[14] Such is the blessing and curse of disciplinarity.

Rhetoric is atypical, however, in its potential for multidisciplinarity—both in formal, academic contexts and in describing a ubiquitous language practice common to all disciplines, traditions, and cultures. That multidisciplinarity has been productive and problematic to the development of rhetoric for several reasons. First, the discipline may have developed to support civic engagement in the Athenian courts, but as the art of persuasive speech, it has infinitely more possible applications. Second, rhetorical studies has broadened to include discourse beyond speech (and even beyond "persuasion," classically speaking) and suddenly is recognizable in every human interaction (and in nonhuman interaction as well). Third, it follows that rhetoricians have begun to look and listen for rhetoric in places, spaces, and modes heretofore underrepresented in the "rhetorical tradition." That development is productive. Such broadening has put rhetoric into conversation with the work of feminist, queer, disability, and critical race scholarships (among a myriad of others). It is no surprise, perhaps, that rhetoric has also been used to perpetuate any number of inequities, from the deeply engrained "traditions" of sexism and racism to the more overt and calculated practices of disenfranchisement and slavery. But an expanded critical repertoire helps us understand how language works in those contexts and, in turn, gives us a better idea of how to counter dubious rhetorics.

The problem, then, comes back to disciplinarity. Due to rhetoric's grand scope, rhetoricians trained in the nomenclature of the Western tradition are given opportunity for broad study and eventually run up against the limits of Western rhetoric's ability to adequately and ethically describe their subject. There is a bit of a paradox when the language a discipline requires for professional ethos and legibility is also inadequate or may even seem inappropriate to the analysis, criticism, or history being produced. Such inadequacy especially occurs when rhetorical work addresses the lives and experience of non-Western traditions, including the several hybrid cultural traditions present in the United States. Surely rhetorical study should not also mean perpetuating the inequity potentially promoted by language orthodoxies and, by extension, disciplinary ones.

Feminist scholars have long provided opportunities to rethink those orthodoxies. For example, Sonja K. Foss and Cindy L. Griffin's notion of "invitational rhetoric" is "rooted in the feminist principles of equity, immanent value, and self-determination" (Littlejohn and Foss 570). Invitational rhetoric presents us with an alternative to the traditional and Aristotelean notion of "persuasion," which can be just another way to describe domination. Invitational rhetoric is grounded in the acts of inviting folks to offer their unique perspectives and creating spaces where those perspectives may be offered freely and safely. Invitational rhetoric recasts disciplinarity's deep grooves and finds value in and across perspectives.[15]

Work in comparative rhetoric also helps to address the orthodoxy problem. LuMing Mao calls disciplinary malaprops "incongruities" and invites us to see them as "the very condition of possibility for new spaces of meaning-making" (210–211). Drawing on Walter D. Mignolo's work on postcolonial discourse, Mao presents those incongruities as "loci of enunciation" that "can help promote narratives that are neither revisionist nor aimed to tell a different truth, but 'narratives geared toward the search for a different logic'" (211). He encourages us away from the urge to search for "what is the most authentic of authentic detail or what is the most native of native knowledge" (211), and toward the utilization of alternative logics to complicate Western rhetoric and to destabilize its authority, if not its insights. Further, Mao posits,

> As we continue to cross borders and to inform and enrich our understanding of other rhetorical practices across language, culture, and time, incongruities of similar kind are bound to crop up [. . .] Directly assessing these incongruities will help us to see through our own blind spots and overcome biases, binaries, and borders that have clouded our visions of the other and ourselves. (211)

While incongruity is not necessarily a virtue, recognizing and working with and, where possible, through incongruity has radical implications for the future of rhetorical studies. Though we will probably continue to refer to those studies by the term *rhetoric*, that term's transdisciplinary potential can only strengthen and give deeper meaning to our critical work. As incongruity gives way to innovation, the tradition itself will transform (turn, turn, turn).

Transformation is a good thing. We need tradition, and we also need traditions to change. Further, if we are to claim the noble goal of revising and resounding tradition (and, by extension, our attending disciplines), we must

> pay more attention to how political, economic, and sociocultural exigencies help determine local contexts or particular performances and how the other's social, political, and linguistic affiliations and affordances can in fact help us rethink and interrogate our own modes of thinking and being. (Mao 217)

Throughout this book, I seek to strike a balance in which the theory, concepts, and logics of Western rhetoric are present but are usually paired or triangulated with those of other traditions.

For example, to substantiate a study of folk music within rhetoric, I feel a certain responsibility to show rhetoric in concert with rhythmic, sounded traditions in ancient Greece. Doing so does not merely pay lip service to the discipline (though there is a bit of that) but reveals an important connection between music and rhetoric in the latter's earliest history. However, *aretē* and *epideictic*, the terms I trace in movement III below to make those connections, are limited in their usefulness mainly because they are words used to describe ancient attitudes and abilities. Movement IV introduces alternative concepts that hail from different traditions but intone a similar idea, albeit in a different disciplinary key. Folkness, which has been my guiding example of this kind of interdisciplinary harmonizing, will appear again in that movement, to help introduce the old and new members of the band I am assembling.

Here, a second tenet of sonic rhetorical theory emerges: sonic rhetorics are multidisciplinary and therefore are often described in different traditions and by different terms. Multidisciplinarity tracks as a sonic rhetorical value as it brings into practice the contrapuntal polyphony Alexander explored in Glen Gould's sound work, but the multivocal elements here are disciplinary. The various disciplinary terms of sonic rhetoric are instructive to our broadening understanding of rhetoric, though the act of traversing disciplines and different traditions should never be done as a kind of terminological colonizing for rhetoric. Instead, resounding the rhetorical tradition across multiple (and often dissonant) traditions should destabilize and delink a single-voiced notion of rhetoric from the hegemonies and certainties of its Western colonial past, introduce noise, and thus create conditions for a multivocal decoloniality where no single rhetoric can dominate.[16]

Movement III: Turning (for a Moment) Toward Ancient Rhetoric

In Plato's dialogue *Protagoras*,[17] the Sophist who gives the dialogue its name engages with Socrates in a discussion over whether or not virtue, *aretē*, can be taught.[18] As the conversation unfolds, Plato's Protagoras argues that the reason Socrates may not be aware of the teaching of *aretē* is because of its ubiquity, not its disparity. "[E]veryone," says Protagoras, "is a teacher of *aretē* so far as he is able, and so you don't notice any of them" (*Protagoras* 327e; Gagarin and Woodruff 184). Preceding that comment is a discussion about the likely sources of such teaching.

> [W]hen the children have learned the alphabet and are ready to read . . . then the teachers put works of good poets before them to read at their benches, and require them to learn by heart poems that are full of good advice, and stories and songs in praise of good men of old, so that the child will be eager to emulate them, and will yearn to grow up to be a man like them. (326a; Gagarin and Woodruff 182)

Plato's Protagoras then makes an important comparison to musical training, another conspicuous source for instruction in virtuous living.

> Musicians do much the same when they teach the lyre; they try to foster Soundness of Mind, and they keep the youngsters out of mischief. Besides that, once the children have learned to play the lyre, they are taught more poetry by good lyric poets. Then the music-teachers set those poems to the music of the lyre, and make sure that rhythm and harmony dwell in the souls of the children, so that they will grow more gentle and their speech and their behavior will improve as they gain grace in rhythm and harmony, for all human life needs the grace of harmony and rhythm. (326a–326b; Gagarin and Woodruff 182)

Plato argues that civic virtue, wisdom, and shared cultural values—the unity of which his Protagoras called a "soundness of mind"[19]—are constantly being taught, reemphasized, and revised as new knowledge emerges from the experience of everyday living. Plato epitomizes the mind-body disciplining nature of *aretē* as that found in the memorization and recitation of poetry, storytelling, and musical performance, each of which contribute to a state of "rhythmic grace" and "harmonious" living. While ancient Greek virtuosity extended well beyond the habituated practice of rhythmic oral traditions, Plato's evocation of it in this context is not unlike the concept of folkness introduced above. Both folkness and *aretē* indicate a kind of value-laden, situated rhetorical practice embedded into everyday life. In both cases, music and rhythmic oral tradition is part and parcel to that embeddedness, affect, and distribution.

Like folkness, the teaching of virtue does not have an easily articulated, logical system for public distribution. *Aretē* is something better understood in the doing than in the saying. It is participatory and embodied. It is therefore distinct, but not altogether separate, from the various arts, or *techne*, that require *aretē* to be developed. Due to the breadth of practices *aretē* embodies, it can have no formal methodology. *Aretē* is less a body of knowledge than it is shared, embodied knowledge—a social agreement about the "normative poles" of virtue and vice (Cohen quoted in Hawhee, "Agonism" 187). In chapter 9 of his *Rhetoric*, Aristotle teaches that *aretē* is an ability "that is productive and preservative of goods, and an ability for doing good in many great ways," adding the hyperbole "actually in all ways in all things" (1.9.1366a36–1366b1).[20] He offers that definition as commentary on epideictic rhetoric, specifically epideictic's relationship to *aretē* or the "points of reference for praising and blaming" virtue and vice (1.9.1366a). Alongside the genres of deliberative and judicial rhetoric, epideictic (or demonstrative rhetoric) is the third "species" (*ediē*) of rhetoric. As George Kennedy notes, it "is the most problematic of the species and has remained a problem in rhetorical theory, since it becomes the category for all forms of discourse that are not specifically deliberative or judicial" (47). Perhaps epideictic is problematic because its potential opens theoretical doors, rather than closing them as is typical for rhetoric under the Aristotelian paradigm.

That said, Aristotle's description of epideictic as funeral oratory encompassing the praise and blame of "virtue and vice and [the] honorable and shameful" (1.9.1366a) is useful here in its simplicity. As noted above, Aristotle emphasizes and begins to theorize the important relationship between epideictic and *aretē*. Epideictic functions in the service of *aretē*; it reinforces, in words of praise and blame, the "abilities" related to excellence, honor, and virtue. Also, Aristotle categorized his three species along a temporal line, with deliberative oratory useful for addressing future events, judicial for the past, and epideictic for the present. As such, epideictic has no specific argumentative "end," or *telos*; its influence is felt in the moment—or, more accurately, at all moments—and it directs present choices according to the cultural norms it reinforces. Epideictic is constitutive of lifestyle; it is less about the persuasion of others and more about the persuasion of self.

Jeffery Walker's book *Rhetoric and Poetics in Antiquity* (2000) delves into the prehistory of rhetoric and can be added to other work interested in what Thomas Cole (1991) called "protorhetoric" and what Richard Marback (1999) summarizes as "the unsystematized and uncodified persuasive and oratorical tactics of the sophists and the poets" (6). Walker shows how rhetoric developed alongside the poetic tradition and how, even with the collation of the disciplines into separate arts, their histories and ends were and remain inextricably connected. Further, he shows that rhythmic poetics, as epideictic containers of value and virtue for a community, are the engines that give rhetoric its power. Civic rhetoric, Walker argues, "necessarily depends on and appeals to the beliefs/desires that epideictic cultivates" (10). That cultivation is sweeping:

> "[E]pideictic" appears as that which shapes and cultivates the basic codes of value and belief by which a society or culture lives; it shapes the ideologies and imaginaries with which, and by which, the individual members of a community identify themselves; and, perhaps most significantly, it shapes the fundamental grounds, the "deep" commitments and presuppositions, that will underlie and ultimately determine decision and debate in particular pragmatic forums. As such, epideictic suasion is not limited to the reinforcement of existing beliefs and ideologies . . . [it] can also work to challenge or transform conventional beliefs. (Walker 9)

Closely following, Walker makes a compelling argument for epideictic as "the central and indeed fundamental mode of rhetoric in human culture" (10). An important exigence to a broader study and a deeper understanding of the genre is its ability to cultivate belief and desire, to create and sustain worldviews, and—important to this study—to be both conservative in those respects but also a tool for challenge.

Walker's explication of epideictic's progressive potential is an update from the view held by Chaïm Perelman and Lucie Olbrechts-Tyteca. While those authors of *The New Rhetoric* (1971) acknowledged epideictic's "central part of the art of persuasion" (49), they also stated that it functions more as a "possession" than as a tool useful in the "struggle" for which other rhetorics arm us (51). In Perelman and Olbrechts-Tyteca's view, epideictic is practiced "by those who, in a society, defend the traditional and accepted values, those which are the object of education, not the new and revolutionary values which stir up controversy and polemics" (51). The mistake in their rendering is the notion that "new and revolutionary values" are not prompted by epideictic rhetoric. Even when new or revolutionary, values still distill from epideictic experiences, be they discursive or something more rhetorically elusive. As Charlotte Hogg argues, "Epideictic rhetoric is more sneakily rhetorical because it is less traditionally apparent as an argument, resulting in it going more unrecognized or under the radar, providing great rhetorical power in its subtlety and malleability" (427). Hogg's observation of what she terms epideictic's "everyday" qualities (425) leads us back to the *Protagoras* and beyond. Epideictic rhetoric is always with us, in various guises and recognized in other traditions by other names. Epideictic is subtle, sneaky even, in its ability to motivate excellence (*aretē*) in both the performance of traditional ideals and revolutionary change (turn, turn, turn).

In this movement, I have demonstrated ways in which my work draws exigency from concepts and theories rooted in the ancient Western tradition of rhetoric and thus demonstrates sonic rhetoric's deep roots in that tradition.[21] I am not arguing, however, for the wholesale application of those notions into a contemporary North American setting. The terms *epideictic* and *aretē* should be heard as a signal to conceptual and disciplinary recognition and legibility—a familiar tune—rather than as a definitive attempt at establishing a kind of ontological conceptual stronghold for the emerging field of sonic rhetoric. Indeed, for my work to be characterized in the sonic rhetorical frame I introduced above, clear signals should not offer certainty. A noisy reverberance beyond academic, historical, and disciplinary borders is needed. The tenet to be gleaned here is that the relationship between sonic rhetorics and traditional rhetorical theory, terminology, and methodology is suspect if offered as the final or definitive word. Sonic rhetorical theory should work to move beyond such disciplinary refuges, acknowledging the use of familiar melodies, but always working to modulate and improvise on them. To that end, the following movement names a possible sonic rhetorical concept with all of the theorizing power of epideictic but with a particularly US resonance.

Movement IV: Turning to and with the Blues

The purpose of this introduction has been to key the reader into a way of thinking about rhetoric that grants new space, dynamics, and frameworks for the sonic. I have asked for a reevaluation of several terms to make that argument, foremost among them the term for Aristotle's rhetorical mode, *epideictic*. I argued not only that the traditional rhetorical disciplinarity that gives us epideictic is useful (and inextricably intertwined with poetic and musical traditions) but also that "epideictic" is just one way of talking about culturally constitutive discourse. Folkness is another, used here and throughout as a stand-in (or even deliberate replacement) for epideictic aimed at orienting the reader toward the appreciation (only implied by Aristotle) of an everyday rhetoric, used by common people—folks—to communicate cultural ideals, values, beliefs, humiliations, and traumas. But we need more terms, because folks do not generally use the languagings of Western rhetoric to describe their cultural experiences and because Western rhetoric, since its inception, has so profoundly failed a significant number of people, particularly folks on the margins.

In this movement, I forward another term, both incongruous (to use Mao's term) and analogous with *epideictic* and *folkness*, but with a more specific and deliberate (and even radical) tuning to US sonic/musical culture, especially the cultural history and everyday vernacular rhetorics of African Americans. That term, of course, is *blues*. Putting *blues*, *folkness*, and *epideictic* in concert is one more way to enact the multivalent "contrapuntal" method that a sonic rhetorical theory should encourage. Doing so celebrates both the harmonic resonances and the noisy dissonances generated when these terms are sung together.

Though the "precise time and manner of the emergence of the blues are lost in the irrecoverable past" (Levine 221), there is general consensus that by the turn of the 20th century, blues was being named as a recognizable style in the Deep South region of the United States (Evans 33–35). Jazz pianist Jelly Roll Morton claimed, for example, to have first heard blues in New Orleans in the year 1902. The musical style has West African roots and developed in and through the violent tragedy of African slavery, the hope of emancipation, and the confusion and relapse of the Jim Crow era. As an amalgam or matrix of work songs, religious "spirituals," minstrelsy, and a number of other musical styles (including those of European dissent), blues eventually settled into a somewhat stable and recognizable musical mode: 12 bars, *aab* line structure, and three repeated chords (tonic, subdominant, dominant seventh). In contrast to its earlier, more communal antecedents, Southern blues music and performance was profoundly individualistic, an expression of an author's "completely personal life and death" (Baraka 67), and dealt with a number of topics and emotions, not (as is sometimes thought) just sorrow and protest.

Though I will take up some of these formal elements in subsequent chapters, I want to emphasize here the significance of blues beyond its structure, subject matter, or exportability into other musical styles. To understand blues in the same key as terms like *epideictic* or *folkness* is to hear blues as an attitude, a representative power, and a sonic rhetoric of resistance and resilience. It is also to understand blues as part of the larger mythos of race and racial history in the United States. As a distinctive "Black music," blues comprises part of what Ronald Radano calls the "tenacity of belief in [a] black musical essence" (*Lying Up a Nation* 3).[22] That belief "represents a crucial mode of musical coherence that reflects the constituting role of sound in the formation of racial subjects" (3). Black musical essence is a powerful myth that "gives texture and meaning in the making of our worlds" but also "forestalls consideration of the interracial background from which ideologies of black music developed in the first place" (3). Black music, blues included, has been constitutive of the "broader emergence of race in American public history and culture" (4). In other words, belief in blues as "black musical essence" is yet another way the demarcation of racial difference has been perpetuated as an enduring value in the United States. Blues, then, has something to teach us about epideictic modes beyond Aristotle and in a finer grained detail than is expressed in Charles Seeger's folkness. Blues demonstrates the ways that rhetorical activity, here packaged as musical sound, constructs and propagates multivalent virtue and value systems that are imbued with and wrapped up in the contradictions of the cultures that produce them. In short, blues reminds us that values themselves are not signal but noise.

In his book *Blues, Ideology, and Afro-American Literature: A Vernacular Theory* (1987, Houston A. Baker Jr. explores blues in that broader rhetorical sense and argues that blues can be a tool for complex cultural analysis. Baker understands the potential of blues as noise. "Rather than a rigidly personalized form," he writes, "the blues offer a phylogenetic recapitulation—a nonlinear, freely associative, nonsequential mediation—of species experience" (5). In blues, Baker hears a synthesis of the ongoing "experiences of Africans in the New World," a "forceful matrix in cultural understanding" that brings to mind the "black blues singer at the railway junction lustily transforming experiences of a durative (unceasingly oppressive) landscape into the energies of rhythmic song" (7). The details of that trope flesh out Baker's theory, where the term *blues* names not only a musical distillation of certain dominant aspects of African American cultural reality but a trope for America more generally. Blues can help us get beyond notions of "essence" and toward the "junctures" of African and Anglo-European cultures. Baker uses the image of crossing locomotive tracks as a metaphor: "[P]olymorphous and multidirectional, scene of arrivals and departures, place betwixt and between (ever *entre les deux*), the juncture is the way-station of the blues" (7). It follows that a better understanding of blues, including its roots and antecedents, leads to a more nuanced understanding of race as a persistent American mythos composed within that juncture. In this polymorphous, multidirectional mode, blues invites a complicating of racial categories such as "Black" and "white," even as it reinforces the multifarious value systems from which notions of "Blackness" and "whiteness" emerged and codified as typifying racial rhetorics.

This purposefully paradoxical assertion might find transitory clarity in a consideration of the legacy of blues as a musical genre. A hybrid musical form from the beginning, but one most often associated with Blackness, blues would become foundational to most, if not all, forms of popular American music (and Western music more broadly). Genres from jazz to rock and roll to hip-hop contain a number of recognizable blues forms, which are engrained into the fabric of US popular music so deeply that it is difficult to imagine US history without them as the soundtrack. But are jazz, rock and roll, or hip-hop "Black" or "white" music? The temptation toward that kind of binary questioning and the bewildering answers it might evoke get at the ways that blues both reinforces and refigures racial tropes in and across US history. Blues therefore represents the foundational cultural presence of African Americans in the United States (with the attending rich social, intellectual, and artistic contributions), as well as the abiding othering, transience, and homelessness that continue to haunt African American life.

Blues is a symbol of unresolved social and historical problems—and, by extension, rhetorical ones. It is a key useful to understanding and exploring the rhetorics of in-between, paradox, and contradiction I have been describing throughout this introduction. Blues somehow communicates both sorrow and resilience, devastation and jubilation, the beautiful and the terrible. As a complex signifier, "the blues" hints at both origins (*mythos*) and ends (*telos*), without ever definitely describing either (H. Baker 8). Blues resonates meaningfully in the moment. Like epideictic and especially when extended through the concept of folkness, blues is affected by past circumstances and casts an eye to the future but is grounded in the present. A sonic rhetorical approach, it follows, orients us toward terms like *blues* with both deep cultural resonance and ties to the sounded world.

Turning to the 1930s

In the preceding movements, I discussed ways in which traditional music and rhetoric are connected. That connection has been described in various ways across time and diverse cultures—as epideictic, folkness, and blues. In those modes, music orients the disoriented, provides a sense of empathy through desperation, and can unify the isolated around a common value or experience. Folksong, then, is a cultural commodity—both a resource for coping with crisis and also, when viewed from a rhetorical perspective, a powerful tool for creating and maintaining values, beliefs, and ways of being.

Studying this rhetorical phenomenon historically helps us understand not only the contours and limits of folksong as sonic rhetoric but also the ways that such rhetoric helps shape broader movements and might aid in the shift of long-standing cultural circumstances. The 1930s, an epoch interposed, in the United States, by the various crises and conflicts of economic depression, provides an apt historical moment for such a study, as the tension between traditional ideals and social realities then reached a pinnacle. Those accustomed to trusting that hard work was the logical antecedent to prosperity were left with the paradox of not just layoffs but rampant joblessness, poverty, and even hunger. As Terry A. Cooney writes, we are best poised to understand the 1930s in "the tensions within and between values, ambitions, ideas, and circumstances" (xiv). But the stark cultural contrasts of the 1930s also provide an opportunity to understand the rhetorical function of folk music as a representation of the various tensions that exist within society at any historical moment. Cooney continues,

> The desire to move in more than one direction at once, to have it both ways, to live with or to resolve contradictions, appears during the 1930s in the most broadly public spheres as well as in the narrower territories of individuals defining their beliefs and families furnishing their homes. (xiv)

The cultural contradictions Cooney describes have only continued to expand in complexity over the last nine decades, so while my focus remains situated within the cultural milieu of the conflicting ideals of the 1930s, a larger goal of this book is to provide a theoretical framework useful for scholars of rhetoric, music, and vernacular culture (which has, of late, become digital culture) who are studying any historical moment.

Listening to the Lomax Archive sets in motion a study to find new scholarly pathways for thinking sonically. The political, cultural, and historical circumstances that rhetorical scholars have become expert at examining will increase in depth and sophistication as rhetorical analysis and criticism is expanded across the sensorium. While rhetoric's sonic dimensions have always been there, the field's current and ongoing expansion into multisensory realms provides a renewed exigence for this study and other expansive ones exploring sound's profound rhetorical multivalences, a soundscape I have only begun to map above. A turn to sonic rhetorics is not unlike a folk revival.

As with any revival, there is a pressing need for fresh and sustained conversations—in this case, about the contours and complexities of those sonic dimensions. Despite the perceived disciplinary neglect I mention earlier in this chapter, there is significant evidence of such sonic revival in rhetorical studies at multiple levels—in conference talks and professional workshop sessions, in "special" print and electronic journal issues,[23] and in conversations around multimodal pedagogies.[24] In fact, the shear expanse of those sounded rhetorical potentials may be partially causal of any ongoing claim of neglect; such radical openness is not usually the stuff on which subdisciplinary foundations are constructed and maintained.

Listening to the Lomax Archive will add some rhythm to that expanse. With chapters that locate the sonic dimensions of rhetorical concepts already reverberant within the field, I hope to make the sonic rhetorical landscape easier to navigate for future studies. As I have already begun to articulate, the conceptual tools I locate hail from both ancient and contemporary theories of rhetoric and are useful in that they name rhetorical activities and experiences (like folkness) common across all historical epochs. These concepts require a common space in which to animate them and for this study. The 1930s and the work of John and Alan Lomax during that time provide that context.

Except for the first, each main chapter in this book is oriented around groups of recordings and a radio broadcast John and/or Alan Lomax made while associated with the Library of Congress archive between 1933 and 1940. The chapters account for both the content of those recordings and the circumstances around their creation and trace a sonic historical thread related to the Lomaxes' problematic but persistent goal to record African American folkness. Given that I have limited my case studies to three groups of recordings, there are a number of gaps in the narrative. While this book is not an attempt at thorough Lomax biography, the interludes I have included as preludes to the chapters provide some additional biographical and historical context to flesh out those gaps. They also provide an opportunity to juxtapose Lomax happenings with adjacent histories, theories, and figures, which provides further context for the cultural milieu the Lomaxes were working in, while also ensuring that the Lomaxes' lives and experiences do not overwhelm the historical or critical bandwidth.

The first interlude serves as an introduction to John A. Lomax and is accompanied by a discussion of the historiographical reality that archivist and historian worldviews (including their prejudices) are inseparable from the work that they do. Its discussion then turns to Kenneth Burke, a rhetorical critic contemporary with the Lomaxes. Burke's work in the 1930s makes explicit connections between symbol-making and history-making and is also useful in fleshing out the broader historical context of this book. As such, interlude I prefaces chapter 1 wherein I flesh out the methods and implications of a distinctly sonic historiography, one inflected by and shot through with folkness. The succeeding interludes offer similar juxtapositions as the first, with Lomax biography supplemented by theoretical discussions on oral history and education, respectively.

In chapter 2, I chronicle the Lomaxes' journey as emissaries for the Library of Congress to several Southern African American prisons. That episode lays out a common theme of the Lomaxes archival work: it was produced under the coercive auspices of white privilege yet also often provided marginalized people opportunity to perform music for the archive and thus for a national platform. In chapter 3, that theme continues as the focus shifts to pianist and composer Jelly Roll Morton. In 1938, Morton joined Alan Lomax and the Library of Congress in his desire to insert and authenticate himself within the early history of jazz. He did so through deftly articulated sonic rhetorics—virtuosic performances and oral histories—but the recorded sessions brought more fortune and fame to Lomax than to Morton, who died soon after. By 1939, Lomax was hosting a national radio program titled *Folk Music of America* as part of the Columbia Broadcasting System's popular series *American School of the Air*. Chapter 4 is an examination of an episode from that program, titled "Negro Work Songs," where, with a particularly authentic American irony, songs recorded in the prison yard were repurposed for performances by professional musicians and broadcast to suburban classrooms across the country.

INTERLUDE I

Resimplifications

"During the late spring of 1932," records John A. Lomax in his autobiographical *Adventures of a Ballad Hunter* (1947), "at the nadir of the general financial collapse, my fortunes had reached their lowest ebb [. . .] I was worth less than nothing; I was heavily in debt, I had no job" (106). He and his wife, Bess Brown Lomax, had also just suffered a terrible illness, which, to his great distress, she had not survived. John Lomax's experience was becoming more and more typical for Americans. The year 1932 marked the beginning of the third full year of the Great Depression in the United States and would be one of its most devastating. In that year, the gross national product fell a record 13.4 percent, and unemployment across the nation rose to 23.6 percent, leaving 34 million people without an income and with essentially no social safety net.[1] At that time, Lomax was a banker, and banks were failing everywhere. Earlier in his narrative, he writes solemnly of the experience of dejected bond buyers confronting him at his desk in the bank where he worked, aghast because the bonds he had recommended were now worth nearly nothing: "I was forced to sit and take it. The market in New York had gone mad. What could I say? Nothing. And I said nothing" (104).

That spring, Lomax had a hopeful but somewhat desperate meeting in New York with H. S. Latham, president of the Macmillan Company. Having had success with *Cowboy Songs and Frontier Ballads*, a book published by Macmillan in 1910, Lomax was hopeful that his proposal for a new project would be accepted and funded by the company, with an advance against the royalties. He presented several ideas to Mr. Latham and caught the publisher's attention with the last, the ballad "Ida Red," a song John had learned on the Gulf Coast of Texas while doing research for his earlier book. "Ida Red," Lomax wrote later, was a "Negro Bad Men" song (Lomax and Lomax 87). The lyrics are a first-person account of a man who is incarcerated after a petty and foolish crime. In each verse, the man pines for Ida Red, from whom he is now hopelessly separated.

I went down town one day in a lope;
Fooled around till I stole a coat,
Den I came back and done my bes',
Fooled around till I got de ves'—
Oh, weep! Oh, my Ida!
For over dat road Ise bound to go. [. . .]
    Dey had me tied with a ball and chain;
Waitin' all ready for de east-bound train;
And every station we pass by,
Seem like I heard little Ida cry.
Oh, weep! Oh, my Ida!
For over dat road Ise bound to go.
    If I had listened to whut Ida said,
I'd been sleepin' in Ida's bed;
But I pay no mind to my Ida Red,
An' now Ise sleepin' in a convict's bed.
Oh, weep! Oh, my Ida!
For over dat road Ise bound to go.
    I wash my face and I comb my head,
Ise a mighty fool about Ida Red;
When I git out of dis old shack,
Tell little Ida Ise comin' back.
Oh, weep! Oh, my Ida!
For over dat road Ise bound to go. (Lomax and Lomax 110–111)

According to Lomax's autobiography, after hearing "Ida Rose," Latham "laughed" but "was also mopping the lower part of his brow" (*Adventures* 109). That reaction fit Lomax's terse description of the song: "It hits like a rifle bullet. When it is ended, you don't know whether to laugh or cry" (108). Latham authorized Macmillan to contract the book that would, in 1934, be published as *American Ballads and Folk Songs*. Coupled with a small and desperately needed monetary advance, the book contract would give 65-year-old John Lomax new hope and a fresh beginning in the career he'd always hoped to have, as a folklorist. The project would bring about an association with and formal mission from the Library of Congress to collect songs and would pave the way for the later library employment of his son, Alan, as well. For John, it was the opportunity of a lifetime.

By May 1933, John and Alan Lomax were en route to what both considered the most likely place to find authentic African American music like "Ida Red": Southern penitentiaries and prison farms, where they knew they would find an isolated and (literally) captive audience for their project. That attitude sums up the central paradox of the Lomaxes' relationship with the people of color with whom they would work, particularly African Americans. The Lomaxes recognized the richness of Black folk culture and its relative lack of national attention and pursued it with near fanatical energy, yet, steeped in the prejudices of their cultural moment, they were often ignorant to the ways that their own privilege and racism both steered and enabled their efforts as folklore collectors.

Even so, John's "almost obsessive interest in blacks" (Porterfield 298) was not incidental to the collection project or to Lomax himself. In the book *The Man Who Adores the Negro: Race and American Folklore* (2008), Patrick B. Mullen investigates the reach of that attitude, including instances during the interwar period. He traces, in Lomax and others of his ilk, a deep undercurrent—of values and beliefs about social hierarchy, race, and cultural authenticity—that drove projects to collect, represent, and understand African American folklife during the first decades of the 20th century and beyond. Mullen's work demonstrates just how strong notions of cultural evolution and primitivism were at that time, when unsettled sociological, anthropological, and linguistic issues were still being fiercely debated. Many people shared the view of Yale-educated folklorist Newbell Niles Puckett, author of *Folk Beliefs of the Southern Negro* (1926), who "conceived the magic folk beliefs of black people as evidence that African Americans were stuck in an earlier primitive stage of evolution, but that through education they could be pulled out of this state and become civilized" (43). African American author and anthropologist Zora Neale Hurston rejected that perspective. Her training at Columbia University, Mullen notes, "enabled her to view folk beliefs and practices in less judgmental ways than Puckett, although such 1920s anthropological models as functionalism had their own implicit condescension" (44). In both her autoethnographic collection of African American folklore (*Mules and Men*, 1935) and her novel *Their Eyes Were Watching God* (1937), Hurston worked to balance her desire to celebrate Black folklore in a way that "promoted the cultural distinctiveness of the race" without veering into the same primitivistic paradigms common to the era (47). She does so by bringing a politicized romanticism to the texts, especially in *Their Eyes Were Watching God*, where Huston depicts an idealized Southern African American plantation culture as an "independent rural black community . . . existing separately from white middle-class culture and in many ways superior to it" (49).

If Puckett and Hurston represent points on a spectrum of 1920s and '30s thinking on race and folklore, John and Alan Lomax occupy positions between those points, with John closer to Puckett and with Alan closer to Hurston. Though John was Puckett's senior by almost 30 years, his bumpy career as a folklorist happened to be most active after Puckett was working in the field, giving John time for his attitudes about race to develop in slightly less reductive ways than Puckett's. Since at least 1904, three years before the publication of his popular first book (*Cowboy Songs*), John's enthusiasm for African American folksong was noted in personal correspondence and in various publishing proposals.[2] By 1910, he already had evidence that there was a rich storehouse of Black music waiting to be "discovered," if one only knew the right places to look. In 1912, he even delivered a lecture titled "Negro Plantation Songs" for the Modern Language Association convention in Philadelphia (Porterfield 167).

John's attitude and excitement were likely inspired by the belief of his mentor George Kittredge (Harvard English professor and folklorist) "that black folksongs and folklore had never been collected by anyone with a genuine interest in preserving them in their native forms" (Porterfield 168). Black music had been collected and published before, but always in ways that Lomax believed were corrupted, either by white scholars (like Puckett) who "dressed them up for literary purposes" or by literate Blacks who "sought to polish [the songs] in order to present their race in the best possible light" (168). John's particular brand of American nationalism created a romantic racial paradigm, in which his belief that African American folksong was "the most natural and distinctive [music] of any America had produced" (168) was also steeped in paternalistic condescension. That attitude is complicated by the fact that he was also an effective champion of African American folk culture, especially in elitist academic circles where calcified, racial orthodoxies were particularly difficult to penetrate.

Lomax scholar Jerrold Hirsch underscores the complexities of this paradox by relating several examples from John's published work. Each example demonstrates that, as Hirsch puts it, Lomax was trying "to give African-American folksong the status he thought his audience gave to the artistic creations of Western high culture" (191). John accomplished that task through a series of comparisons—allusions "used to give classical status" to contributors to the Archive of American Folk Song (191). For instance, James Baker, one of the incarcerated men Lomax encounters early in the trips he and Alan took to Southern work farms, reminds Lomax of Homer, because Baker "had the quiet dignity and reserve of a Roman" (191). Lomax also compares Huddie Ledbetter (Lead Belly) to Mozart and regards the store of songs kept by another prisoner, Mose Platt, as equal in epic length to the *Iliad*. Hirsch points out how radical and even disturbing those comparisons might have been to Lomax's pious, classically trained audience:

> To some extent this strategy was a radical attack on the prestige attached to high culture produced in the Old World—a prestige that blinded Americans to the value of their own culture. However, it cut more than one way. One implication was that indigenous African-American folksong could only be regarded as art if it could be compared to true art—Western high culture. In this way, this strategy reinforced the prestige of high art forms while revealing hardly anything about the art of African-American folksong or the artists who created it. (191)

John Lomax's interest in Black vernacular culture is hamstrung, most often, between, on the one hand, his desire to respond to a legitimate scholarly gap in knowledge and, on the other, the prejudices typical of a Texas man who came of age at the turn of the 20th century. Put another way, Lomax's adoration of and fascination with Blackness was pursued in the service and protection of his own whiteness. Despite his clear respect for Black culture and even his attempts to change prevailing scholarly opinions around African American art and music, Lomax's relationships with the African Americans who would begin contributing their voices to the Library of Congress's archives most often reveal his implicit belief in their racial inferiority. For John Lomax, the "Negro" was a "simple, emotional, imitative human being [with] a child's eager and willing adaptableness to his environment" (Porterfield 170). Unsurprisingly, then, his research methods were oppressive as often as they were innovative.

As I have been laboring to acknowledge, a close study of the Lomaxes' numerous achievements soon reveals how often those achievements were accompanied by ignorance, questionable ethics, and outright arrogance. (I have singled out John here but will also trace a similar tendency, with some marked improvements, in Alan.) That paradox is symbolic of a broader American cultural reality, a problem we are still laboring to acknowledge, let alone resolve. The problem might be summed up in the following questions: How do we understand and parse the complicated legacies at the heart of the American experience, legacies rife with brilliance, violence, beauty, and horror? Or, in this specific case, what do we do when a magnificent archive is assembled by flawed agents through means that are sometimes dubious?

Those questions will reverberate throughout this book, as they press us toward the potentials of a workable sonic historiography that not only accounts for paradox but makes it central to the methodology. Sonic historiography should sound both the magnificence and the ugliness of the past, both its harmonies and its dissonances. A polyphonous approach to US history might help assuage the ways that history is politicized to fit squarely within a particular ideological paradigm or is used to narrow rhetorical ends. At least, such an approach will offer a different channel to attend.

Kenneth Burke and Resimplification

John Lomax's failings dim but do not extinguish either his significance as a folklorist or the importance of his archive. Lomax's search for an authentic vernacular other was misguided but was not outside (and maybe was even a bit progressive for) the prevailing intellectual character of the day. Another member of that intelligentsia was Kenneth Burke, the Greenwich Village novelist turned critic. Burke was working on similar issues and through similar prejudices at the same time as the Lomaxes. In a reflective prologue to the third edition of *Permanence and Change*, Burke observes,

> This book [. . .] was written in the early days of the Great Depression, at a time when there was a general feeling that our traditional ways were headed for a tremendous change, maybe even a permanent collapse. It is such a book as authors in those days sometimes put together, to keep from falling apart. Not knowing quite where he was, this particular author took notes on "orientation." Not being sure how to read the signs, he took notes on "interpretation." Finding himself divided, he took notes on division (or as he calls it in this book, "perspective by incongruity"). Looking for some device by which to reintegrate the muddle, he asked about the possibility of a "resimplification" that would not be an over-simplification. (xlvii)

The personal anxieties Burke evokes about disorientation, division, and the desire for greater simplification—for new symbols to assist in the navigation of the rapidly changing world—are emblematic of the response many people had to the bitter winds during the uncertain years in the early 1930s. The disorientation was faced in multiple ways across the gamut of American experience, largely due to the tremendous economic unrest affecting a good portion of the nation's "everyday" citizens, but also due to the (not unrelated) movement and upheaval within artistic, political, and even scientific spheres. Burke's observations about the 1930s connect us into developing ideas about art, poetics, and music in that decade's popular, intellectual, political, and vernacular cultures and will help us make sense of where and how those ideas converged around a growing interest in folklore, including folk music.

Burke himself is a bit of a folk hero in rhetorical studies, undeniably influential and perhaps (some might argue) overplayed. Such attention turns up the volume of Burke's flaws. His writing is infamously convoluted and can be difficult to untangle. He is also narcissistic, classist, and mostly unwilling to address the race problems of his day. As a proud member of a community of intellectual aesthetes, Burke generally concerned himself with so-called highbrow art. It is frustrating that despite all of his work in the 1930s exploring "simplification," there is scant mention of vernacular culture. Burke liked music, was an amateur but accomplished pianist, and even worked, for a time, as a music critic for magazines, *The Dial* (1927–1929) and *The Nation* (1934–1936). But he usually only concerns himself with classical composers and the "serious" music of the symphony. He was friends with Ralph Ellison, one of the most important African American writers of the era, yet resisted Ellison's pleas to help address problems of the racial divide.[3] Burke told Ellison that, as a white person, he found the conversation "extremely awkward" (Crable 3). Burke's telling excuse persists, as questions of how white scholars should contribute to ongoing and often tense conversations and scholarship on race continue to hang awkwardly in the air. But Burke's shortcomings are instructive in the same ways as John Lomax's. They discourage a wholesale buy-in of his ideas, but they provide instructive contours to the shape and sounds of progress. In that sense, Burke is more useful as a portal than a lodestar.

Not incidentally, Burke's work on reorientation during the 1930s was also a reorientation for rhetoric. The Depression, along with the greater interwar period that encapsulated it, marked a time when, according to rhetorical historian James A. Herrick, "scientific thinking was [. . .] ascendant, and the methods of reasoning and speaking about contingent matters that had traditionally been studied and taught under the name of rhetoric were derided as decidedly inferior to scientific method" (204). However, that logical positivist approach to civic discourse (which had earlier echoes in both Ramism and Enlightenment rhetoric) failed to prevent financial collapse, devastating war, and dangerous political extremes.[4] George Kennedy notes that the period's emergent works in rhetoric stood as "strong reactions to the circumstances of the 1930s and 1940s: economic depression, fascism, and the Second World War" (295). The novel rhetorical approaches to understanding language, culture, and history that were put forward by I. A. Richards and, in later decades, Richard Weaver and Chaïm Perelman (among others)—now often referenced as the "new rhetorics" movement—responded, in small part, to a growing intellectual suspicion of cut-and-dried empiricism as the answer to the world's social and financial problems.

Burke's work is particularly influential and enduring. The 1930s was "the decade of his most remarkable productivity" (George and Selzer xi), seeing the publication of three of his major works of criticism: *Counter Statement* (1931), *Permanence and Change* (1935), and *Attitudes toward History* (1937). These books reflect his embeddedness in the scrum of the intellectual culture of the time, his attention to issues of socialism and anti-war initiatives, and also contain the genesis of many of Burke's most important ideas about rhetoric. While all three books were culturally oriented, *Permanence and Change* was especially a work of cultural history, aimed at grappling with ways "to keep from falling apart" (133). Burke's desire toward the "possibility of a 'resimplification' that would not be an over-simplification" (xlvii) plays out in that book as a brilliant discussion about the importance of poetry and myth to public culture and politics.

Burkean Thought in the Modernist 1930s

Burke's attempts to lionize art and poetics as a response to the economic, political, and artistic problems of his time left us with a valuable rhetorical perspective of that moment and its various movements. His arguments give us a sense for the ways that poetics came to be seen as valuable and even crucial to the rebuilding of a sustainable US culture after so much loss during the Depression. Ann George and Jack Selzer characterize the years leading up to the 1930s as years of shifting values—of "modernism" as a reevaluation.

> In the final decades of the nineteenth century and particularly in the first two decades of the twentieth, modernism amounted to a dialogue on how people might appropriately respond to the civic and artistic stresses created when various nineteenth-century certitudes about nature and human nature eroded or collapsed. (4)

The endemic certainties they reference were the residuum of post-Emersonian confidence in a God-animated nature, Victorian ideals supporting a "stable, hierarchical civilization," and "nineteenth-century absolutes about law, morality, conduct, and the workings of nature," certitudes beginning to decay under the influence of Darwinian, Kantian, and post-Newtonian ideas about mortality, morality, and science (5). Modernist ideals emerged as a represented desire to disassociate with genteel society and to imagine "radically novel, radically shifting," and "relentlessly experimental" alternatives. It follows, as George and Selzer maintain, that modernist ideology during the interwar period was plural by nature, and those modernisms were often in productive competition (7).

Publications such as *The Masses* (later *New Masses*), *The New Republic*, *The Dial*, *Broom*, *The Smart Set*, *Aesthete*, and *Contact* functioned as both a modernist arcade and as political soapboxes where the various modernisms were articulated both as artistic innovation and as staunch ideological rules of cultural engagement and production. Those journals published the poetry of T. S. Elliot, William Carlos Williams, and Langston Hughes, the fiction of expat authors Gertrude Stein and Ernest Hemmingway, and the criticism of Malcolm Cowley and Kenneth Burke (as well as dozens, if not hundreds, of others)—many of whom "felt they could encourage a new and indigenous American culture that would combine radical politics with artistic experiment" (George and Selzer 34).

Interest in a "new and indigenous American culture" was in the air even before the Depression hit. For example, in 1918, literary critic Van Wyck Brooks published the essay "On Creating a Usable Past" in *The Dial*. In that enduring and prescient critique of US art culture at the beginning of the 20th century, Brooks regarded contemporary American art as flat and lacking rhetorical impact, because it was based on the remote and fading value infrastructure of European models and ideals. "The present is a void," he argued, "and the American writer floats in that void because the past that survives in the common mind of the present is a past without living value." The "common mind" needed to be revitalized, imbued with new traditions and new pasts. "If we need another past so badly," he continued, "is it inconceivable that we might discover one, that we might even invent one?" (339). In broad strokes, American modernism at the beginning of the 20th century was exactly such a response: a search for new values and alternative commonplaces, as well as the fashioning of "new," usable pasts that might inspire a more robust and resilient social infrastructure.

The Depression began with a stock market "crash" that also sounded the tumble of key failures within ideological systems propped up to support those advances. Burke remembered the 1930s and the administration of Franklin D. Roosevelt as "a time when, on every side, there was the feeling that, for better or worse, an earlier way of life had come abruptly to an end" (*Permanence* lvi). That feeling of loss was reflected in anxieties about new, less-familiar ways of life, which now included often dissonant realities formed in the wake of industrialization, mass culture, and other trends made prominent through rapid technological advance.

Within that context, Brooks's call to historical invention was unique in its recognition of the tie connecting artistic innovation, mythopoetic historiography, and what I have been calling "folkness." Like Brooks, Burke took seriously the call of the artist as a composer of shared social symbols. He brought his resolve to the First American Writers Congress, held in New York City by the League of American Writers on April 26–28, 1935. Burke was invited to speak at the gathering, and my brief recounting of that episode here is intended not necessarily to extol his position (a call to a particular communist orientation) but to examine his methods.

The league boasted membership from a wide variety of well-known authors, scholars, and critics—intellectuals interested in exploring the role and responsibility of the artist to society, including "the function of art, especially during times of political and social crisis" (George and Selzer 60). Burke's address, titled "Revolutionary Symbolism in America," was crafted in response to the official call that appeared in *New Masses* on January 22, 1935. The congress was formed to bring together those in "clear sympathy to the revolutionary cause [. . .] who do not need to be convinced of the decay of capitalism, of the inevitability of revolution" (Hicks 20). But while the Marxist ideals implied in that call were promoted religiously by such "revolutionaries," Burke found "Marx's account of economic determinism to be neither realistic nor logically compelling" (George and Selzer 75). Instead, Burke saw the Marxist ideals as "symbols" that helped to make up the larger myth surrounding the developing movement, with potential to inspire new possibilities. The Marxist mythos was a usable past. "'Myths,'" he argued during his controversial speech, "may be wrong, or they may be used to bad ends—but they cannot be dispensed with . . . they are our basic psychological tools for working together" (Burke, "Revolutionary Symbolism" 267).

Among those myths, Burke names "race, godhead, nationality, class, lodge, guild"—each of which make "various ranges and kinds of social cooperation possible" (267–268). Echoing Brooks, Burke describes the rhetorical half-life of such myths: "A symbol [. . .] loses its vitality when the kinds of cooperation it promotes—and with which its destiny is united—have ceased to be serviceable" (268). As an example, Burke suggests a revision to the poetic/political methods of his colleagues who had taken up the Marxist symbology of "the worker" to forward their work toward a new American order. Instead, Burke suggests "the people" as an organizing symbol, arguing that the symbology of "the worker" did not resonate with their audience, most of whom were likely not familiar with communist discourse as it had developed within its European and then Soviet contexts. "I am suggesting fundamentally," he argued, "that one cannot extend the doctrine of revolutionary thought among the lower middle-class without using middle-class values" (269).

Burke's argument is persuasive. The construct of "the people" evokes an experience that has "living value" to Americans who were christened as such by their founding document, the Constitution of the United States ("We the People . . ."). Fascinating about Burke's move is the way that he invents a past where the Constitution might implicitly suggest communism as a viable American ideology. Burke understood well the mythic power of poetic symbols, saying that "a poet does not sufficiently glorify his political cause by pictures of suffering and revolt. Rather, a poet makes his soundest contributions in this wise: he shows himself alive to all the aspects of contemporary effort and thought" (270). His words would cause a bit of a stir at the congress and may be taken as controversial today. As Benedict Giamo observes, however, "By taking up the topic of symbolism, Burke signaled to the audience the importance of communication and rhetoric in broadening the appeal of communism among the American public" (para. 19). In other words, using the poetic and rhythmic power of "the people" as a recognizable and therefore usable past, Burke made communism into a palatable alternative American ideology.

The way Burke's 1935 speech broadened communism's national appeal through the identification of common symbols was an echo of a theory Burke had already begun articulating in *Permanence and Change*, which was published just before the New York congress. In that book, Burke "recommended a 'poetic' orientation as a gentle leaven to the hardcore Marxist interpretive slant" (George and Selzer 22). He saw the myth and symbol-making inherent to poetics as "creating a dynamic superstructure with the potential to transform society both culturally and economically" (89), one where a "better life" could be imagined and articulated symbolically and aesthetically by the writer, gleaned metaphorically by the reader, and then promoted and adhered to as an ideal by an identifying audience. That move from the symbolic language of poetics to the symbolic action of social value agreement is an important part of why Burke saw discursive poetics as "equipment for living," providing an artful rendering of moralistic structures, "various strategies for the encompassing of situations"—that is, situational rules for life (*Philosophy* 1). The central argument in *Permanence and Change* revolves around Burke's perception of the tension between varying systems of morality and how the best ones construct and motivate an orientation toward a "good life" with the widest potential human benefit. Burke believed that a poetic "terminology of motives" is best for finding such a good life (29).

The Sonification of Perspective by Incongruity

In his hyperfocus on literature, Burke never makes the connection between his call for a revaluation of mythic rhetorics and the growing interest in folk culture in the 1930s. Even so, in his own unique way, Burke describes folkness. In his theorizing about the utility of moralistic rhetorics, Burke identified another branch on the tree of epideictic rhetoric. Further, in describing the ways that myths effect possible futures, Burke cues us to the ways that poetics have a powerful, even dangerous potential as a historiographic tool. "Morals are fists," Burke argues late in *Permanence and Change* (243). They motivate and punctuate both good and poor behavior. When the motives behind morals are understood, we can know "*why* people do as they do" and can therefore "know *what* to expect of them and of ourselves," which can then "shape our decisions and judgments and policies" (18). The reverse is also true. When a reliable rhetoric of morals is in place—when we understand the ways that morality is composed—motives become more predictable and can be written back into history for current needs (e.g., "We the People" as a communistic idea). Given his various literary and political preoccupations during the 1930s, Burke's missing of the growing folk movement is an understandable (if disappointing) oversight. His understanding of poetic discourse's potential to forge new histories and, in turn, a new present is still instructive for understanding why folk music would be of interest to a society whose other myths had begun to fail them.

Managing failing myths is the final thread in this Burkean interlude. Burke understood history as having moved through three successive rationalization constructs: magical, religious, and scientific. As an ontological response and challenge to mystery in the human world, each rationalization works as a means of knowledge production and management within its system. Magic and positivistic science based their rationalization on the assumptions that "nature operates through immutable laws" (59) and that those laws can be manipulated by savvy practitioners. Religion is a kind of nonrational logic most useful for understanding and dealing with realities out of human control or on the outside of human understanding. Religious mysticism provides a space wherein paradox—a construct not generally legible within magical or scientific rationalizations—can be managed not only successfully but with significant meaning (and for good or ill).

The distinctions between the magical, religious, and scientific are important for Burke and for us insofar as the ontological systems of rationalization produce a viable ethics—an epideictic scheme of values—for both understanding and critiquing the human motives produced within those systems. Burke is most interested in promoting an ethics that responds to the deep complexity of human motivation, one that is at home with the nonrational elements of religious rationalization but that would provide a vocabulary for developing systems of meaning despite and even through those complexities—a "secular mysticism" (*Permanence* 113). For Burke, the poetic or dramatic metaphor becomes the

> ultimate metaphor for discussing the universe and man's relations to it [. . .] In adopting such metaphor as key, we have a vocabulary of motives already at hand, evolved through the whole history of human thought. Indeed, beginning with such a word as *composition* to designate the architectonic nature of either a poem, a social construct, or a method of practical action, we can take over the whole vocabulary of tropes (as formulated by the rhetoricians) to describe the specific patterns of human behavior. (263–264)

Burke then shows that onomatopoeia, synecdoche, and other rhetorical tropes are themselves methods for representing common human actions and their motives symbolically through language.

For the lost access to the nonrational that religion had provided, Burke's poetic/dramatic dichotomy offers a viable substitution, along with a respite for those in existential/spiritual meltdown. Beyond poetic discourse's ability to represent human emotional complexity, Burke is interested in its symbolic potentials for discovering "new meanings," particularly during crisis, as "the crumbling and conflict of values" (*Permanence* 116) leads to the "breaking down [of] old schemes of orientation" (111) and the need to build new ones. The method he provides for that action is the nurturing of the pseudo-prophetic capacity to "see around the edges of orientation in which a poet or thinker lives" (117). That sight, which he calls "perspective by incongruity," is a nonrational ability to synthesize the conflicts of traditional and progressive ways of thinking and being and to make something generative or even beautiful from the inherent paradoxes and conflicts. Burke maintains that when economic, scientific, and other "accepted terms of authority" have "fallen into disrepute," people "seek in the cosmos or in the catacombs some undeniable body of criteria. They try to salvage whatever values, still intact, may serve as the basis of new exhortations and judgments" (173).

In 1930s America, the humanistic values of ordinary (and often rural) American people sprang to the forefront of the popular imaginary as a place to find renewed or persistent values, and much of that information came in sonic packages. As long-held faith began to give way to skepticism in supernatural benevolence and communication, people were introduced to the technological miracle of other voices singing out through a phonograph speaker or on the airwaves of the radio. Those new voices from the heavens did not promise novel means for prosperity or salvation but, instead, sang of injury, heartache, and also mischief, mayhem, and civil disobedience. For a people in crisis, those vocalizations were sounds of relief.

The present study is an effort to embrace and resound that "perspective by incongruity" in order to demonstrate what sonic archives have to teach us about the rhetorics of history and history-making practices, especially when the subjects come from marginalized populations. Such a resolve pushes this project in several directions at once and through somewhat tangled and dense historical layers. But in this resounding, I hope to emphasize and not shy away from that polyphony, in order to hear, for example, John Lomax's innovations and limitations resonating in the mix together and alongside those of Lead Belly or James Baker, African Americans with equally compelling and complex insights to share.

Chapter 1 advances a methodological approach to the problem of responding to a magnificent archive assembled by flawed agents. It begins with a key and particularly didactic episode from the Lomax archive, one that exemplifies the polyphonic perspective I have been advocating and that brings together the broader themes of the book: rhetoric, folkness, race, and history-making. I relate the story of how Huddie "Lead Belly" Ledbetter sang his way out of prison a second time. The details are a bit convoluted, but the mythology that emerged around the song in question, "Governor Pat Neff," shows how intimate the relationship between folklore, history, and rhetoric can be. That story leads to a discussion of the utility and tyranny of "true" or official histories, particularly as they contribute to the misrepresentation or underrepresentation of people and communities of color. I then outline the historiographic theories and methods that inform my larger work, some contemporary and others that I glean from the 1930s-era modernist milieu within which the Lomax archive was produced.

CHAPTER 1

Sonic Rhetorical Historiography

Reorienting Authenticity during the Interwar Period

> It was as if the American people, just as they were poised to execute more social and political and economic innovation than ever before in their history, felt the need to take a long and affectionate look at their past before they bade much of it farewell, a need to inventory who they were and how they lived, to benchmark their country and their culture so as to measure the distance traveled into the future that Franklin Roosevelt was promising.
>
> —David M. Kennedy, *Freedom from Fear* 256–257

> What do we hear when America sings? What sounds from the disembodied voice of a nation so traumatized and confused by its own racial constitution? What might the music tell us that we fail to discern in other artifacts of culture?
>
> —Richard Radano, *Lying Up a Nation* 2

Lead Belly and Lomax: History-Making and the Folkness of Forgetting

♫ LEAD BELLY: Oh!
Oh Mary, sweet Mary
Yes, miss Mary, Oh Mary
Nineteen hundred and twenty-three,
When the judge took my liberty away from me
Nineteen hundred and twenty-three,
When the judge took my liberty away from me
I left my wife wringin' her hands and cryin', sayin'
"Lord have mercy on that man of mine"

I left my wife wringin' her hands and cryin', sayin'
"Lord have mercy on that man of mine"
Told my wife before I left the land,
if I never no more see her, do the best she can
I told my wife before I left the land,
if I never no more see her, do the best she can
Goodbye, Mary, sweet Mary
Oh Mary, ooh ooh
I know my wife would jump and shout
when the train rolls up, I come a-stepping out
I know my wife would jump and shout
when the train rolls up, I come a-stepping out
Say, "What you gonna say?" Oh, hello Mary! Sweet Mary
Oh, Mary, ooh ooh
Had you, Governor Neff, like you got me,
I'd wake up in the mornin', I'd set you free
If I had you, Governor Neff, like you got me,
I'd wake up in the mornin', I would set you free
If I had you, Governor Neff, like you got me,
I'd a-wake up in the mornin', I would set you free
"Where you going?"
I'm goin' back to Mary, ooh ooh
Oh Mary, ooh ooh

In January 1935, *Time* magazine's music section offered a story titled "Murderous Minstrel." Juxtaposed conspicuously alongside a more typical-to-form article about famed composer Igor Stravinsky, "Murderous Minstrel" was accompanied by several verses from the song "Governor Pat Neff" and by a photograph of a middle-aged African American man, wearing worn overalls and strumming a patched 12-string guitar. The article begins in a racially charged and sensationalized vernacular common to the day: "In Texas a black buck known as Lead Belly murdered a man" (50). That crude and racist statement referred to a 1918 incident that led to Lead Belly's imprisonment in the penitentiary in Sugar Land, Texas. The story continues, recounting a simplified version of the circumstances that led to his release in 1925 and return to prison by 1930.

> [Lead Belly] sang a petition to Governor Pat Neff and was granted a pardon. Back in the Louisiana swamplands, where he was born

> Huddie Ledbetter, his knife made more trouble. He was in State Prison at Angola when John A. Lomax, eminent ballad collector, stopped by last summer and asked the warden if he could please hear Lead Belly sing.
>
> John Lomax arrived in Manhattan last week to lecture on ballads and with him was Lead Belly, wild-eyed as ever. The Negro had been pardoned again because Mr. Lomax had made a phonograph record of a second petition and taken it to Louisiana's Governor Allen. (50)

That account and many other reports of Lead Belly's second pardoning—a compelling but disputed detail related to the circumstances surrounding his release from Angola prison—is part of a fascinating historical problem that, as biographers of both Lead Belly and Lomax have acknowledged in different ways, remains "a central element of Lomax-Leadbelly lore" (Porterfield 331).[1] John Lomax writes about the event in he and Alan's published compilation *Negro Folk Songs as Sung by Lead Belly* (1936): "I met [Governor Allen's] secretary, who took the aluminum record and promised to play it for his chief. On August 1, thirty days afterward, Lead Belly was across the Mississippi River and headed for Shreveport. In a paper bag he carried a carefully folded document. Governor Allen's pardon had come" (33). What was actually on the paper Lead Belly carried has become the subject of a historical dispute, as a second pardoning likely never occurred.[2] The most compelling evidence against it is a 1939 written response from Angola warden L. A. Jones to New York's probation department, the latter of which had requested information about Lead Belly's release.

> This man has been the recipient of wide publicity in various magazines of national circulation, the story usually being that he sang or wrote such moving appeals to the Governor that he was pardoned. Such statements have no foundation in fact. He received no clemency, and his discharge was a routine matter under the good time law which applies to all first and second offenders. (Wolfe and Lornell 120)

Untangling the timeline of what was and was not known about the alleged pardon (and by whom) has not been easy. In October 1934, several months before the *Time* article's publication, Lomax appears to have believed that his trip to Baton Rouge with Lead Belly's recorded request to the governor was successful. In a handwritten letter to Oliver Strunk, Lomax's supervisor and the head of the music division at the Library of Congress, John reported on his recent experiences with Lead Belly:

> My driver and assistant [. . .] is a Negro ex-convict, Leadbelly by name, who two months [ago] sang a petition for pardon on a record, addressed to Governor O.K. Allen. I carried the record back to Baton Rouge a hundred miles away. The Governor listened to it and then pardoned Leadbelly. He came on to Texas and attached himself to me. He says that I will never again have to tie my shoes if I "don't want to." When I come to Washington in January I'll bring him along and give you and Mrs. Strunk a specimen of Negro music as interpreted by a real Negro. (Lomax to Strunk, October 1, 1934)

Lomax's report compresses the time between events and glosses the circumstances related to the supposed pardoning. For example (as Lomax wrote in the above recollection), when Lomax arrived in Baton Rouge, the governor was in a meeting, and the phonograph disc was left with the governor's secretary, causing Porterfield to conclude, "There is no evidence that 'musical Governor Allen' ever actually heard it" (331). If we take the other parts of the letter at face value (which, of course, we cannot), it is possible that Lomax thought Lead Belly had been pardoned because Lead Belly had told him so. The origins of the mythic second pardon may have come from Lead Belly jumping to conclusions about the circumstances of his release, believing that John Lomax had something to do with it. Or Lead Belly may have simply understood the utility of attaching himself to Lomax (a man of influence and position who had shown a genuine interest in the convict) and made a compelling plea to Lomax for employment.

We will never really know. The specific details were lost in the shuffle of contradictory accounts and foggy memories or possibly left out intentionally by one party or another. The murky historical circumstances rehearsed above, pieced together using several primary sources and the best attempts of those intent on understanding them, reveal three rhetorical contours of the historiographical process. First, we are reminded that the writing of history (and therefore "history" itself) is messy and distributed rather than linear, logical, or completable. Second, we get a sense for the flexibility and fluidity of history. Third, forgetting here surfaces, again, as an inevitability and even a necessity within the historical process. For Lead Belly and Lomax, the presentation of a folk history, one shot through with some useful uncertainties, was crafted for their mutual benefit and was also the best mode for presenting their story to the American public.

That story is history, and recorded history is always, to one extent or another, lore. Histories are composed to abstract, codify, and give circulation and rhetorical force to the otherwise confounding nature of the past's multiplicity and opacity. There is no such thing as "true" history in a strict, objective sense. Professional historians are not ignorant of this fact, and it would be unfair to suggest that they are not concerned with preparing careful renderings in which past events, people, places, and circumstances are represented with as much empirical veracity as possible. My claim regarding history's subjectivity is merely meant as a reminder that the realities of representing the past are always met with constraining exigencies—some ideological, others disciplinary, and still others pragmatic. Those infinite historical contingencies remind us that if a well-composed history provides any certainty about the past, that accomplishment is the triumph of the rhetorical skill of historians as much as of their ability to manage and present documentary evidence.

With that caveat in mind, we can more easily accept folklore as a viable historical mode or, at least, as doing important historical work. The important difference between professional or academic history and folk history is that the latter is more up-front about its subjectivities. Rather than focusing on relating accurate historicity, folklore's various modes—folksongs or folktales, for example—distill or even invent the past and imbue it with poetry, synecdoche, metaphor, and a host of other rhetorics. Those rhetorics are indicative of the value and virtue inherent to a particular historical epoch. In this way, folklore can contain truths about the past without being a "true" or even accurate representation of it. Folklore is history without the righteousness of certainty. Or, more precisely, folklore is a history of ideals and ideas rather than of exact events.

Rendering it from that direction, we might understand folklore as history for the present, lived moment. Folklore is our most enduring genre of epideictic rhetoric. Historical folkness is the history we hold in our minds during everyday life—our sense of the past's contribution to current "reality." This reality or nowness is concerned less with details than with symbols—stand-in notions or general renderings of how "the way things were" contributes to the present moment. With the more open understanding that history works as an always-in-progress composition, it is easier to accept that John Lomax most likely did not help get Lead Belly out of jail with a carefully placed phonograph, though Lomax may have thought he did for a time. Either way, the pardon story utilized the power of Lead Belly's song "Governor Pat Neff" as a sonic rhetoric in a new set of historical circumstances and as a kind of sequel to previous events, but with a different governor. Lead Belly's and Lomax's retellings of the events surrounding the second pardoning were crafted to have utility beyond (or even because of) the contradictions and messiness of discoverable "facts." They present a folkloric rendering of the past as a "history" in service to their shared rhetorical goals.

That artful, practical rendering of lived experience into a circulating dynamic narrative is an example of history infused with folkness. It is not objective history but, rather, a historic turn—a logical possibility offered as "what happened," rendered through the rhetoric of folklore and activated through the strategic use of folksong. For better and worse, history is bound up in such turnings. The historicity of Lead Belly's second pardoning is thus both false and true. Historical turning like I am describing broadens the bandwidth of historiography (making it more than just a pursuit of empirical facts) and allows productive paradox and unknowing into historiographical methodology. I relate the episode involving Lead Belly and Lomax as an example of history rendered through a sonic rhetorical historiographic methodology. The paradoxes that surround that particular moment and the folksong at the center of it show sonic rhetoric's historical possibilities. Those paradoxes are key moments of rhetorical invention, both for the subjects involved and for rhetorical historians interested in sound's potential as a historical tool.

Toward a Sonic Rhetorical Historiographic Methodology

This book explores broadening the historical bandwidth through turning to folkness. The goal of this chapter is to explicate a methodology for ratifying that practice. Such a methodology has a number of possible uses. It gives us ears to recognize practical in-the-moment applications of sound as history (e.g., those used by Lead Belly and Lomax) and also might be organized as a set of critical tools for understanding and articulating complex or contradictory realities that are historically contingent. Sonic rhetorical historiography accounts for those results, as well as any number of others, in the octaves between practical art and critical tool. Unpacking the term *sonic rhetorical historiography* provides a more general framework for the methodology.

The term *historiography* names the historian's art, which includes the employment of a diverse body of disciplinary methods and the practical work of research using archives and primary/secondary evidence in the service of producing a historical text.[3] Historiography can be accurately (if not commonly) thought of as the rhetoric—that is, the artful composition—of history. The term *rhetorical historiography* generally describes the art of composing rhetorical history, which has its own methods but similar ends. Rhetorical historiography adds a particular emphasis (rhetoric) to the same practices (archives, evidence, composition). Its focus—whether on mapping "the history of rhetoric" (a common disciplinary interest) or on rhetorics as crucial components within history—is the prerogative of the researcher.[4] (While there is a nod to the history of rhetoric in this book's introduction, this project is more centered on rhetorics in and of history.)

A sonic rhetorical historiography operates within those parameters. It takes as its subject matter sonic rhetorics and how they are or might be used to compose histories, including the ways that sound has been used as rhetoric in history. Emphasizing sound should include a shift from visual to sonic objects as the primary or, at least, the favored means of historiographical evidence. Such a shift offers a different wavelength (both literally and figuratively) for doing historiography, one that leans hard into the contingencies that sound invites us to acknowledge. Given sound's capacity for polyphony and multivalence, a sonic rhetorical historiography might most effectively be used as a methodology for revising—or resounding—history to better acknowledge people, events, and places marginalized by traditional methods of composing history. It may have its greatest potential when infused within the feminist, queer, disability, and/or BIPOC (Black, indigenous, and people of color) rhetorical historiography already in circulation in the field.

The project of revising historiographical methodologies in rhetorical studies toward greater inclusivity has been in progress for at least three decades.[5] That work has sought to shift the conversations and practices of and about what "counts" in history, toward marginalized communities, rhetorics, and rhetors. Some of the new methodologies draw on the roots of established rhetorical theory but then recast those theories head over heels, engaging their radical implications to help build something new.[6] Others approach rhetoric through developments in adjacent fields—from the sciences, to gender and sexuality studies, to (in my case) music and sound. When the stakes of rhetorical history change—when we begin to acknowledge the ways that privileging certain history-making processes over others shapes current lived realities—the work of historiography takes on a dramatically different importance. An outpouring of new historiographic possibilities have emerged, putting new methodologies of composing and understanding rhetorical history alongside completely revised and resounded historical epistemologies and ontologies.[7]

However, even in our attempts to recover, remember, and memorialize, new forgettings always emerge. Thus our attempts require ongoing theorizing, including retheorizing through the production of what Michelle Ballif calls an "excluded third methodology" (4). Rhetorical historiographic methodologies that account for the "excluded third" in society not only encourage the ongoing search for "other" rhetorics but also reorient how we think and write about history itself. New methods that are adopted should push us beyond the remembered/forgotten dichotomy and toward the composition of histories that account for otherness and forgetting on their own terms and thus as a crucial part of (and with particular rhetorics suited for) history.

Listening to the Lomax Archive finds its exigence in that movement. History, it turns out, is not what we often think it is. History is not the past reassembled through the pursuit of clear and discoverable empirical evidences or a carefully lit stage of coherent, logical events. We might do better to imagine our histories as plural, overlapping, and contradictory, like a hall of echoes—reverberant, cacophonous, and at times overwhelming and enveloping. History is an ocean instead of a stream. One way of responding to Ballif's call is to theorize new rhetorical historiographical methodologies that better reflect/resound history's contingencies rather than righteously forwarding its certainties.

A sonic rhetorical historiography is resonant within that movement. As a broad methodology, it should bring a concern of the "excluded third" out from the margins and into the forefront of the stage. In that sense, it is corrective. It should push back against history's tyrannies and provide new space and novel ways to both create and think about history. Beyond that guiding thematic, such a framework may include some variation of the following elements: (1) a historical epoch to interrogate, (2) a viable sonic archive of material from or relating to that epoch, (3) a historical problem or issue that a sonic rhetorical approach helps to parse, and (4) an ethic of careful listening. The use of this or another methodological framework might be formal or not. This chapter, for example, purports to offer a sonic rhetorical historiographic methodology, but it is not quite a formal "methodology chapter." Instead, I have been building the scaffolding of my methodology all along, and that work will continue beyond the confines of this chapter.

Similarly, rhetorical historians might emphasize some of the above historiographical methods more or less than others or add unique elements of their own. In fact, beyond my general list, I have several other methods at play here. For example, where possible, I utilize sound-related vocabulary to set a tone in this book, in hopes that it will prompt readers to think differently from (or at least notice) the typical visualist epistemological paradigms that prevail in the English language. Additionally, I feel it is important to recognize and account for the methodological trajectories currently at play within the broader discipline of sound studies and how sonic rhetorics might reverberate within or against them. As I stated earlier, I also think that not only contemporary theories but the theoretical and rhetorical ideas circulating within a historical context are useful historiographic tools and often facilitate the connections between sound, history, and rhetoric that are of most interest to me. The following sections continue in that vein, with a short discussion of contemporary theoretical trends in sound studies, followed by sections that examine 1930s-era authenticity, the archive, race, and listening. In and through each section, the four methodological elements named above come into play, though most often as part of a chorus rather than as distinct solos. My hope is that such an approach brings into the scholarship an echo of the materiality and phenomenology of sound itself.

Sonic Materiality versus Sonic Phenomenology

In the chapters that follow, African American folk music from the Lomax archive is the primary subject of analysis. Throughout my study of recordings of prison work songs, jazz piano performance, and the sounds of such music on the radio, I am interested not only in Black music's rhetorical impact within its historical context but also in the ways that we might fashion new histories in and through the sonic rhetorics of that music. Thus far in this study, I have been working to lay a foundation for how the consideration of folk culture and folk music might be useful in complicating received histories. But more work is needed to prepare for a careful listen to the Lomax archive.

As before, I feel some responsibility to orient this work within the grooves of already spinning records and traditions. Sound studies methodology generally positions critical sonic work as being from either a phenomenological/psychoanalytic or a Marxist/material genealogy. Gunn et al. describe a tension between "those who examine mental or psychical sonic experiences ('interiors')" and "those who are interested in sound's historical and material contexts ('exteriors')." As Greg Goodale writes in *Sonic Persuasion* (2011), materialist writers (among them not only Marx but also Adorno and Attali) "provided a way of thinking about music as a product and how that product's manufacture, sale, and consumption produce or reflect alienation, the division of labor, false consciousness, and so on." "Phenomenological and psychoanalytical studies," he continues, "tend to focus on the voice, though these occasionally move into music" (144). Further, such work "emphasizes epistemologies and heuristics, or, in other words, how we know and how we resolve problems" (144–145). To sum up, under the materialist orientation, scholars work to understand sound and music's contribution to lived reality and to ontological questions of being. Phenomenological sound studies deal more with questions of knowing (epistemology), experience, and identity and have traditionally privileged the voice and speech.

"The best work on sound has consistently been written from the Marxist tradition," Goodale argues, and he surveys persuasive evidence in his book (144). Jonathan Sterne's work falls within that group, but Sterne also has axes to grind. In his monograph *The Audible Past* (2003), he works to establish a hierarchy (or invert a previous one) between the material and the phenomenological, one that moves "the speaking subject away from the center of sound theory" in order to disrupt the "philosophical privilege of dialogue" (including hearing and speech) popularized by Marshall McLuhan and Walter J. Ong during the 20th century (345).[8] "It is not the voice that orients our theories of sound," Sterne writes, explaining that "the voice is a *special case* of sound" (343). Sterne's work has thus encouraged an approach that moves from the outside in when working with sound. He and others, such as historian Emily Thompson and compositionists Jonathan Alexander and Byron Hawk, bring a materialist bent to their sound studies projects that demonstrate sound's power and affect as an object in the world, often beyond human ears. Objectifying sound in that way invites a broader sense of historical composition that decenters the human or that at least reminds us of the broader ecologies and relationships present in the world (Hawk 7).

In this project, my emphasis on history, historiography, and technology advances that materialist tradition. Listening to the African American folk music of the Lomax archive, however, is a human activity in which discussions of experience, identity, and subjectivity prevail, if not preside.

I am, therefore, reticent to pick sides. Sound creates, composes, and contributes to traditions of both being and knowing. I therefore take up a mixed-methods approach, where materiality and phenomenology intersect in both harmony and dissonance and in both the realities and the histories they compose. A sonic historiography demands the attention of both intellectual approaches, especially in a study of the mid-20th century, where external material conditions drove so many to a more careful study of interiority. A pluralist orientation invites us to think about music both as an extension of humanity and as an object that participates in and influences various ecologies and economies, both monetary and moral.

Among sound's various phenomenologies and materialities, rhythm strikes me as offering insights to both orientations within sound studies and rhetoric. Literally a continuous material striking—sometimes explicitly sounded as a "beat," sometimes inherent to a larger work in motion—rhythm also has interiorizing attributes. It organizes, temporalizes, and often even brings a sense (and presence) of genre and thus audience to a piece of music. If music is tonal, rhythm sets the tone. Rhythm exists as an organizing force beyond music as well—as predictable regularities in the natural world and cosmos, symmetry in life cycles, and theorems and algorithms that underlay complex feats of science and computing (to name just a few)—the proverbial "ways in which" ways do their whiching. In fact, rhythm may be yet another way to imagine folkness, itself another way to imagine epideictic, itself another way to imagine the deep and organizing structures that set the tone of human (and nonhuman) experience and understanding. In that sense, rhythm is much of the reason blues (to return to the example discussed in this book's introduction) can be understood as both a music and a worldview. Blues is interior and exterior. Similarly, folk music is both rhythmic and part of a larger effort to bring rhythm (regularity, predictability, and beauty) to everyday life. Folk music is both experience and infrastructure, both phenomenological and material.

In the following sections, I examine two distinct but synchronous rhythms of the interwar period, authenticity and race. While neither notion is inherently sonic, I will show how each, in its relationship to and proclivity toward sound, demonstrates the range, depth, and embeddedness of sonic experiential and material infrastructure within history. Interjected between those examinations is a brief trip to the archive, the American Folklife Center at the Library of Congress. A locus of power—where authenticity and race is collected, codified, and redistributed—the archive can also be a site of radical transformation. The Lomax archive is an example of both.

Depression-Era Authenticity: Resounding the Past as a Tool for the Present

The creation and maintenance of folklore is a tradition as old as any in human society. But the formal collection and cataloging of Western folklore began in Europe in the late 18th century, with the publication of several collections of old poems and songs. By the 19th century, "ballad collecting" was a popular practice in both academic and nonacademic circles, valued as an act of both artistic and historic preservation and as an opportunity to nostalgically remember an idyllic vernacular past. In the early 20th century and into the 1930s, many of those notions were still commonly held. For some, however, folklore collection began to take on a different tenor, with a shift from the "endangered relic" paradigm to one that recognized the living and vibrant utility of vernacular artifacts being produced in the present. As is implied in the phrase "folk revival," interest in vernacular traditions is often cyclical and generally emerges to meet a reoccurring necessity of renewal: the desire to find stability during or following a period of uncertainty, a search for a sense of permanence despite continued change. The renewed interest in folk music during the 1930s was part of a trend emergent during the period between World War I and II—especially in the midst of the Depression—to seek out "real" or "authentic" aspects American culture during a moment of shared crisis. As Regina Bendix asserts, "The quest for authenticity is a peculiar longing, at once modern and antimodern." "[Authenticity] is oriented," she continues, "toward the recovery of an essence whose loss has been realized only through modernity, and whose recovery is feasible only through methods and sentiments created in modernity" (8).[9]

In the 1930s, those "methods and sentiments" were tied to technological advances in the instruments of representation (including photography, audio recording, and film), as well as to a popular sentiment fascinated with representations of emotional "humanness." William Stott writes, "The adjective 'human' recurs throughout the thirties literature as a synonym for emotional, or touching, or heartfelt" (6). He cites an example of a critic who praised Virgil Thomson's score to *The River* because it borrowed folk melodies and hence was "full of the emotional content inherent in anything essentially human" (6n2). Technological advances provided a larger population immediate and accessible ways to document or experience representations of the "everyday." Stott quotes Warren Susman's essay "The Thirties": "The whole idea of documentary [was that it makes possible]—not with words alone but with sight and sound—to see, know, and feel the details of life, to feel oneself part of some other's experience" (Susman quoted in Stott 8). Authenticity might be described, then, as the complex phenomenology of identity-making that occurs through the imagined identification with the people or ideals (or both) of a mythic past. In a like manner, Charles Taylor wrote that authenticity maintains a kind of nonrational ethic of "what it means to be true and full human beings" (26). Whether that ethic circulates as part of the soul-enhancing paradigm of the "good" (according to Plato), as a road to God (according to Saint Augustine), or even as nontheistic (but romantic) assumptions of an earlier and higher moral plane, it serves the same purpose: "Our moral salvation comes from recovering authentic moral contact with ourselves" (Taylor 27).

Such formulas begin to express authenticity's potential for power, as it is evoked through the competing representations of moral humanness and individuality that translate into a workable "ethics." The development of an ethics of authenticity is epideictic in its effort to determine and enact a value scheme, or what constitutes the goods and ills within a society. Taylor rightly identifies the culture of authenticity as one engaged in rhetorics of difference. The authentic individual is "original" (wholly unique), and "otherness" therefore becomes a subject to mine within authenticity. In the 1930s, that kind of thinking led to a cultural paradigm shift where the "primitive" vernacular other (which included the racial other) held new public interest. As historian Paul McCann writes,

> [T]he market crash and subsequent Depression engendered a new cynicism toward the institutions of Anglo-American culture. Instead of being viewed as a threat to civilization, the primitive became its potential savior—the means by which a decadent West could restore its lost vibrancy. The threat was no longer primitive insurgency but the random cruelty of a whimsical marketplace and the government's inability to resolve a domestic crisis. (61)

Authenticity, then, is both powerful and problematic. At best, a search for authenticity is also the review and scrutiny of values made vulnerable in and through crisis and is, as such, a process of revaluation. At worst, however, it is a search for a dichotomous "self" and "other," motivated by an impulse for cultural gatekeeping and executed through the moral (and racial) self-aggrandizement of essentializing difference.

Like other folklorists of the interwar period, John and Alan Lomax were not innocent of those kinds of reduction, though their perspectives grew more nuanced over time. In particular, the Lomaxes came to understand folklore in general and vernacular music in particular less as endangered relics and more as substances with living and vibrant utility, which elevated their status from artifacts to rhetorics. Along with other New Deal folklorist/scholars, the Lomaxes promoted what historian Benjamin Filene summarizes as "new ideas about what constituted authentic folklore, how to preserve it, and what role it should play in contemporary society" (137). Those ideas posited a functionalist view of the authentic, rejecting the popular notion that modern(ist) society had evolved beyond the need to use "primitive" mythopoetic cultural constructs to define itself.

Kenneth Burke's modernist notions of "substance" and "consubstantiality" are useful here in parsing the ways that authenticity might be rendered more ambiguously, beyond its idyllic or essentializing capabilities. Those ideas, in development in the 1930s and published in 1945, forward "substance" as that which "stands beneath or supports the person or thing" (Burke, *Grammar* 22). Substance is the complex arithmetic between personal and cultural identity: one's "roots." In comparison, "consubstantiality" is the identification between two or more substances with intent to create mutual understanding, an "act of unification" (188). Those ideas and ideals that were at the heart of rhetoric for Burke also reverberate through the work of the Lomaxes. At their best, John and Alan Lomax sought out the substance of America through the collection of folksongs in order to promote national consubstantiality or a more democratically rich understanding of US national identity. In their less-than-best moments, they fell into a common trap, confusing "substance" with an essentialized "primitive" other, which limited who they would consider as subjects appropriate to be recorded for the archive.

Listening in the Lomax Archive

Even so, the vast and remarkable Lomax archive easily outstrips the limitations of its curators' methods. The Library of Congress reports, "The entire body of Lomax material at the American Folklife Center encompasses more than 100 collections and includes 700 linear feet of manuscripts, 10,000 sound recordings, 6000 graphic images, and 6000 moving images" ("Lomax Family at the American Folklife Center").[10] There is material in the collection to sustain any number of robust and diverse research projects almost indefinitely. The AFC was created in 1976 and is housed in the Library of Congress's iconic Jefferson Building, in a room around the corner from the building's grandiose Great Hall. In contrast to the Great Hall, the AFC has the vibe of a community library, with large tables, a few listening stations, and three or four rows of stacks. A hammer signed by Pete Seeger hangs in a case on one wall, and an old guitar belonging to folksinger Burl Ives sits unlabeled on a shelf. Given the austerity of the AFC's reading room, it is hard to believe that it houses over six million items, of which the Lomax material represents but a fraction.

The Lomax Family Collections are curated by Todd Harvey and managed meticulously by him and other members of the AFC's staff. With their assistance, during visits to Capitol Hill, I worked with two types of Lomax archival materials. First, I sifted through hundreds of documents from its 700 linear feet of manuscripts. The documents consisted of correspondence, newspaper clippings, concert programs, and other textual and visual ephemera, most of which was produced by, about, or for John and Alan Lomax. Second, I listened. Opportunities to listen to the Lomax archive abound, in a variety of formats. Many of the vinyl records and compact discs made from Lomax recordings and released by Folkways Records (later Smithsonian Folkways) are at hand. Patrons like myself are more likely to come in to listen to content that has not seen formal release, and I listened to hours of such recordings on reel-to-reel tape machines and on CDs that contain digital transfers of content from the original acetate discs.

The contrast between my visual and sonic experiences with the archive led to an obvious but essential observation: unlike the documents in the archive, the recordings are not about the Lomaxes. John and/or Alan made the recordings, and their voices appear on them frequently, but it is the other voices and music on the recordings that make them worthy of being stored in a national archive. Significantly, there is a conspicuous lack of a paper trail for many, if not the majority, of the people on the Lomax recordings. Whatever documentary history those individuals might have produced—letters, receipts, journals, and so on—are mostly lost. Only their sonic histories remain. Realizing that loss led me to some key questions about sonic rhetorical historiography. For example, what happens when the traditional means of historical composition are absent? What might it mean to write histories when archival sound—in this case, folksong—is the primary historiographical material? Composing this book has been a long process of tracing the contours of those questions.

A lack of visual, documentary evidence is detrimental to the traditional historiographic process. It presents various problems for event mapping, reconstructing biography, and numerous other activities typical to historical research and composition. But it also presents new opportunities for thinking about history and through historical problems. The "folks" the Lomaxes were most interested in recording lived in remote areas and often in tight-knit communities. They were often poor, and many were people of color. All those elements contributed to the subjects' presumed authenticity and, therefore, to their value to the Lomaxes and the archive. While the details a more robust paper trail would provide are absent, the historical sounds of complex social realities—community, desolation, poverty, religious belief, and race (to name just a few)—ring out.

The observations inspired by the Lomax archive provide a key methodological point for rhetorical (or any other) historiographers using sonic archives to compose histories. Using the knowledge of sound's dense and polyphonic materiality as a guide, the sonic archive provides a means for parsing complex and multivalent historical experiences (e.g., the social realities listed above) that traditional historiographical means might not. Learning to listen to history in that multivalent key is one of the critical tools crucial to that process. While vernacular music is only one type of sonic material that might be found in the archive, it offers an ideal place to practice such listening. Folksongs communicate complex sociohistorical experiences and values in a seemingly simple package, heightening the historiographical multitonality. Regardless of the sonic historical object, however, the sonic archive offers the means for hearing and then writing dissonance into histories that more accurately represent the various contradictions of everyday experience.

The Sound of Race and/as Authenticity

Few areas promise to benefit more from the kind of productive and purposeful complication offered by a sonic archive than the study of race in the United States. Race is a mythic, multivalent historical experience, capable of inspiring both expansive and reductive ideas and ideals. Like vernacular music, with its repeating rhythms and themes vibrating along the complex root system of "tradition," race has a folkness of its own. Further, race is utterly fabricated—composed, during its genesis, to uphold the profitability of colonial invasion and trade. As W. E. B. Du Bois writes,

> The economic foundation of the modern world was based on the recognition and preservation of so-called racial distinctions. In

> accordance with this, not only Negro slavery could be justified, but the Asiatic coolie profitably used and the labor classes in white countries kept in their places by low wage. (52)

Race is a historical fabrication with dubious beginnings, but that fabric—sometimes shoddy, sometimes exquisite—is now part of a vast collection of cultural, rhetorical, and historical tapestries. In the United States, race is a persistent orthodoxy, a folktale we all contribute to and maintain, whether consciously or unconsciously.

As I have been describing, one of the many ways that US culture was shifting in the 1930s was in the development of novel or revised conceptions of race and racial history, with new fabrications and new rhythms including changing notions of both Blackness and whiteness as identity markers. Those conceptual developments were particularly audible around a growing (if often misguided) effort to know and experience the "real" or authentic histories of ordinary people, including people of color. One can hear that pining for vernacular culture in the words of John Lomax as he expresses his desire to find, through Lead Belly, a "specimen of Negro music as interpreted by a *real* Negro" (Lomax to Strunk, October 1, 1934). That notion of realness—of African American life truthfully or authentically presented—is a problematic venture. But the effort was indicative of an initiative, in the Progressive Era, to recompose America and, by extension, American ideals, after earlier ideologies so utterly failed to produce sustainable economies and culture. That initiative included a revaluation and reconstitution of authentic Blackness. In the face of so much disruption and despair, authenticity was fetishized with unprecedented vigor during the Great Depression. The US government's effort to locate and then record "authentic" depictions of race and racial experience for a national archive is just one evidence of that fixation.

In the 1930s, there was also a need for updated and alternative histories. North America's 300 years of slavery had produced a vastly disproportionate archive of traditionally "viable" historical artifacts (textual, material, geographical, etc.). One result of the dearth of accurate African American history was the circulation of African American identity and culture in caricature. The racist accoutrements of decades (if not centuries) of popular culture, from blackface minstrelsy's Zip Coon and Jim Crow to the persistent happy field hands and housemaids embodied by characters like Uncle Tom and Aunt Jemima, had produced a mythologized version of African American history that few questioned as veracious. Those stereotypes "were so familiar that few people had any notion that they degraded black Americans. Most people thought the caricatures were simply funny" (Lemons 102). Part of the impetus of creating an archive of "real" African American culture can be heard as a response to that ignorance. The process of correcting those problems was fraught from the beginning, but acknowledging that difficulty is not to say that the process was fruitless or did not leave its mark on the rhetorical and cultural history of the United States.[11] While the sonic archive produced as one response to that regrettable predicament was instrumental as both a repository and a tool for more progressive racial compositions, it also created new stereotypes, including new reductive and even racist histories that privileged only certain aspects of African American culture as authentic. Racism's sad tradition is to reconstitute itself in new ways and shrewd guises again and again.

The growing interest in vernacular culture in the 1930s, which can be understood as a poignant response to crisis, included both a longing for representative mythopoeia and a willingness to rethink and refashion long-held beliefs and ideas—in this case, around race and the racial imagination. New and revised notions of Black subjectivity that were being introduced at the national level through a wing of the US government (the Library of Congress) included a shift in the popular understanding of African American identity. Rapid changes and updates to sonic technology aided those ontological and epistemological shifts. Advancing and increasingly mobile technologies enabled music from remote areas to be recorded, as the quality and fidelity of recordings themselves improved dramatically with every passing year. The connection between advancing technologies, African American subjectivity, and sound is of primary interest to Alexander G. Weheliye in his book *Phonographies: Grooves in Sonic Afro-Modernity*. Weheliye writes that "the 'sound of blackness' articulated through constantly shifting sonic technologies represent a crucial signifying locus for the formation of (black) subjectivities throughout the twentieth century" (13). Weheliye recognizes music as a central element in that process:

> Music as it is transmitted through different sound technologies provides alternative spaces for the articulation of "diasporic citizenship" and offers avenues for present-day black musical artists to envision and sound their multiple sites of political and cultural membership. (15)

I agree with Weheliye's observation and add that what is true in the present was also true in the past: Black music's potential for political and cultural orientation/interaction has been a crucial rhetoric for African Americans as long as both have been present in the United States—that is, always.

The unsurprising irony is that Black music also shapes and always has shaped white political and cultural membership in the United States. Whiteness depends on Blackness to define, nurture, and propagate it, and in the United States, sound has always been a part of that process. As Jennifer Lynn Stoever writes,

> Sound both defined and performed the tightening barrier whites drew between themselves and black people, expressing the racialized power dynamics and hierarchical relationships of chattel slavery through vocal tones, musical rhythms, and expressed listening practices marked by whites as "black" and therefore of lesser value and potentially dangerous to whiteness and the power structures upholding it. Functioning as a medium, sound enabled race to be felt, experienced, and affected by white Americans as a collection of fixed sonic desires and repulsions that are taken into the body and radiate out from it. (31)

Stoever's insights press for a consideration of how sonic authenticity and "desires and repulsions" of racial difference circulated as both material good and experience/affect during the interwar period. Technology plays an important role in that equation, as sound reproduction, fidelity, and broadcasting all contributed to the reach and thus the depth of rhetorical impact that African American folk music could have during that time.

Careful Listening in the Sonic Archive

Learning to listen to the sonic archive in order to compose new histories is a lofty goal that I think we are capable of with a little guidance and rehearsal. I find it useful to frame such efforts by using metaphors for sonic experience and practice. Thus far, I have referenced "blues," "polyphony," and "rhythm," for example, as producing the kinds of sound I think we should be listening for in the sonic archive. As a metaphor for the methodology introduced in this chapter, I imagine an auditorium with a stage set for a variety of interacting instruments—with some in melodious conversation and with others, no doubt, in cacophonous competition. That metaphor holds and is transferable if we recognize, as does David Byrne in *How Music Works* (2012), that "the space . . . 'makes' the art, the music, or whatever"

(14). Byrne discusses how the music heard in various auditoriums—from symphony halls to New York's famed (but now defunct) club CBGB—is played in those spaces because that is where it sounds best. A punk band at Carnegie Hall would certainly sound, but it would be both aesthetically and musically mismatched to that space. My particular auditorium was constructed in a modernist, depressed 1930s context, guided by the ethic of Ballif's "excluded third" method of rhetorical historiography. Resounding onstage are the concepts and theories I have curated above (epideictic, mythos, folkness, poetics, authenticity, and race, among others), emphasized to give the listener of the Lomax archive tools for best understanding both the context and the content of the archive. Other sonic rhetoricians and historians will build different auditoriums and set stages with the concepts and theories that will resound best there. I have sought to construct an auditorium attuned to the rhythms (both material and phenomenological) of African American sonic traditions, and within that context, I bring one final method and metaphor to the stage, in order that we might learn to listen carefully.

Listening to the Lomax Archive is an exercise in listening to many layers of historical composition, where African American folksong became a sonic rhetoric of both progressive and reductive understandings of and reconstructions of race. The practice of careful listening that I advocate is not unlike the contemporary practice and expertise of disc jockeying, which is an act of literate, attentive listening, made material in performance through the deft curation and/or layering of adjacent sounds. The listening work of the disc jockey (DJ) runs from cohesive and creative playlist creation to the professional art form of sampling, remixing, and scratching, over a rhythmic backbeat perfected within the hip-hop tradition. Referencing disc jockeying as a model for careful listening thus also roots us firmly within the African American traditions at the heart of this study. The hip-hop DJ and master of ceremonies (MC) revolutionized (again) American music and brought African American culture into the mainstream (again). As records spin on turntables, my earlier evocation of revolution continues to reverberate (turn, turn, turn).

Adam Banks argues that "the DJ provides the figure through whom African American rhetoric can be reimagined in a new century" (2–3). The DJ is "the current manifestation of the griot," and the griot is an author of folkness, being "canon builder," "time binder," "rhetor extraordinaire," "keeper of the culture," and "a master of both words and music who is a storyteller, praise singer, and historian" (3, 22–23). Griots are DJs are historians, writing with sound. Paul D. Miller (aka DJ Spooky) makes the connection explicit: "Dj-ing is writing, writing is Dj-ing. Writing is music, I cannot explain this any other way" (57). In his book *Rhythm Science* (2004), he points out the musicality and rhythm in compelling prose. Further, Miller identifies writing as a kind of sampling, "the way you pick up language from other writers and make it your own" (57).

Disc jockeying, then, is an act where listening and composition (and recomposition) are happening simultaneously, rooted in the past but created in and for the present moment. As such, disc jockeying requires *aretē*/virtuosity: the best DJs mix a practical and embodied skill with an encyclopedic understanding of music and curate the LPs in their crates to match the needs of a particular gig. Before a performance, a DJ has prepared with hours and hours of listening, and such listening builds up as a knowledge store of possible mixes and sonic combinations before the show ever starts. At the gig, DJs "drop" that "ka-knowledge" (to borrow some language from the Beastie Boys)[12] as samples—sonic material culled from their collections—in a virtuosic rhythmic performance set over a backbeat. Careful listeners need not be DJs, but they should curate a similar listening ethic. Indeed, the more practiced the listener is, the more rewarding and revolutionary the listening can be. Careful listening in the archive requires commitment to being attuned not only to the sounds, rhythms, and people on the recordings but also to the ways that those sounds reverberate and have relationship with other soundings (historical, cultural, political, etc.).

Granted, that the historical narrative of this book is far removed from the era when disc jockeying came into its own artistically is a recipe for possible methodological anachronism. Maybe imagining the Lomaxes as early DJs is a stretch, but they were certainly jockeying discs around the country. In the early 1930s, the Lomaxes' method for field recording was a "portable" 130-pound disc recorder made by the Presto Recording Corporation and carried in the back of their car. The discs used with the recorder "were coated with an acetate lacquer and had a core base, which could be made from either glass or aluminum" ("Making and Maintaining the Original Recordings"). With microphones set up and 50-pound batteries attached, recording commenced as the record revolved, turning on its plate. The Presto machines produced instantaneous records, etching grooves directly into the discs by the steel or brass needle. The Lomaxes may lack the virtuosity and style of later DJs, but their knowledge and interest in the vernacular culture they were recording was vast, and their ability to listen carefully grew with each field recording. That their recording equipment and the quality of their recordings may seem primeval to us now is an opportunity to check our presentism. The Lomaxes were on the cutting edge of what recording technology had to offer in the 1930s.

Coda

Resounding throughout this chapter has been the argument that the typical historiographic tools for understanding and writing rhetorical histories of and about race in the United States are inadequate. The methodology presented here seeks to address that disparity, offering the combination of sound, sonic archives, and careful listening as a possible remedy. That methodology represents an eclectic playlist and therefore threatens a bit of cacophony, but we need multiplicity of theory and methodology to understand the complexity of rhetoric's sonic possibilities, especially in relationship to race and racial composition. While there is an abundance of historical scholarly work attempting to make sense of race, there is much less work examining how sense makes race.

The struggle to reconcile the Lomaxes' progressive race work with their variegated racism is symbolic—or bears overtones—of the antithetical unresolvability of racial politics, including both our historical and our current embodied relationship with raceness. I return to that struggle again and again in this book, because, like the Lomaxes, we continue to be confounded by race, struggling with even devising a stable definition of racial categories. As Manning Marable, historian of US racial politics, writes,

> [T]he boundaries of "whiteness" and "blackness" have never been fixed. They have been continually rearticulated and renegotiated as the political economy of American society was transformed successively from agricultural to industrial production, and as civil society and political institutions were increasingly forced to incorporate racialized minorities as participants in democratic life. (55)

John and Alan Lomax were engaged in that renegotiation. In their struggle to advance new racial ideas and beliefs in the United States, I find a model for the possibilities and predicaments of such work. It would be a mistake to think that the Lomaxes did not learn anything as a result of their efforts. In 1981, at 66 years old, Alan Lomax looked back across nearly 50 years of work and said, "I realized that the folklorist's job was to link the people who were voiceless and who had no way to tell their story, with the big mainstream of world culture" (Lomax and Cohen 94–95). The next chapter starts in 1933, at the beginning of the journey that led to that conclusion.

CHAPTER 2

Rhetoric, Representation, and Race in the Lomax Prison Recordings

> [B]lackness indicates . . . existence without standing in the modern world system. To be black is to exist in exchange without being a party to exchange. Being black is belonging to a state organized according to its ignorance of your perspective—a state that does not, that cannot, know your mind.
>
> —Bryan Wagner, *Disturbing the Peace* 1

> The Lomaxes were in rebellion against what Zora Neale Hurston derided as "the spirituals dressed up in tuxedos": black culture dressed up for national consumption in the pretentious garb of European high cultural forms. Rather than disguising or denying the folk roots of black music, the Lomaxes sought to present to the American public the results of their wanderings: an authentic black folk figure performing authentic black music. However, what exactly constituted this authenticity was determined and defined by the Lomaxes themselves.
>
> —Hazel V. Carby, *Race Men* 102

Listen Carefully

♫ *(recording begins with pulsing static)*

JOHN LOMAX: *(spoken)* This is the Levee Camp song sung by John Gibson, Chattanooga Tennessee.

JOHN GIBSON: *(spoken)* Lord, this Levee Camp song is mighty bad to sing. But I'm going to sing this old Levee Camp song for you old boys. It's hard down here on this levee camp.

GIBSON: (*singing*) Captain, Captain [. . . ?]
And I'm trying to play bad
I'm going to take it this morning, if you make me mad
LOMAX(?): (*prompts*) must be cross
Captain, Captain, (*mutters a question*) must be cross
I see[?] they coming and it won't knock off
(*indistinct prompting*)
Rear mule crippled and my lead mule blind
I'm not gonna call off till they go stone blind
(*indistinct prompting*)
Wake up in the morning, gotta wash my face
Gotta eat my breakfast in the same old place
Oh Lord. (*tape echoes*)
I been wheeled off[?] and I worked on pain
Lord, it must be heavy for the light we main[?]
Oh Lord
(*indistinct prompting*)
Captain, Captain, don't kill our old boy
Lord it might be—
(*recording skips and cuts off*)
(*indistinct music heard before recording ends*)

When John Gibson first met John and Alan Lomax, he had just begun serving a 20-year sentence in the state penitentiary in Nashville, Tennessee. At that meeting, Gibson (also known as "Black Samson") asked the Lomaxes to help facilitate his release (J. Lomax, *Adventures* 151). Perhaps that was why, despite his reluctance, Gibson allowed himself to be recorded for the Library of Congress archive. In December 1934, a little more than a year later, a remembrance of John Gibson by John Lomax was published, with the song "Levee Camp Holler," in the Lomaxes' 1934 book *American Ballads and Folk Songs*.

> This song is the workaday of the Negro behind a team of mules. [. . .] Black Samson, whom we found breaking rocks in the Nashville State Penitentiary, admitted that he knew the song and had once sung it; but since he had joined the church and had turned away from the world, he no longer dared sing it. All our arguments were in vain. The prison chaplain protested that he would make it all right with the Lord. But Black Samson replied that he was a Hard-

> shell Baptist and that, according to their way of thinking, he would be in danger of hell-fire if he sang such a song. At last, however, when the warden had especially urged him to sing, he stepped in front of our microphone and, much to our surprise, when he had made sure that his words were being recorded, said: "It's sho hard lines dat a poor nigger's got to sing a worl'ly song, when he's tryin' to be sancrified; but de warden's ast me, so I guess I'll have to." And he did. But he had registered his protest before the Lord on an aluminum plate, now filed in the Library of Congress at Washington. (49)

John Lomax's frankness about Alan and his involvement in persuading Gibson is astounding, but the added detail of their having exerted pressure from ecclesiastical and institutional authorities is dumbfounding. Obviously, such machinations were once tolerated, but there can be little doubt that the Lomaxes exploited John Gibson's desire for freedom by exhorting him, despite his pronounced and explicit reluctance to sing, an act of inducement that, almost 90 years later, we can readily call coercion.

Listen again, carefully. Knowing some of the details that surround John Gibson's circumstances inspires multiple listenings. Most listeners are already equipped with some musical listening skills or literacies, even if they have come as a result of casual listening—to genre, style, time period, or artist. Causal listening yields enough experience with the sonic to warrant listening critically, but more developed and nuanced sonic literacies are needed. Listening to the Lomax archive will require more than casual listening. "Levee Camp Holler" and other music produced for the Lomaxes in Southern African American prisons in the early 1930s became a means for both racial understanding and the problematic codification of historical African American identity in the United States. Listening to the voices on the records in a rhetorical key offers a way to understand more fully the multiplicities of meaning and the paradoxes inherent to racial representation. As Jennifer Lynn Stoever argues, "[L]istening operates as an organ of racial discernment, categorization, and resistance in the shadow of vision's alleged cultural dominance." She observes, further, that sound is "a critical modality through which subjects (re)produce, apprehend, and resist imposed racial identities and structures of racist violence" (4). In concert with Stoever, I argue, in this chapter, that careful archival listening should reveal the complexities she lists and provide a more nuanced understanding of the complications and politics of representation during the interwar period.

A careful listen of the Gibson field recording should reveal details a casual listen does not. For example, "Levee Camp Holler" begins with an introduction from John Lomax, followed by a short protest from Gibson: "Lord, this levee camp song is mighty bad to sing." It is unclear why Gibson's words do not match up better with the Lomaxes' published rendering. The track is convoluted; there are starts and stops during the recording, and another, muted voice can be heard prompting Gibson with forgotten lyrics. (Making that observation took several listens.) Gibson seems not to know the song well or to act as if he does not. Also, the recording of "Levee Camp Holler" cuts out abruptly during the middle of the ninth stanza—compared to the 28 stanzas that appear in *American Ballads and Folk Songs*.[1] The aluminum recording discs were cut in real time with a diamond-tipped needle and could only fit about 15 minutes per side. Recordings frequently ended midsong, the way that "Levee Camp Holler" does, but those songs usually were rerecorded on a fresh disc. Perhaps Gibson could not be persuaded into a second take.[2]

Though the dialectic is captivating, there is more to listen for on the recordings than the drama between present and muted voices. It is impossible not to notice the sound of the recording materials themselves—the scratch and glitch of technology's age and decay as well as the buttressing residues of preservation. The revolving swoosh of the original aluminum disc is decipherable in an ebb and flow of static and a needle skip, caught and cut off quickly at the end. There is also evidence of the transfer by Library of Congress technicians, decades ago, from disc to magnetic tape. One can hear a hiccup in the audio—a faint echo of Gibson's voice as magnetic tape folds over onto itself momentarily in the mix. Finally, though much more difficult to detect, the song was transferred into the binary code of a compact disc, where all previous imperfections codify forever in the digital version. Compressed again as an MP3 and stored in a database, "Levee Camp Holler"—a song John Gibson never wanted to sing—is available in ubiquity, streaming from that database and also in other places on the World Wide Web, from Spotify to YouTube.

Attending to the multiple layers of Gibson's "Levee Camp Holler" is what I mean when I say "careful listening," and such listening might go even deeper. For example, I mentioned sonic and nonmusical clues of the material and historical conditions present during and after the recording, but I did not address more traditional sonic components, such as sung lyrics, tone, and melody, which are perhaps more intuitive (and which I will model in the presentation of later recordings). My emphasis here has been on the modest practices of care and attention. The presentation below of the song "The Angels Drooped their Wings and Gone on to Heaven" offers another opportunity to listen. "Angels" is a spiritual, sung by a group of incarcerated men. Its bright message of redemption and its beautiful four-part harmonies belie the context of its recording. Listening closely to the prison archive means listening to "Angels" in concert with "Levee Camp Holler" (as well as the Lomaxes' other prison recordings), to hear the depth of circumstance, emotion, and suffering and even small joys as the men coped with their incarceration. Listening to a sonic archive is an exercise in exploring the breadth and the depth of the historical field, bringing sensation to the historical record in ways that traditional historiography might otherwise ignore.

Prison Moan

♫ GROUP OF PRISON FARM LABORERS: (*tuning*) Hmmmm
All the angels drooped their wings and
Oh Lord in heaven Lord the angels drooped their wings and
Oh Lord in heaven Lord the angels drooped their wings and
Oh Lord in heaven
My Lord: Carry the news
Great God: Carry the news
My Lord: Carry the news on high
Oh the angels rolled the stone away
Oh Lord in heaven Lord the angels rolled the stone away
Oh Lord in heaven Lord the angels rolled the stone away
Oh Lord in heaven
My Lord: Carry the news
Great God: Carry the news
My Lord: Carry the news on high
Oh my mother got the news and
Oh Lord in heaven Lord my mother got the news and
Oh Lord in heaven Lord my mother got the news and
Oh Lord in heaven
My Lord: Carry the news
Great God: Carry the news
My Lord: Carry the news on high
Oh the angels rolled the stone away
Oh Lord in heaven Lord the angels rolled the stone away

Oh Lord in heaven Lord the angels rolled the stone away
Oh Lord in heaven
My Lord: Carry the news
Great God: Carry the news
My Lord: Carry the news on high

Gibson's travails were not atypical. Recording for the Lomaxes offered a unique opportunity, but one with spiritual and ethical consequences for both the participants and the Lomaxes. In the acknowledgments for *American Ballads and Folk Songs*, John Lomax writes,

> I must place that group of Negro "boys" who this summer, cheerfully and with such manifest friendliness, gave up for the time their crap and card games, their prayer meetings, their much needed Sunday and evening rest, in order to sing for Alan and me—that group whose real names we omit for no reason than to print the substituted picturesque nicknames. Those black "boys" of Texas, Louisiana, Mississippi, and Tennessee by their singing removed any doubt we may have had that Negro folk songs are without a rival in the United States. To Iron Head, Clear Rock, Chin Scooter, Lead Belly, Mexico, Black Samson, Lightnin' Eyes, Double Head, Bull Face, Log Wagon, Creepin' Jesus, Long Distance, Burn Down, Steam Shovel, Rat, Black Rider, Barrel House, Spark Plug, to two "girls" Ding and Bat, and others who helped without giving their names, and to many another the thousands we saw, in happy memory tinged with sadness, I offer grateful thanks.

In that lengthy remembrance, Lomax's small sadness goes unexplained, but the reader soon learns that each person mentioned—from Iron Head to the women Ding and Bat—was incarcerated. John and Alan Lomax traveled to 11 Southern African American prisons in the summer of 1933 with plans to record the "folk song of the Negro." That music, John later wrote, was "in musical phrasing and in poetic content . . . most unlike those of the white race [and the] least contaminated by white influence or by modern Negro jazz" (J. Lomax, *Adventures* 112). Prison farms, a form of penal servitude, had returned to popularity in the United States after the 13th Amendment was ratified, especially in Southern states. On the farms, men and women alike were engaged in menial and often backbreaking labor. Only thinly vailed as carceral recompense, various insidious forms of slavery continued on the farms, as chain gangs and fields patrolled with guns and dogs served as a renewed way of enforcing unpaid human labor.

In the prisons, the Lomaxes hoped to find people cut off from the general public, isolated from both the physical and technological influence of popular culture—particularly radio, records, and the cinema. Imprisoned African Americans might be possessors of generations of otherwise lost folksongs. No access to the radio or cinema meant that they had not been exposed to contemporary popular music, which muddied the proverbial authenticity of a good folksong. By that logic, both John and Alan understood the vernacular music of the isolated African American as a protected and preserved remnant of slave and, by extension, Black culture—a mysterious world that, for most white citizens in the United States 70 years after emancipation, was only just beginning to receive sustained public and scholarly attention. Their work that summer produced over 100 aluminum discs of recorded material, most of which the Library of Congress continues to preserve.

The prison performances and the subsequent records offered a few of the musically talented convicts a new (if complicated) rhetorical agency and yielded lasting effects on how African American culture circulated within the United States. Portals to a remote, unfamiliar subculture, many of the songs that the Lomaxes archived would eventually contribute to a mainstream (largely white) public reception that African American vernacular culture had not previously enjoyed. Yet a tension emerges from the knowledge that scholarly work reliant on the Lomax archive (including, frankly, the present study) is scaffolded on early 1930s social realities, which included a fascination with racial difference as well as concomitant objectification of the Black subject/prisoner as historical material. Prejudice's power is, in that way, a paradox; it both motivates and constrains our ability and capacity for understanding and identification. The Lomaxes and other white scholars interested in cultural preservation shaped the reception of that history in profound, often problematic ways. The recordings thus remain a rich yet thorny resource for scholarly and popular inquiry to the extent that they indexed both Black experience and the ongoing production of whiteness in the United States.[3] We receive the Lomaxes' prison project, then, within the dissonant complexity of both prejudice and progress. They understood themselves as part of a progressive initiative far ahead of their time. That time has long passed, however, and a contemporary point of view makes moral demands on the Lomaxes that may well have been incomprehensible to them. The irony of progressive thought is that it will be regressive soon enough.

In acknowledging that paradox, I hope to sidestep some of the pitfalls of working with material like the Lomax archive. Such material is flawed from the beginning and cannot be otherwise. To be certain, the Lomaxes' collection of prison recordings assembles important historical sonic artifacts, and listening carefully to them can be a harrowing experience. The sounds of the prisoners' toil, sorrow, and longing are preserved as vocal specters on the records. They are thus easily fetishized, as they were by the Lomaxes, as somehow "authentic" or exemplary of some essential component of African American life or experience. As I listen to the men singing in the recordings, I get caught somewhere in the historian's dilemma mentioned above. I am faced with choosing which narrative to make my focus. At one moment, I am grateful to the Lomaxes, whose recorded work is nothing short of a national treasure. In the next, I recognize their piracy and see that their treasure is ill-gotten, despite what they thought of as worthy means. I hear unmistakable humanity in the disembodied voices of the men on the recordings, some of whom died in prison nearly 75 years ago. In my experience—one impossible without the agonism at the center of the two conflicting narratives—a kind of resolution emerges. It is really more an antiresolution (at least in the harmonic sense), as the descriptor most apt for describing my experience is "dissonance." I am familiar with dissonance as a musical experience of notes in tension, and it is apropos that dissonance becomes the rhetorical frame that best represents the historical tensions of the prison recordings in the Lomax archive.

The dissonances particular to the early 1933 and 1934 prison recordings are made more comprehensible through conceptual framings that lend themselves well to managing ambiguity. The first framing is a guiding principle of revisionist historiography—one cued to the both/and-ness of historical "fact" (as explored in this book's first chapter) and to music's power to capture the layers of that dissonance. Along with the notion of a conflicted representative historiography, another instructive dissonance reverberates instructively across the prison recordings: that of rhetorical voice. As a theoretical concept, voice already enjoys a rich literature within rhetorical and sound studies, which I contextualize and expand on below. I trace three coalescing agencies of personal, communal, and political voice and describe how traditional subject/object representative relationships within and among those agencies in the archive blend together within the sonic. Interested as I am in the agency of those in prison—particularly the new agency that a chance to perform for the archive afforded a few of the most talented among them, I also wish to complicate the notion of agency to understand its inherently discordant contradictions.

Thomas Rickert has recently invoked the term *ambient rhetoric* to describe the "attunements" among those complex interrelationships, and I draw on his insights as well as those of several others whose work in race, material rhetorics, and rhetorical agency guides the task of deeper rhetorical listening. Reference to "rhetorical listening" invokes Krista Ratcliffe's widely recognized work on the subject, particularly the idea that practiced rhetorical listening involves "a stance of openness that a person may choose to assume in relation to *any* person, text, or culture," even (or especially) when those relations are troubled (17). That stance is a meticulous enactment of Kenneth Burke's theory of identification, a call to radical empathy, which Radcliffe pushes to its limits.[4] Since I, too, am interested in the ways that listening draws out opportunities for empathetic identification between and across political, cultural, and racial difference, I deploy rhetorical listening in that sense across two undergirding planes. First, the prison recordings do bring about a more nuanced understanding of African American experience in the United States in the 1930s. Yet the number of those who heard the recordings before their release in the early 1940s was limited to those with access to the Library of Congress, and even then, interest in them was likely limited to scholars and, later, musicians looking for ideas and inspiration. John and Alan Lomax were, in a sense, the delegated listeners for the country, and because of their positions of national power, their limited capacity for rhetorical listening turned out to be particularly influential. Our historical understanding of the Archive of American Folk Song (as it was then called) is thus filtered through the Lomaxian identification rendered historically in the recordings and books they produced. In that second sense, the theoretical ideal to reach toward through sonic rhetorical analysis is dissonance, not the more comfortable "harmony" that "understanding" (identification's ideal) often evokes.

The careful listening that I describe above can help to reveal the dissonant nature of the individual, communal, and political agencies at play among the prisoners themselves. Listening carefully requires attentiveness to the materiality of sound and how it might articulate simultaneity, dissonance, and multiplicity, and much of this chapter draws on materialist methods in an effort to push beyond typified phenomenological notions of voice. The chapter's exercises in listening to the Lomax archive will lead to discussion of how historical sonic artifacts such as those in my study productively complicate our understanding of racial formation and the ongoing racial project of reifying notions of racial otherness in the United States. Some of the songs I present here from the prison archive are the subject of close analysis, while others, such as "The Angels Drooped Their

Wings and Gone on to Heaven" above and "Good God A'mighty" below, are meant both to set the tone of this chapter and to give readers//listeners a broader sense of the archive's offerings. Sentient listening to the particular grouping of archival music collected here can often be an affecting experience, and some recordings are more difficult to listen to than others. Part of the challenge results from material conditions present at the time of the recording as well as from the way that technology's decay obscures their clarity. More poignantly, perhaps the most exacting difficulty in listening lies in the content of the recordings themselves. The prison recordings echo a despicable past of de jure segregation—resounding with evidence of oppressive injustice, systematic cruelty, and omnipresent prejudice. Each of the listening observations and experiences they offer are important and lend themselves to a more nuanced understanding of sound's rhetorical impact.

Dissonant Voices

♫ "LIGHTNIN" WASHINGTON AND GROUP: (*singing, call-and-response*)

[. . . ?] morning
Ah my Lord Lord
I went to the bottom
Good God A'mighty
I went to the bottom
Ah my Lord Lord
With a big found diamond
Good God A'mighty
With a big found diamond
Ah my Lord Lord
Saw the captain riding
Good God A'mighty
Saw the captain riding
Ah my Lord Lord
Oh Captain won't you help me
Good God A'mighty
Oh Captain won't you help me
Ah my Lord Lord
I'm down in trouble
Good God A'mighty
I'm down in trouble

Figure 1. "Lightnin'" Washington singing with a group of unnamed prison laborers in the woodyard at Darrington State Farm, Texas, 1934

Ah my Lord Lord
I don't want to see Julie
Good God A'mighty
I don't want to see Julie
Ah my Lord Lord
Now Julie had the baby
Good God A'mighty
Now Julie had a baby
Ah my Lord Lord
Well go get the sergeant
Good God A'mighty
Now go get the sergeant
Ah my Lord Lord
Well [. . . ?]
Good God Amighty

Well [. . . ?]
Ah my Lord Lord
I cross big [. . . ?]
Good God Amighty
I cross big [. . . ?]
Ah my Lord Lord
I'm going to see the baby
Good God A'mighty
I'm going to see the baby
Ah my Lord Lord
That baby's worried
Good God Amighty
Well the baby has a worry
Ah my Lord Lord
She's worried about her daddy
Good God Amighty
She's worried about her daddy
Ah my Lord Lord
I'm down in trouble
Good God Amighty
I'm down in trouble
Ah my Lord Lord
Ain't got nobody
Good God Amighty
Ain't got nobody
Ah my Lord Lord

After being refused admission to the Texas State Penitentiary at Huntsville and rebuffed by a negative experience at Prairie View State Normal and Industrial College (now Prairie View A&M University), John and Alan Lomax made their first real headway in recording African American prisoners when they visited the Central State Prison Farm in Sugar Land, Texas. At "Sugarland," the Lomaxes encountered two aging men who would become central to the prison archive. One was 71-year-old Mose "Clear Rock" Platt, who had been jailed for 47 years on a murder charge. A master improviser, Platt could sing the same song with seemingly infinite variations and just as easily devise new songs on the spot, making him, as John Szwed has written, "a folklorist's dream" (*Alan Lomax* 41). The other singer central to the archive, James "Iron Head" Baker, was 64 and knew so many songs that John Lomax would later refer to him as a "black Homer." John Lomax recalls first meeting Platt and Baker in the hospital building on the Sugarland complex, while recording a convalescing man named Mexico. Baker was watching the recording session with interest and said (in John's rendering), "I'se Iron Head, I'se a trusty. I know lots of jumped-up, sinful songs—more than any of these niggers" (J. Lomax, *Adventures* 165). He recorded with the Lomaxes for the rest of that night and throughout the next day, taking turns singing with his "pardner," Platt.

The Lomaxes observed that the songs produced at Sugarland were of immense diversity. There were "rhythmic, surging songs of labor; cotton-picking songs; songs of the jailbird," as well as "songs of loneliness and the dismal monotony of life in the penitentiary; songs of pathetic longing for his 'doney,' his woman" (J. Lomax, *Adventures* 166). Above all, the Lomaxes averred, the "words, the music, the rhythm, were simple" and the result of the "natural emotional outpouring of the black man in confinement" (166). The music is remarkable, but its description as a "natural outpouring" tells us more about the Lomaxes than it does about the men whose singing was recorded, leaving us to ask what might be understood about the prisoners' circumstances through careful and more informed listening.

Listening and Voice: Mose Platt

Below, I move within the narratives on which the Lomaxes collaborated with Platt, Baker, and other prisoners, to demonstrate sound's relationship to the oral/aural process of personal, communal, and institutional/political agency and remembering. Such processes can be understood as useful nuances of rhetorical voice. While the theoretical concept of voice has been employed to various (and sometimes disparate) ends,[5] Eric King Watts usefully frames a way of understanding the theoretical potential of voice within the sonic mode. Watts distinguishes a "middle road" between the "ontic and symbolic" potentials of voice, drawing out the tensions between "speech as a sensual, personal, and 'authentic' phenomenon and language as an abstract impersonal symbolic system" (180). Those tensions are ever-present in the prison recordings and show up in the relationships and rhetorics at play at each level of the rhetorical situation.

An example of one end of that tension can be heard in James Baker's singing voice, which, in concert with the material clues on the recording and the Lomax book excerpt, is a powerful reminder of his humanity and the reality of his subjugation. In comparison, "Levee Camp Holler"—the song John Gibson sung under duress—was interesting to the Lomaxes as a symbol expressing African American prison life and, by extension, an even more abstracted symbolic slave culture. Within that symbolic paradigm, John Gibson himself is unimportant. For the rhetorical listener, there is a merging of the components of the recording that are in tension—the seemingly distinct ontic components (concerned with being—in this case, human being) and the symbolic components. One cannot exist without the other. The presence of a listener (us) opens up other possible meaning relationships between the recordings, the voices on them, and the institution that produced and distributed them.

Agency is both contingent to and emergent from the rhetorical situation that produced the recordings and has various meanings dependent on which relationship is emphasized. I find a framing from Thomas Rickert useful in getting at this kind of rhetorical nuance. Following the work of Jenny Edbauer Rice and others, Rickert encourages an "ecologic" rhetorical approach that embraces complexities so that "the interactions of numerous agents mutually form and condition a chaotically dynamic system" (xiv). For Rickert, rhetoric is ambient and does its work "responding to and put forth through affective, symbolic, and material means, so as to . . . reattune or otherwise transform how others inhabit the world." (162). Music performs that ambience well, particularly because its affective, symbolic, and material aspects reveal tensions and dissonances that occur within the rhetorical process and that require an understanding of rhetoric in its complexity, rather than as a tool for clear or incisive determinate persuasion.

An example of those various tensions and dissonances can be found in the voice of Mose Platt, who, unlike Gibson, willingly participated in the Lomaxes' field recordings. His voice can be heard on at least 12 distinct recordings, which encompass solo performances as well as a number of collaborations with other prisoners, including his friend James Baker. Platt has a deep, distinctive, baritone singing voice. His seemingly effortless vocal and pitch control indicate years of practice and performance. When other men join in singing with Platt, their ease and enthusiasm reveals participatory singing as part of a deeply embedded culture, not just a shared casual pastime among the prisoners.

I have selected two of Mose Platt's recordings for a close listen. Both are about slave escape and capture. Presented here in preface to the second song, "Ol' Rattler," is the song with the dubious title "Run Nigger Run."[6]

♫ MOSE PLATT: (*singing and clapping on beat*) . . . the nigger flew
The nigger lost his Sunday shoe
Run nigger run, the [?] ok
To run, nigger run. You better get away
Nigger run, the nigger flew
The nigger lost his Sunday shoe
Run nigger run, the [?] ok
To run, nigger run. You better get away
Nigger run, by my gate
Wake up nigger you slept too late
Run nigger run, the [?] ok
To run, nigger run. You better get away
Look down yonder what I see
[?] big nigger behind that tree
Run nigger run, the [?] ok
To run, nigger run. You better get away
Nigger run, the nigger flew
The nigger lost his Sunday shoe
Run nigger run, the [?] ok
Run, nigger run. You better get away
(*voice in crowd shouts in encouragement*)
Let me tell you what I do
I'm gonna buy me a Sunday shoe
Run nigger run, the [?] ok
To run, nigger run. You better get away
Nigger run, nigger flew,
The nigger tore his shirt in two
Run nigger run, the [?] ok
To run, nigger run. You better get away
Let me tell you what I see
I'm going to hide behind that tree
Run nigger run, the [?] ok
To run, nigger run. You better get . . .
(*break in the recording*)
un behind that [?]
Nigger run, but he run too slow
Run nigger run, the [?] ok
To run, nigger run . . .

"Run Nigger Run" evokes the long tradition of slave escape. A song with a nearly identical refrain can be connected to Nat Turner's slave rebellion in Southampton County, Virginia, in 1831 (Lomax and Lomax 228). But when listening to Mose Platt sing his version, it is difficult to mistake the enthusiasm in his voice as he performed it proudly for the Lomaxes, the warden, and an audience of his peers. Halfway through the recording (43), we even hear several voices encouraging Platt to keep singing. Clearly, a song about escape sung in prison had meaning in harmony with the tune's historical context. In a sense as much transgressive as comic, there is dissonance between the two renderings, one historic and symbolic, the other kairotic and salient to the moment. Platt had a dark sense of humor.

We hear that humor again in another song about slave escape, "Ol' Rattler," named for its subject, a mythic prison watchdog. The dog's job, to chase and maul any escaping prisoner, was presumably tied to a longer tradition of slave capture. In the following discussion of that song, I attempt to make the humanistic/symbolic dichotomy explicit by comparing recorded sound in varying shades of abstraction, from recorded vocal singing to its abstract visual/textual rendering. To make my point, I work backward—from most abstract to least. At the far end of that trajectory are Mose Platt and the recording's other voices, which present a striking, unmistakably human contrast to the other representations. But in that most "present" and least abstracted space, I pause to complicate the move toward championing the salience of the voice or its ability to access or understand deep humanity. A voice on an archival recording is still an abstraction, and there is still an insurmountable distance between that recording and the people who made it.

In *American Ballads and Folk Songs*, race is represented visually in the text of the sheet music for "Ol' Rattler," through lingual dialect and in the short, excerpted quote at the top from Mose Platt. Both textual and musical elements of that discursive artifact potentially racialized the interpretation of the content. Lyrics rendered as dialect and grace notes in four of the five opening measures are attempts to represent the sound of Mose Platt's voice, with one approximating his vocal style and with the other seizing on the vocal nuances of his sung musical intervals. The lyrics to the song, printed on the opposite page, also approximate (and do not always match) with the recorded version. Nevertheless, they depict a bleak reality of African American prison life, defined by its invisible and insurmountable rural borders. Ol' Rattler did not simply keep prisoners from escaping, since, as

American Ballads and Folk Songs

OL' RATTLER

Mose Platt ("spells it P-L-A-W-P [P-L-A-double T], jes' lak you plait a whip"), alias Big Foot Rock, tells how he ran away from prison upon a time, how "ol' Rattler, de fastes' an' de smellin'es' bleedhoun' in de South" trailed and treed him.

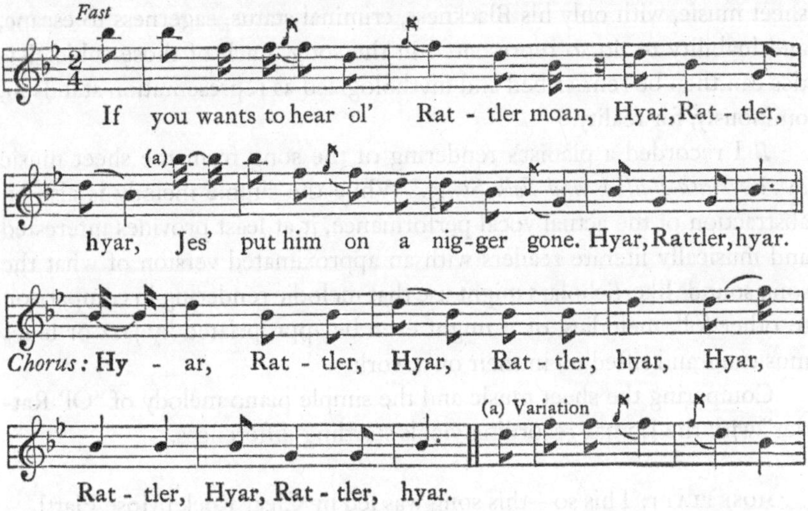

Figure 2. Sheet music for the song "Ol' Rattler," as printed in *American Ballads and Folk Songs*

one lyric relates, those who made the attempt would not survive his attack: "If I trip this time, I'll trip no more." A close reading of the lyrical texts reveals several elements that, when paired with an analysis of other songs in the collection, reveal a complex association of fear, oppression, back-breaking labor, and the constant threat of death and violence—punctuated here and there with a cathartic line of comedy or bawdy tale of sexual conquest. The Lomaxes' meticulous inclusion of the lyrics allow for careful analysis and, even in dialect, give the interested reader an opportunity to reflect on the experience of captivity and the terror of attempted escape:

Now I run till I'm almos' blin'
I'm on my way to de long-leaf pine.
I didn' have no time to make no thimpathee
My nighes' route was up a tree. (Lomax and Lomax 67)

Yet the various visual, musical, and textual renderings of the transcription contain several significant elisions. They tell us very little about Mose Platt. (We are fortunate to have his name at all, given that many of the recordings are attributed merely to "unknown prisoner.") Platt is caricatured in the sheet music, with only his Blackness, criminal status, eagerness to escape, and inability to do so represented in the song. Each of those subjectivities can then be reinscribed and mythologized as representation stands in, ominously, for reality.

♫ I recorded a pianist's rendering of the song from the sheet music in *American Ballads and Folk Songs.*[7] While the simple melody is also an abstraction of the actual vocal performance, it at least provides interested and musically literate readers with an approximated version of what the song sounds like. Scholars might use that melodic rendering in comparison to other folk melodies, or it might even be appropriated by jazz or blues musicians and riffed on in their own work.

Comparing the sheet music and the simple piano melody of "Ol' Rattler" with the Lomax recording yields startling differences.

MOSE PLATT: This so—this song was led by Clear Rock [Mose Platt], assisted by Iron Head [James Baker] on this central state farm, Sugar Land, Texas.

(*Platt leads and Baker accompanies him on the refrain.*)

♫ MOSE PLATT: (*singing*)
Hey Rattler
Hey Rattler, Hey
Hey hey Rattler
Oh, b'lieve to my soul, there's a nigger gone
Hey, Rattler, hey
B'lieve to my soul, there's a nigger gone
Hey, Rattler, hey
Oh, he went right through the corn
Hey, Rattler, hey

I heard ol' horn blow
Hey, Rattler, hey
Going: Get the dog, man
Hey, Rattler, hey
Going: Get the dog, man
Hey, Rattler, hey
Run that nigger to the river side
Hey, Rattler, hey
Run that nigger to the river side
Hey, Rattler, hey
Going: call ol' Rattler
Hey, Rattler, hey (*howls*)
Call ol' Rattler
Hey, Rattler, hey
Oh, Rattler coming yeah pen[?]
Hey, Rattler, hey
Oh and call ol' Rattler
Hey, Rattler, hey
Oh, Rattler coming yeah pen[?] (*howls*)
Hey, Rattler, hey
Oh, Rattler coming yeah pen[?]
Hey, Rattler, hey
Oh, put that nigger right up that tree. (*howls*)
Hey, Rattler, hey
Ol' rock couldn't get to three[?]
Hey, Rattler, hey
Oh spent so long with the sympathy
Hey, Rattler, hey
Oh, run that nigger right lost his mind.
Hey, Rattler, hey
Oh and call ol' Rattler
Hey, Rattler, hey
Oh and call ol' Rattler
Hey, Rattler, hey
Oh he run that nigger till he went stone blind
Hey, Rattler, hey
Oh, 'crosst the river to the long-leaf pine
Hey, Rattler, hey
Oh, run him so far he didn't leave no fine

Hey, Rattler, hey
Oh, the baby here got a baby's there
Hey, Rattler, hey
Oh, believe in my soul that [. . . ?]
Hey, Rattler, hey
Oh, they didn't allow no black folks there
Hey, Rattler, hey
Oh, trip this time, I'll trip no more
Hey, Rattler, hey
Oh, going to the North where you can go
Hey, Rattler, hey
Oh, and ring the sergeant
Hey, Rattler, hey
Go and ring the sergeant
Hey, Rattler, hey
Oh, ride them this and ride them that
Hey, Rattler, hey
Believe in my soul that there's another one gone
Hey, Rattler, hey
Oh, to hold it up you hold right on[?]
Hey, Rattler, hey
Run that nigger right through the corn
Hey, Rattler, hey
Oh, big foot rock[?] he sure did gone
Hey, Rattler, hey
Oh, big foot rock[?] he sure did gone
Hey, Rattler, hey

Platt's voice is rich and expressive compared to the piano's monotones. Variations on the melody are noticeably present on the recording, even within the few verses captured. Platt's phrases sometimes garble together; it is difficult to understand his every word, as often occurs in everyday encounters. His singing companions emerge as important pieces of the song's arrangement, while their parts go unrepresented in the sheet music. In contradistinction to a prescriptive understanding of rhetoric as logical clarity in persuasion, the most powerful aspect of voice rendered here or anywhere else is not the clarity of its communicative potential but its variety, nuance, and multiplicity.

Another powerful aspect of an "ontic" listen of recordings like "Ol' Rattler" is that it momentarily diverts attention away from the heroic narrative of a white savior, so prominent in Western culture, and demands attending to the person's voice on the recording. Symbolic meaning is laid aside for a moment, and we are reminded of Roland Barthes's characterization of the voice's uncanny ability to connect us with the human. For Barthes, that human essence is the "grain of the voice"—or language "in its very materiality" (506). If, as John Durham Peters reminds us, "the voice is a metaphor of power," tied distinctly to the experience of embodied identity, then "[e]ach person's voice is a creature of the shape of one's skull, sinuses, vocal tract, lungs, and general physique. Age, geography, gender, education, health, ethnicity, class, and mood all resound in our voices" ("The Voice and Modern Media" n.p.). We hear each of those aspects in the recorded voice of Mose Platt—evidence of his distinct humanity and, even though he was incarcerated, his power and agency. However, in line with Derrida's critique of the metaphysics of presence, the humanistic qualities of Platt can only reach out so far.[8] Eventually, his voice gets lost in the mix of the earlier representations, and under scrutiny, the recording cannot bear the weight of a true *present*ation of the subject. As the recording—which has a grain all its own—reminds us of the disconnection and temporal distance between his human body and mechanized historical reproduction, Mose Platt suddenly becomes a ghost.

Iron Head Blues: Secular and Spiritual Communion

Platt's singing companion James Baker ("alias Iron Head," as he was wont to say on the recordings) had lived and worked as a prisoner in the Central State Prison Farm near Sugar Land, Texas. Tall and quiet, he had a reputation among fellow inmates as having a large repertoire of songs. John Lomax devoted a whole chapter in his autobiography to Baker, who the folklorist got to know well over several years of acquaintance. As mentioned before, Lomax called Baker a "black Homer," because Baker knew hundreds of songs and because his abilities for improvisation and on-the-fly composition may well have matched the genius of ancient epic poets. That comparison is more apt than even Lomax would have imagined. Baker's rhythmic facility contributed to his popularity with and also to his respect among fellow inmates. Baker said he got his nickname "Iron Head" when an oak tree fell nearby while he was cutting wood on the Ramsey State Convict Farm, a work prison in Angleton, Texas: "Some limbs hit my head, an' it broke 'em off; didn't knock me down, an' it didn't stop me from working" (J. Lomax, *Adventures* 169).

Baker referred to himself as "De roughest nigger what ever walked de streets of Dallas. In de pen off an' on fo' thirty-fo' years" (J. Lomax, *Adventures* 166). After six convictions, Baker identified as an "H.B.C.—habitual criminal, you know" (166). Lomax comments, however, that Baker did not really look the part, that his dignity and tenderness far outshone any residual evidence of hardness in his face. By Lomax's description, Baker seemed a solemn and honest figure, one whom "unlike the other Negro convict[s] [. . .] confessed that he was guilty of other crimes than those that had put him in prison": "Mos' of de times dey didn't catch me," Lomax quotes Baker as saying (168). Baker had a familial relationship with other inmates. One night while he was recording for the Lomaxes, his colleagues crowded the room and shouted requests. One of those requests, Lomax writes, caused a bit of a rise out of Baker. They urged him to sing "Shorty George," a song about "the short passenger train that ran from Houston to the farm once a month on a Sunday, bringing visiting wives and sweethearts" (168). They begged until Iron Head had to shout at them, "You niggers know dat song always tears me to pieces. I won't sing it." He then walked away, stood in the corner shadows, and motioned for Lomax, saying, "I'll sing dat song low for you."

♫ Ah well the Shorty George
Ain't no friend of mine
Ah well the Shorty George
He ain't no friend of mine
He takes all the women
And left the men behind
    Oh well I'm going to Galveston
They're going to Maryland
Oh well I'm going to Galveston
They're going to Maryland
Oh baby, you can't quit me
Ain't no need you tryin'
    I've got a letter
all [. . . ?]
Well I've got a letter
all [. . . ?]
To come home at once
And lovin' be deceived[?]
    Oh well, I've got the train

And the train went a flying
Oh well, I've got the train
And the train went flying
My baby she wasn't there
But she slowly died
    Oh when your baby ain't dead
But she slowly died
Oh when your baby ain't dead
And she slowly died
Oh tell me how can you blame
A poor man (*recording cuts off*)

"It makes me restless to see my woman," Baker confided in Lomax about the song, adding, "I'se a trusty an' I has a easy job. I could run down one o' dem corn rows an' git away, any day. But when de law caught me, dey would put me back in de line wid de fiel' han's. I'se too ol' for dat hard work" (167).

In the spring of 1936, after corresponding with Baker a few times, Lomax returned to Sugar Land and arranged for Baker's parole. The conditions of his release were that he would work for Lomax as a chauffeur and as an ambassador in the prisons, "acting as a go-between with black musicians and demonstrating the kinds of songs Lomax was looking for" (Porterfield 375). After the recording trip concluded—and if Baker cooperated—Lomax would help him set up a business doing the work he had done in prison. Lomax tried unsuccessfully to teach Baker to drive, but Baker was more successful in his second role. "Feels sorta like home," he remarked after a stop at the prison known as Parchman Farm (J. Lomax, *Adventures* 172). While they drove, the man who called himself Iron Head would often sing his favorite song, "Go Down, Old Hannah," which Benjamin Botkin describes as "one of the best known of the slow drag work songs sung by Negro prisoners in South Texas." According to Botkin, Baker claimed to have first sung it in prison in 1908, "on long hot summer days, when about three o'clock in the afternoon, the sun (Old Hannah) seemed to stop and 'just hang' in the sky" (5). The symbolism in "Go Down, Old Hanna" is polyphonic, with both the sacred and secular represented. In the recording of the song made by the Lomaxes in 1933, Ernest Williams and Baker sing with (according to the Library of Congress reference card) "a group of Negro convicts."

ERNEST WILLIAMS, JAMES BAKER, AND UNNAMED OTHERS: (*singing*)

Go down, old Hannah,
Won't you rise no more?
Go down, old Hannah,
Won't you rise no more?
Lawd, if you rise,
Bring judgment on.
Lawd, if you rise,
Bring judgment on.
Oh, did you hear
What the captain said?
Oh, did you hear
What the captain said?
That if you work
He'll treat you well,
And if you don't
He'll give you hell.
Go down, old Hannah,
Won't you rise no more?
Go down, old Hannah,
Won't you rise no more?
Oh, long-time man,
Hold up your head.
Well, you may get a pardon
And you may drop dead.
Lord there's nobody feels sorry
For the life-time man.
Nobody feels sorry
For the life-time man.

The imprisoned men generally considered songs like "Go Down, Old Hannah" and "Shorty George" to be "sinful." Like John Gibson, many refused or had to be persuaded to sing them. That did not seem to be the case for Mose Platt or James Baker, who sung them frequently and without much prompting, often (as the anecdote above reveals) as part of the daily experience of living. "Sinful" songs are part of a rich tradition of secular African American songs that, unlike the "Negro spiritual," were sung for pragmatic rather than religious purposes. As a product of an antebellum

African American consciousness, Lawrence Levine writes, such African American secular music was "occasional music" and "as varied, as narrow, as fleeting as life itself" (19). Spirituals, he argues, were the best source for understanding the Black worldview during slavery, because "slaves used it to articulate their deepest and most enduring feelings and certainties" (19). Despite those differences, Levine concedes that the two styles of music had unmistakable similarities: "In both the temple and the field, black song was for the most part communal song" (217).

One gets that sense when listening to James Baker's songs in the Lomax archive. He was a master of both the secular and the sacred, and in his case, the two styles often merge. It can be difficult to tell if a song is meant for working or worshiping. "Go Down, Old Hannah" is a prime example. The song was a "slow drag work song" used in the field for laborious work with a hoe or other ground tilling implement. When one listens to the song, the slow but intense rhythm of that work is manifest, but so is the depth of the tune as an emotional petition to the sun, Hannah, to "rise no more." Despite its seemed secular content, the song is sung in a distinctly spiritual style and in the traditional call-and-response, or antiphonal, structure of sacred songs. The antiphony was intentionally communal and, as Levine and others have shown, residual of African life and sociality (33). In the case of "Go Down, Old Hannah," both the secular and the sacred are present. For Baker and his fellows, Hannah (the sun) is a source of both suffering and light. Her persistent rising and falling is a reminder of the rhythms of prison life, hard work, and the lack of hope for the "life-time man." The escape of death is welcomed and characterized here in the petitioning of the sun to "raise no more." However, the line "Lord if you rise, bring judgment on" could as easily be part of a hymnal. The connections to the sacred may go even deeper than just style. Christians often see Hannah, the Old Testament mother of the prophet Samuel, as a type and shadow of Mary, mother of Jesus (see 1 Samuel 2). Like Jesus, Samuel's birth was miraculous; the rising and setting "sun" Baker sings of—one explicitly connected to judgment in "Go Down, Old Hannah"—is reminiscent of the other, homophonic "son." For the inmates, the song has both a functional, practical, communal purpose and a more implicit, symbolic one. Still, the rhetorical complexity of the song makes it hard to classify as either secular or sacred. We can understand "Go Down, Old Hannah" as an amalgam of enmeshed rhetorical components—material, practical, spiritual, historical, and, for Baker, even sentimental.

Lead Belly and the Sonic Politics of a Pardon

The ontic and symbolic meshing of sound as voice had rhetorical implications for personal and communal meaning-making for incarcerated men in Southern Jim Crow prisons. Through multivocal nuances within those two modes, voice in song cuts across easily classifiable rhetorical ideals, leaving them always in tension, always dissonant, and always decentered. Even as voice is significant to personal identity, Gibson's, Platt's, and Baker's individual identities are easily subsumed by the symbolic in even the most carefully drawn attempt to focus in on ontological individuality. An intentionally symbolic understanding of voice, while a more familiar rhetorical positioning, is also complicated by that multivocality. Songs can be abstracted from their original voices and be given new meanings by external parties for specific institutional, nationalistic, or racial purposes, but the same music can also be richly symbolic for its originating users. Institutionalized or nationalistic symbolism codifies African American experience (and race itself) into a reduced and simplistic monotone. The institutionalization of the prison recordings has the same effect as their digitization: compression, distortion, and the codification of various imperfections. Yet the sonic symbols at play within the vernacular context of the song itself—represented well in the antiphony of call-and-response—are the symbols of community, sympathy, and shared struggle. The former symbolization is reductive, the latter productive.

In the final case study in this chapter, I discuss political voice, which, along with the personal and communal voices, rounds out the three agencies or rhetorical modes sonically discernible in the prison recordings. As I have asserted, the differences between those modes do not necessarily differ in the ways that they sound; rather, they work together in concert and, reach out to meet one rhetorical need or another, depending on context and on what the moment requires. Perhaps one of the most exciting and frustrating elements of studying music rhetorically is that music is rife with significance. Any one voicing can have a multitude of rhetorical implications. John Lomax understood that significance and used the music from the prisons (as well as the prisoners themselves when he could) to further his career. That opportunity was part of the political environment of the prisons while the Lomaxes were on-site making records. They were not just there to gather recordings philanthropically, for the greater good of the country. Occasionally, prisoners also took advantage of the opportunity the recording project afforded, when they recognized the political possibilities of their involvement with the Lomaxes and others from whom they could leverage privilege.

In the preceding section, I mentioned that John Lomax helped to arrange James Baker's parole. Lomax then employed Baker as a traveling companion, until they parted company when their relationship and tolerance for one another dissolved. Lomax encountered Baker a few years later, back in prison in the Ramsey State Convict Farm, where he was working on the garden squad. "I should have left him at Sugarland to weave from corn shucks horse collars and rugs for Captain Gotch and Captain Flanagan," Lomax later wrote (*Adventures* 177). As much as Lomax laments the ultimate results, Baker's release was a significant political triumph for both. Recall that John Gibson also hoped that his interaction with the Lomaxes would lead to his release. In a rhetorical situation where privilege is so unevenly distributed, the political agency of the incarcerated would be limited to the few things that might set them apart, like good behavior and cooperation. In Baker's case, when the Lomaxes arrived, his talent as a singer gave him sufficient agency to negotiate release—even though his freedom would not last long.

Baker's story is reminiscent of the much more famous example of Huddie "Lead Belly" Ledbetter's prison releases, from Sugarland in 1925 and from Louisiana's Angola prison after an encounter with the Lomaxes and their recording machine in 1934 (see chapter 1). Both John Lomax and Lead Belly claimed that Lead Belly's second release occurred due to a pardon from the state governor. The second pardoning was a likely fiction that never actually occurred, but Lomax and Lead Belly both used the tale to advance their commercial and professional success.

Lead Belly's first pardon, however, is a fact of record, a remarkable example of how music was one of the few political tools afforded prisoners serving in Southern African American prisons at the beginning of the 20th century. "Governor Pat Neff (Sweet Mary)" was the name of Lead Belly's sung petition, for which Lead Belly drew on a number of rhetorical tactics to accomplish his goal of release. For example, knowing that Neff was a devout Baptist, Lead Belly wished to appeal to the governor's religious sensibilities. Lead Belly's girlfriend was named Mary, but calling Mary his "wife" in the song conflated his situation powerfully with the symbolic Mary of scripture: "I put Mary in it, Jesus's mother, you know. I took a verse from the bible, around about the twenty-second chapter of Proverbs, around the fourteenth verse: if you will forgive a man his trespasses, the heavenly father will also forgive your trespasses" (Wolfe and Lornell 86).

That compositional choice was part of a larger, more carefully composed process for Lead Belly. He did not usually write down his compositions, but he wanted to be precise in his petition: "If I had you like you have me, I'd wake up in the morning and set you free."

As in the example of "Go Down, Old Hannah," the lyrics of "Governor Pat Neff" complete the sonic argument being made. On their own, lyrics only get the musician/rhetor so far, but when placed (literally) in concert with Lead Belly's musical talent, his persistence, his correct assessment of audience, and his timing, the lyrics bring a critical and legible edge to the sonic materiality at play. Even so, I hesitate to go further in this particular analysis, as one cannot point casually to any one combination of those factors as leading to Lead Belly's pardon by Governor Neff. That indeterminacy is part of the larger rhetorical decentering that occurs within sonic rhetoric. A close listen paired with a careful historical analysis reveals several resonant and contributing details that point toward causality, but they also raise several unanswerable questions. Like his second "pardon," what is unknown about the release of Lead Belly from Sugar Land in 1925 is as interesting as what is known. One question that looms large for this study, for example, is to what extent the lore of Lead Belly's pardon resonated with Mose Platt and James Baker, captives of the same prison complex in 1933, the year the Lomaxes arrived. Their likely acquaintance with the story of Lead Belly—the man who had sung his way to freedom—may very well have influenced Platt and Baker's decision to engage with John and Alan Lomax.

Toward a Sonic Rhetoric of African American Vernacular Culture

To speak of "vernacular culture" is to consider how highly particularized experiences of quotidian folklife are everyday represented and codified both as a shared cultural identity and as a means of presenting and differentiating that identity from other, sometimes competing vernaculars. For Margaret Lantis, a more complete rendering of that idea might be the "vernacular aspect or portion of the total culture" that expresses the notions of "'native to . . .' or common of a locality, region, or, by extension, of a trade or other group: the commonly used or spoken as distinct from the written" (203). Vernacular culture, then, is more readily found in the currency of everyday experience (not only in speech and, by extension, song, but also in the "handmade" and material). The residue of tradition is represented within everyday practices, but the traditional need not mean antiquated.

Indeed, Lantis's entomological analysis of the word *vernacular* reveals that the "Latin does not seem to suggest traditional or primitive but rather 'of one's house,' of the place. This is the connotation we want: the culture-as-it-is-lived appropriate to well-defined places and situations." Lantis continues, "Since speech is not only essential but an important essential of situationally structured behavior, it is quite all right if 'vernacular culture' suggests first speech, then an extension to other behavior" (203).

Though the Lomaxes were not necessarily the first investigators drawn to African American study, their interest in collecting the musical vernacular artifacts of African American prisoners is distinguished by their pioneering attempt to understand and give structure to an obscure, distinctly racial history of slave and postbellum culture through the study of recorded, speech-based vernacular artifacts. Though the Lomaxes saw their work as one of cultural preservation—of locating and preserving a distinct and authentic African American musical past—we can understand it as one exploring both racial difference and racial formation through the collection and distribution of African American vernacular music. The proto-blues music that the Lomaxes and others recorded in the South carried with it vernacular evidence of what some took to be a "new race," forged in the blending of African extraction and American emancipation/reconstruction. Amiri Baraka underscores this point in his influential study *Blues People*, arguing that the "African cultures, the retention of some parts of these cultures in America, and the *weight* of the stepculture produced the American Negro. A new race" (7). Baraka makes music the "persistent reference" of his study, because "the development and transmutation of African music to American Negro music (a *new* music) represents . . . this whole process in microcosm" (7–8). The Lomaxes' work, then, might be understood in terms of what Michael Omi and Howard Winant call a "racial project," which is "simultaneously an interpretation, representation, or explanation of racial dynamics, and an effort to reorganize and redistribute resources along particular racial lines." They explain, furthermore, that "racial projects connect what race means in a particularly discursive practice and the ways in which both social structures and everyday experiences are racially *organized*, based upon that meaning" (56). Omi and Winant thus call attention to the linkage between social structure and representation in the processes of racial formation. Those two elements can be understood in the same terms as the contrasting but linked elements discussed above as related to voice, where both internal/social and external/representative rhetorics are in circulation.

In the prison recordings, the vernacular genres of African American life on the sharecropping farms of the Jim Crow South elucidate distinct types of behaviors within African American experience during that era and likely, as the Lomaxes suspected, much earlier eras as well. They also provide a keystone in our understanding of African American music's progression from the 19th century to the 20th. As well as presenting the rhythm of work life in the prisons in 1933, work songs such as "Levee Camp Holler" or "Pick a Bale o' Cotton" can be understood accurately enough as "the immediate predecessors of blues" (Baraka 18). As I have sought to show, spirituals characterize the merging of American and African superstitious/religious traditions, and secular or "sinful" songs like "Ol' Rattler" or "Run Nigger Run" were expressions of sorrow, rebellion, sexuality, and playful levity. Each of those genres carries what Henry Louis Gates Jr. has famously named "Signifyin(g)" elements.

Though dated, Gates's theory remains a poignant descriptor for African American artistic, rhythmic, and poetic culture. Signifyin(g), which is the "black trope of tropes, the figure for black rhetorical figures" (Gates 75), can be found in the African American linguistic stylings of (among others) trickery, half-truth, innuendo, boasting, and playful circularity. Understanding that the manipulation of those "classic black figures of Signification" created African American agency—the opportunity for "the black person to move freely between two discursive universes" (Gates 76)—helps us to understand Lead Belly's political petition. His music successfully Signified both African American suffering and virtuosic creativity—a kind of masterful pairing of everyday Black experience and white genre expectations. That both/and sonic rhetorical appeal allowed both he and James Baker to secure freedom from prison. Even when release was not the end result, all of the examples I have discussed above showcase vernacular African American music's rhetorical power. We have heard that power in the voices of the imprisoned engaged in everyday (and often personal) activities and emotions, in the symbolic cadence of community, and as a decontextualized representation of African American culture appropriated by the powerful voice of institutional authority. Though we now see the cracks in the Lomaxes' methods and ideologies, their recordings had, for a time, significant progressive impact on scholars and, later, a (largely white) middle class, by nuancing previously held views of racial difference through an increased understanding of African American experience during and in the decades immediately following slavery.

As a racial project, then, the Lomaxes' work within African American prisons had two significant opposing ideological consequences—one expansive, the other reductive. On the one hand, the sounds of toiling, worshiping, and otherwise Signifyin(g) prisoners helped to redraw the racially coded parameters of African American vernacular culture for white audiences comfortable with paradigms drawn from other long-held Black cultural representations.[9] Theorists within critical race studies call that process "rearticulation."[10] On the other hand, those representations became tropes of typical African American life in the South—codified as the "African American tradition"—and therefore limited and even re-essentialized public understanding of the complexities and always-evolving nature of African American culture in the United States.

The study of folk music as rhetoric offers various possibilities for understanding cultural formation and difference, especially when the vernacular is part of a racial project, because of vernacular music's ability, as a discursive practice, to express multiplicity concisely. As I have expressed throughout this book thus far, the seeming paradox of concision/multiplicity should be a heralding attribute of a sonic rhetorical approach. Listeners of the prison recordings hear what seem to be a simple expression of lived experience. But, as I have explored in this chapter, careful listening reveals interpretation, representation, and historical explanation of racial experience, in various complexities inherent to racial dynamics in the United States (Omi and Winant 56). Through careful listening, rhetorical meaning is derived not through so-called persuasion but from the difficult, often painful dynamics of working through and against difference— both working toward a sustainable understanding of otherness and working from the other side, out of obscurity, discrimination, and subjugation and toward equality. In the 1930s, African American vernacular music was beginning to be understood not just as a body of artifacts to be collected and indexed for the archive but as a discourse engaged in changing understanding of race and racial difference. During the interwar period, some began to realize, as Baraka argues, that African American music was not just representative of Black cultural experience "from slavery to 'citizenship'" (x) but could be understood as being symbolic of American culture itself.

INTERLUDE II

Oral History's Exigence

With the 150 field recordings that John and Alan Lomax collected during their Southern journeys (including the precious prison recordings), the holdings of the Music Division at the Library of Congress nearly doubled. However, bureaucratic ills, loss of an important grant from the Carnegie Corporation, and dealings with an ornery and conspiring supervisor, Oliver Strunk, worked together to make John Lomax feel undervalued in his work and put him on the brink of quitting his honorary position as curator of the Archive of American Folk Song (Porterfield 384). Lomax was worried that if he did not quit, Strunk would find a way to push him out, for what the former was reporting (cruelly) as a "relatively small accumulation to date of your two years' efforts" (Porterfield 536n3). In reality, the archive was thriving. By 1935, it grew by over 500 recordings, almost solely due to the Lomaxes' fieldwork.

Fortunately, John Lomax was well connected. Through the influence of his friends on Capitol Hill—particularly Texas senators Morris Sheppard and Tom Connally—he was able to plead his case before the head librarian of the Library of Congress. As a result, John was given the opportunity to renegotiate the grant that funded the Lomaxes' field trips and was able to secure new recording equipment. John was also provided traveling expenses, a secretary, and a new vehicle for travel (Porterfield 385). He was then named the head of the archive, which finally added some authority and prestige to his position, despite his yearly salary of one dollar.

The good fortune continued when John was offered two new opportunities with the government that would dovetail with his work at the Library of Congress. Both new jobs were initiatives of the New Deal's Works Progress Administration (WPA), one with the Historical Records Survey (HRS) and the other with the Federal Writers' Project (FWP). Those positions indicate that the fieldwork in which John, Alan, and other folklorists were engaged was not only growing in popularity but beginning to be seen as having powerful capital, culturally and (perhaps more significant) nationally. John's work with the HRS (under fellow Texan Luther Evans) was to oversee and advise a project then underway, "involving a national survey of historical records in county courthouses and the collection of interviews with several thousand ex-slaves" (Porterfield 386). During his first few weeks working with the FWP and as the national advisor of folklore and folkways, John worked to expand existing research on the subject of slave life. Given the task of writing instructions for HRS fieldworkers who were interviewing former slaves, he issued them a list of "detailed and homely questions" designed to "get the Negro thinking and talking about the days of slavery" (Mangione 263). As Porterfield notes, "With his lifetime interest in blacks and their way of life, Lomax was well prepared for the task and came up with a set of questions that elicited valuable information" (388). John's questions were aimed at developing a more comprehensive understanding of African American life before emancipation, by asking for minute details on everything from clothing to food, living accommodations, and even childhood games and traditions.

Lomax also encouraged interviewers to inquire after information that might aid future readers in understanding living conditions, relationships with plantation-based and other slave owners, and, as Porterfield notes, "the manner in which [an enslaved person] was informed of his freedom" (388).[1] Porterfield reports that the project produced "more than two thousand vivid and comprehensive narratives that provide an invaluable eyewitness account of slavery and its terrible ramifications" (388). The interviews would eventually become the large anthology *Lay My Burden Down: A Folk History of Slavery* (1945), compiled and edited by Lomax's colleague and fellow folklorist Benjamin Botkin.

John Lomax's detail-oriented interviewing method, paired with the deft skill of his (second) wife, Ruby Terrill Lomax, in handling language, transcription, and record keeping,[2] informed another widely acclaimed collection of folk history, the 1939 publication *These Are Our Lives*. That book's appendix includes the interview instructions given to the relief workers compiling the life stories. Titled simply "Instructions to Writers" and perhaps written or at least directed by John Lomax, they include an outline on how life stories might be encouraged from interview subjects. Collecting

Figure 3. John A. Lomax, Doc Reed, and Richard Amerson conducting an interview at the home of Mrs. Ruby Pickens Tartt, Livingston, Alabama, 1940

an "authentic" story is stressed, as the interviewer is instructed to "discover the real feeling of the person consulted" and to "record this feeling regardless of [the interviewer's] own attitude toward it" (418). The list includes instructions on what kinds of story contain the highest degree of potential human interest and on the importance of knowing when to veer from the outline in order to allow fruitful side-stories to emerge. Built throughout all the instructions is encouragement for the interviewers to be sensitive—to keep personal opinions and feelings in check and to refrain from acknowledging distain related to poor living conditions or other undesirable circumstances that interviewers encountered.

Like the collectors of slave narratives, the editors of *These Are Our Lives* were charged with recording the stories of average citizens in various contexts in the American South: on the farm, in textile mills and factories, in service occupations (business, dentistry, law enforcement, etc.), and in WPA relief work. "The idea," wrote project director W. T. Couch, "is to get life histories which are readable and faithful representations of living persons, and which, taken together, will give a fair picture of the structure and working of society" (ix). Belief in the importance of offering a "faithful" and "fair" representation of otherwise underrepresented America not only embodied the work of the narrative and *Lives* projects but ran through the entire Federal Writer's Project, which had its source in the headwaters of the executive office. "So far as I know," Couch continued, "this method of portraying the quality of life of a people, of revealing the real workings of institutions, customs, habits, has never been used for the people of any region or country" (ix). For the most part, it had not been used in the ways being developed by the WPA. While, as noted in the previous chapters, the soundness of some of John Lomax's methods has received scrutiny over the years, the expertise and experience that he brought to the FWP had a significant impact not just on the greater project and mission of the WPA, through the projects mentioned above, but on oral history or life history and ethnographic practices in general.

In his introduction, Couch touches briefly on those impacts, by pointing to several advantages of oral history and implicitly acknowledging a shift in the exigency related to an emerging public understanding of its usefulness. Life histories, Couch argues, offer a different perspective—"certain possibilities and advantages"—to traditional histories or historical but fictive portraits of vernacular America (x). By compiling a history of the people, the "folk," in their own words, a historian avoids the composite and homogenized character present in popular fiction and also retains a sense of individual humanity—something often lost in the socioscientific model of the case study. John Steinbeck's *Grapes of Wrath* (published in April 1939, the same year as *Lives*) may be implicated in the former critique. In the latter, socioscientific approaches "treat[ed] human beings as abstractions," robbing subjects of the nuances of personal identity (Crouch x). Abstraction particularly threatened minority voices, which is one reason John and Alan Lomax's pioneering work in the Southern states (especially their work in the prisons), the narrative project, and the work overseen by Couch were so revolutionary. Those projects were not the only of their kind, but they pointed toward a slightly revised historiographical methodology that was open and inclusive rather than reductive and/or empirical. That work, when combined with the technological advantages of new methods of audio recording, revolutionized how Americans might hear and, by extension, understand themselves, as well as, perhaps more important, how they might understand others. On that point, Couch's serious sentiment is instructive still: "This is no trivial matter. The People, all the people, must be known, they must be heard. Somehow they must be given representation, somehow they must be given voice and allowed to speak, in their essential character [. . .] Here, then, are real, living people" (xiii–xiv).

Even so, oral history remains suspect for some academic historians doing the "serious" work of empirical social history. The privileging of hard, written documentation relegates oral history to a secondary status. One problem is that oral history provides a singular perspective offered as uncorroborated memory. Oral history is as likely to contain folklore as to convey facts. If the evidence oral history provides is a mixture of facts, misremembered details, mythologized self-narratives, and outright fabrications, is it history? Jazz historian Burton W. Peretti argues that it is and that the ambiguity of oral histories can be "stimulating" (118). Sometimes, as is the case in the history of jazz—a subject that Peretti says academic historians ignored "for decades" (122)—oral history far exceeds the documentary evidence left behind. Under those circumstances and when "used with care," Peretti declares, oral histories "are almost priceless sources" (122). Corroboration—with other oral histories and with the scant documentary evidence left behind—is still possible, if definitive veracity is the goal. But oral histories offer history in the mode of folkness. "Folklore," Peretti continues, "has always favored oral traditions (in direct opposition to history's penchant for written sources)." He argues further, "In interviews, what is seen and heard is 'truth' of a phenomenological variety, expressed in cadences, gestures, rhetorical strategies, and statements of the subject [. . .] Even lies, willful distortions of the truth, are a form of 'truth' expressed in a peculiar way by the performer" (127). Oral histories are thus an alternative, if not a challenge, to traditional empiricism; they invite interpretative (rather than starkly empirical) strategies—sonic rhetorical analysis, for example. More often than not, in the rush to produce textual history, oral history's status as aural history is completely disregarded.

Oral/Aural History: The Democratization of History through First-Person Rhetorical Narrative

By and large, the life stories collected by the fieldworkers in the Federal Writers' Project were accomplished by interview and transcription. While transcribers made efforts to represent subjects' unique voices through the careful alphabetic rendering of dialect (in the way that literary renderings of African American Vernacular English often appeared), Lomax's predecessor Sterling Brown urged that "truth to idiom be paramount and exacting truth to pronunciation secondary" (quoted in Mangione 263). Textual renderings of spoken interviews, be they idiomatic or in dialect, represent a remediation that, while rendering the discursive "data" more easily transferred, also repurpose the audience's experience of the words, in addition to extracting them from the phenomenological sphere created by a speaker's voice. Transforming voices into text reduces (if not eliminates), the aural cadences and rhythm of spoken dialect but also eases its redistribution as data—for any number of scholarly, commercial, scientific, or personal uses. In the case of the New Deal projects, the benefits of oral history rendered as printed text are undeniable. Print is more easily reproducible, more easily circulated, and more accessible. With relative ease, a large audience had access to the life stories of a widely diverse group of fellow Americans—some, like the formerly enslaved, who never had an audience before. Textuality (through print technology) efficiently met perceived demands of a consumer public in the process of discovering their interest in themselves as a people. But what might it have meant for the voices textuality left behind and what might have been the reception if *These Are Our Lives* had it been produced as a series of phonograph recordings and then sold or produced for a national radio broadcast?

While music was always their primary goal, John and Alan Lomax recorded several spoken stories, sermons, personal histories, and yarns. Those oral histories were rarely heard by the public, and most remain in the ephemera between the more popular element of the recordings, the songs. For the Lomaxes, the nonmusical recordings were likely deemed less marketable or just less remarkable than the music that typically accompanied them. A carefully edited book collecting the most striking and sensational stories would likely be more interesting to the commercial market: Alan Lomax's books *Mister Jelly Roll* (1950) and *The Rainbow Sign* (1959), for example, were distillations of recorded oral histories. The aural nature of recorded history may also be less accessible to a general public because of the difficulties and effort involved in listening. Those difficulties range from receiving the actual sound of the recording—its affective materiality—to understanding the regional accents and dialects of both rural white folks and people of color. Those listening practices represent consumer work less present in textual renderings, especially if a text has been heavily edited and linguistically codified for a large public audience.

The advantages and potentials for attention to sonic renderings of oral/aural histories in rhetorical criticism is a subject only just beginning to receive explicit attention, often in the work of digital rhetoricians working with found or reappropriated aural artifacts.[3] That emerging work underscores how listening to oral/aural history enhances our understanding of historical individuals but also emphasizes oral history as a "co-constructed process of narrative composition" (Anderson, "Olive Project," para. 1) Such co-construction is made explicit in the transformation of oral history from audio recordings into cohesive narrative artifacts, as in the above examples. Attention to oral history as it is rendered from aural to textual artifacts requires attention to the ways that movement within modalities shifts both meaning and experience. That process also calls attention to how mediation transforms the message and reforms the rhetorical situation.

Knowing a bit about the methods and practices that John Lomax and his colleagues at the WPA employed in compiling oral history is key to understanding the oral musical history of jazz musician Jelly Roll Morton that is central to chapter 3. In the next section, leading up to that chapter's discussion of the making of dialectical oral history by Morton and Alan Lomax, I discuss briefly how the making of oral/aural histories, especially the stories and narratives central to them, has been taken up in rhetorical studies and related disciplines. The goal of that discussion is to highlight that oral/aural historiographical practice is indeed rhetorical and that some scholars consider it centrally so. The discussion works as an important interlude between the above, more general history of the WPA, FWP, and John Lomax's work as an oral historian in the early 1930s and the next chapter's more specific discussion of the work of John's son and predecessor, Alan, in the Archive of American Folk Song near the end of that decade. Alan's sessions recording oral history with Jelly Roll Morton and the variety of mediated artifacts resulting from those sessions represent a compelling example of sound recording's paradox as a medium in "seeming abstraction from the social world even as it [is] manifested more dynamically within it" (Sterne, *Audible Past* 6).

Constitutive Rhetoric and Rhetorical Criticism's Narrative Paradigm

History, including biography and autobiography, is most often represented and mediated through and within a narrative structure. Wayne Booth recognized his work as a literary critic and rhetorician as dealing directly with narratives as they are represented through the "presentation of time-ordered or time-related experience that in any way supplements, re-orders, enhances, or interprets unnarrated life" (14). He recognized that "re-ordering" extended even to self-making and that making sense of ourselves as actors within the paradox of lived experience—its simultaneous chaos and monotony—was an act of story-making. The appeal of oral history to a study interested in sonic rhetorics is related to that grand tradition of narrative creation but also to the nature of storytelling as an oral/aural practice. Oral history—especially when recorded using audio technology—retains both its narrative and its aural characteristics and allows the researcher to consider what the presence of a sonic component contributes to the rhetoric of the message being related.

While much of our storytelling has moved into literate, multimediated, and even digital spaces, the act of story-making has remained a practice with goals of dialogic resonance and of identification through shared experience. Unsurprisingly, narrative as a rhetorical practice has been the subject of Western scholarly inquiry and debate since ancient Greece. In his *Poetics*, Aristotle emphasized the importance of plot in his discussion of the elements of tragic narrative (the other elements being spectacle or setting, character, thought, diction, and melody). The tragic dramas that Aristotle was interested in theorizing were important to the culture not as depictions of actual events but as still "real" or imitative renderings of various types of value-laden potential—experiences that audiences would find compelling. As such, plot was important both as a way of setting up the chronology of events but also as creating a structure of meaning around the events depicted, in a way that presented their mimetic or imitative "reality" as something from which general causality and reason/rationality might be extracted. In other words, plot created a narrative structure for understanding the important morals and ethics of a community, "what [they] consider[ed] important, trivial, fortunate, tragic, good, evil, and what impel[ed] movement from one to another" (Martin 87).

Modern and ancient storytelling—be it in Aesop's fables (which predates Aristotle by several centuries), African Yoruba mythology (which included the use of the signifying monkey), Greek or Shakespearean drama, or radio, television, or film—draws on the epideictic power of mimetic narrative as a means of value sustaining and constituency. As James Jasinski (2001) relates, during the 19th century's turn toward Romanticism, the utility and primacy of the imitation paradigm in rhetorical narrative would find a rival in a growing interest in personal expression as the most important function of artistic narrative production:

> The Aristotelian-Romantic tension—the question of whether literary art (and all discursive practice, for that matter) functions primarily to imitate or reflect the world or to express or evoke the inner world of the author—remains a topic in aesthetic and discursive theory. (392)

Those two sometimes-competing paradigms are rounded out holistically by musical discourse, especially vernacular and, more widely, "popular" music. Pop music both combines mimetic literary/narrative elements and attempts to depict and imitate the emotional tenor of the moment through musical tropes.

The study of narrative as a rhetorical device or mode addresses that tension in the way it draws together and creates meaning around the effects of rhetoric, be they aesthetic/visceral, instrumental, or constitutive. When a narrative works rhetorically, "it functions aesthetically to create a vivid, memorable, and compelling world" (Jasinski 393). That world can be inhabited, presented, or both. As a world-making agent, narrative functions constitutively, and within that mode, narrative as rhetoric can "shape and transform how a community understands its world" (393), through a process that Maurice Charland (1987) argues happens before persuasion. He observes that constitutive rhetoric contributes to "the production of ideology" or "the constitution of the subject" (213), that "[n]arratives 'make real' coherent subjects," and that "this making real is a part of the ontological function of narratives" (221). The "real," however, is an illusion. As Charland explains, ideology is, necessarily, a useful illusion of "a unified and unproblematic subjectivity" (221), and "[s]ubjectivity is always social, constituted in language, and exists in a delicate balance of contradictory drives and impulses" (222). Constitutive rhetoric, then, is a part of the larger discourse of epideictic rhetoric. It is value-laden and used to create and sustain values within a worldview. Constitutive narratives are built to provide structures in which characters can dwell, and once lived in for long enough, those structures have the potential of becoming part of the rhythmic fabric of a culture's discursive body. In this way, narratives achieve the status of "reality" and, as Charland puts it, a stature "beyond the realm of rational or even free choice, beyond the realm of persuasion" (214), where choices related to social identity, religion, faith, and race or ethnicity can seem predetermined and embedded within the meaning, making myths of "the way things are and always have been."

Narratives also work instrumentally to persuade internal and external audiences. In those cases, the goal is to prove or maintain a belief in the efficacy of the internal logic of a certain understanding/opinion of the way things are or should be. Within Walter Fisher's theory of narrative paradigms, each narrative structure relies on an internal rationality, constructed by the rhetor, as part of a functional understanding of the world. Potential conflicts arise when competing ideological narratives come into contact. Narrative is used instrumentally in order to respond to the exigencies created by such conflict, to negotiate the contours of those conflicts through appeals to the audience's internal logics, and—where possible—to find common ground, common values, common stories. Fisher argues that "prevailing theories of human communication and logic—ancient, modern, and contemporary—do not answer these questions adequately" and that human values have gone largely ignored as a resource for understanding the "constitution of knowledge, truth, or reality" (xi). A result of that misstep has been the "unquestioned superiority" of technical discourse over the rhetorical and poetic, leading to gross social and political misunderstandings from both internal and historical perspectives.

To address that problem, Fisher argues for a reconceptualization of humans as primarily storytellers (or *Homo narrans*). Fisher's perspective leads to an understanding of human communication as chiefly storymaking—as "symbolic interpretations of aspects of the world occurring in time and shaped by history, culture, and character"—with "good reasons." Within his narrative paradigm, reason and, by extension, rationality are contextual constructs with internal logics that reflect "values or value-laden warrants for believing or acting in certain ways" (xi). Those logics depend not on scientific rationality (or historical empiricism) but on the fidelity of the story to existent narrative structures within a cultural or subcultural rendering and on a story's resonant fidelity within those constructs. From that perspective, rhetoric can be a way of subverting the violence and/or subjugation that occurs when opposing paradigms come into contact and conflict with one another.

For example, contemporary critiques of anthropologic and ethnographic practices have centered largely on the acknowledgment that levying external scientific logics or judgments of "rationality" about the internal "realities" of a subject's culture or discourse community can be damaging to the population or individuals studied. Narrative logics might be understood as producing their own

> rationality . . . determined by the nature of persons as narrative beings—their inherent awareness of *narrative probability*, what constitutes a coherent story, and their constant habit of testing *narrative fidelity*, whether or not the stories they experience ring true with the stories they know to be true in their lives. (W. Fisher 65)

The existence of external or competing story sets (along with their competing logics) does not go unacknowledged within the narrative paradigm. Rather, Fisher explains, those stories "must be chosen among in order for us to live life in a process of continual re-creation" (65).

That way of thinking about rationality undermines the idea that some forms of communication are superior to others, or that "true knowledge" exists universally outside of the constructs of culture. From Fisher's rhetorical perspective, "truth" can exist within cultures in complete opposition to outside logics or empirical/scientific renderings of what constitutes true knowledge. What matters is coherence and fidelity within the internal logic of the systemic story structure that undergirds the society. The stakes for an application of that kind of open, nonrational epistemology for truth may seem untenable—particularly in courts of law, scientific labs, or other knowledge paradigms where truth is determined logically or with carefully established empirical (or even spiritual) methods. Historical rationality is always already fiction, but that does not mean we should jettison truth as an ideal altogether. Historical inquiry requires a different, more porous understanding of and patience with truth—particularly considering the ways in which individual truths about the past contradict as often as they coalesce.

As I address Jelly Roll Morton's story in the next chapter, several notes from the above discussion should hang sustained in the air in relative harmony. First, his oral history—his version of jazz's inception—is "true." Second, Morton's tale is itself constitutive of history. Third, that constitution is most powerful when it is most musical. Morton's take on what happened to him in New Orleans around the turn of the 20th century is true in the sense that it is presented as part of a relatively coherent narrative with an internal logic. For the listener, that logic reveals Morton as the mythic prophet in his rendering of the jazz narrative/mythos. As a mythmaker, Morton asserts certain assumptions, truisms, and conflations of the historical ground he covers, but throughout his narrative, his argument rings true: he was the "originator of jazz, stomps, and swing."

CHAPTER 3

Inventing Jazz

Jelly Roll Morton and the Sonic Rhetorics of Hot Musical Performance

> Jazz was the hybrid of hybrids and so it appealed to a nation of lonely immigrants. In a divided world struggling blindly toward unity, it became a cosmopolitan musical argot. This new musical language owes its emotional power to the human triumph accomplished at the moment of its origin in New Orleans—a moment of cultural ecstasy.
>
> —Alan Lomax, *Mister Jelly Roll* 122

> We had all nations in New Orleans.
>
> —Jelly Roll Morton quoted in Lomax, *Mister Jelly Roll* 122

The "Originator of Jazz, Stomps, and Swing"

It is difficult to overstate the influence and popularity of jazz during the 1930s. "Swing" music, as it was often called, had dominated almost two decades of popular US culture—in the clubs, on phonograph record releases, and on the radio. Jazz was so ubiquitous that Alan Lomax had grown suspect and seemingly sick of it. Both Alan and his father, John, had avoided recording jazz musicians during their many recording trips across the country. They were weary of how the jazz commercial juggernaut dominated radio, sheet music, and record sales. Even the budding film industry had produced *The Jazz Singer* (1927) as its first "talkie" (a film with a synchronized audio track).

Popular jazz upset the Lomaxes' sense of racial propriety and authenticity. They were uncomfortable with the ways white performers had long appropriated and changed the genre to make it more accessible to white audiences. Jazz was, at worst, a bastardization of real African American music and, at best, an overblown and passing fancy that had overstayed its welcome. "At that time," Alan later said, "jazz was my worst enemy. Through the forces of radio, it was wiping out the music I cared about—African traditional folk music" (Szwed, "Doctor Jazz" 122). But in 1938, Alan changed his mind. He had been working for a year as "assistant in charge" of the Archive of American Folk Song at the Library of Congress, when he became acquainted with a man who called himself Jelly Roll Morton, who said that he "wanted to correct the history of jazz" and that he was the "originator of jazz, stomps, and swing." Lomax recalled, "I looked at him with considerable suspicion. But I thought, I'd take this cat on, and . . . see how much folk music a jazz musician knows" (9).

Morton, born Ferdinand Joseph Lamothe, came of age in the first decade of the 1900s, during what might be considered the final cacophonous refrain of Old New Orleans—the city's blistering coda. Starting at age 14, Morton cut his musical teeth playing piano in the honky-tonks and brothels of the port town. In that context and for a number of years, Morton played several clubs a night, developing his skill and repertoire along the way. We now know Jelly Roll Morton as a jazz virtuoso. Alongside Buddy Bolden, Sidney Bechet, and Freddie Keppard, Morton is regarded by jazz historians as one of several key musicians tied to the emergence of New Orleans jazz at the beginning of the 20th century.[1]

Morton left New Orleans in around 1905 and traveled the country as a vaudeville pianist and singer, also working in other professions (Szwed, *Alan Lomax* 121). Like many New Orleans jazzmen seeking their fortune, Morton eventually ended up in Chicago, where he worked from 1923 to 1930. There, in a kind of jazz boiler room, he joined the likes of the New Orleans Rhythm Kings, Joe "King" Oliver and his Creole Jazz Band, and even Louis Armstrong. In 1920s Chicago, the "jazz age" was in full swing, and Jelly Roll Morton was one of its many benefactors. Competition motivated everyone toward excellence and innovation. Armstrong said that his move to Chicago was when he "got good" (Reich and Gaines 80).

While in Chicago, Morton had his first hit, with "Wolverine Blues" (or "The Wolverines"; ♫ "Wolverine Blues" https://doi.org/10.3998/mpub.98710978.cmp.17).[2] Sheet music for the song was published by Melrose Brothers Music, which would go on to release dozens of Morton's arrangements and compositions. Morton also recorded for the popular "race" record label Okeh, and in 1926, he signed a record contract with the Victor Talking Machine Company. At Victor, Morton and his band Red Hot Peppers recorded a number of what today's listeners consider classic jazz "sides," such as "Doctor Jazz," "Black Bottom Stomp," and "Jungle Blues" (Szwed, *Alan Lomax* 121). In those most successful years of his career, Jelly Roll Morton accumulated both fame and a small fortune.

♫ "Jungle Blues" (https://doi.org/10.3998/mpub.9871097.cmp.18).

But by May 23, 1938, when Morton came to visit Alan Lomax at the Library of Congress, jazz tastes had shifted dramatically. Morton was all but forgotten. Though he had tried to maintain a place in the public eye, Morton was out of money, in poor health, and in desperate search of an audience. The Depression had hit the recording industry particularly hard, and with radio offering a free listening alternative, record sales dwindled. To make matters worse for Morton, his publisher, Walter Melrose (of Melrose Brothers Music), had stopped paying Morton's share of royalties. After months of unanswered correspondence, Melrose finally sent Morton a pittance ($86.94) and said the publisher's debts were settled (Reich and Gaines 168). Morton was furious. After a final failed attempt, in New York City, to recapture interest in his music, he relocated, dejected, to Washington. When hopes to begin a new career there in prizefighting management went nowhere, he relegated himself to working as a bartender, bouncer, and piano man for a ramshackle one-room tavern, the Jungle Inn.

A few months before his visit to the Library of Congress, Morton was listening to Robert Ripley's nationally broadcasted radio show "Believe It or Not!" and heard W. C. Handy announced as the "originator of jazz, stomps, and blues." Handy, a songwriter and publisher of orchestral pieces, was a celebrated early adopter of jazz and blues forms and was "perhaps the most widely respected African American in the United States" at the time (Szwed, "Doctor Jazz" 13).[3] He was not, however, a true "jazzman"—at least not by Morton's standards. At best, Handy was a benefactor of the jazz movement. He was most certainly not its inventor.

With the help of his friend Roy Carew, Morton wrote a letter in protest and correction to Ripley, in what might be seen as a first move in Morton's last serious attempt to recapture his place in jazz's emerging public memory. After a polite introduction, Morton made a now-famous assertion.

> In your broadcast of March 26, 1938, you introduced W. C. Handy as the originator of jazz, stomps and blues. By this announcement you have done me a great injustice, and you have also misled many of your fans.
>
> It is evidently known, beyond contradiction, that New Orleans is the cradle of jazz, and I, myself, happened to be creator in the year 1902, many years before the Dixieland Band organized. Jazz music is a style, not compositions; any kind of music may be played in jazz, if one has the knowledge. The first stomp was written in 1906, namely "King Porter Stomp." "Georgia Swing" was the first to be named swing, in 1907. (Morton, "I Created Jazz")

In the letter, which goes on for nearly 1,500 words, Morton defends his position with a litany of arguments.[4] Most striking is Morton's insistence that jazz is not a group of compositions but a style in which "any kind of music may be played." That assertion would be central to the narrative Morton would weave during his sessions with Alan Lomax.

♫ "King Porter Stomp" (https://doi.org/10.3998/mpub.9871097.cmp.19).

This chapter chronicles the time Morton and Lomax spent together recording those sessions in the Library of Congress. Using audio excerpts from their long musical conversations, I exhibit Morton's sonic rhetorical approach for reinserting himself into a tradition that had seemingly forgotten him. Alan Lomax also had hopes for the sessions' output, and his agenda would shape Morton's story as well. Most important, however, I show how Morton's arguments diverge rhetorically from those he forwarded in the letter to Ripley. His argument remains the same on the surface, but his rhetorical toolbox expands once he is behind a piano, when his arguments take the form of both oral storytelling and performed music. Morton was a master of both, and his argument is strengthened by oral performance and by his piano playing, which he describes as "hot." Morton, who signed his letter to Ripley as "World's Greatest Hot Tune Writer," emphasizes the term *hotness* as a designator for true jazz playing. The argument he makes for his authenticity as an author of jazz's origins depends on a careful articulation of what hotness is, where it comes from, and what it sounds like. That argument required Lomax and the eventual, broader audience of the sessions to listen carefully, and we are obliged to do the same to hear the nuances of the sonic argument Morton performs.

Morton's demonstration of hotness is the key to his argument and is also a particular kind of virtuosic and racial performance. His argument for authenticating himself included a rather unique portrait of racial experience in early 20th-century New Orleans, one that would be a challenge to the Lomaxes' notions of Black musical essence. Embedded in the performance of Morton's desperate attempts to bring himself back into the national spotlight is a radical complication of jazz, as a source of Black musical essence and, therefore, as part of the ongoing infrastructure of the racial divide. As Morton discusses race and race mixing as a typical part of the emergent jazz scene in New Orleans, he seems to argue that hotness was a distinct element of African American essence. Morton's stories, performances, and embodied status as a Creole of color communicate a different message. As I retell the story of Jelly Roll at the Library of Congress, my own argument is that Morton's sonic rhetorics and his musical articulation of hot jazz resonate as a challenge to Black essentialist (and therefore white supremacist) historiography.

Mythos, Virtuosity, and the Roots of Epideictic Rhetoric

Jelly Roll Morton's unique burden of proof raises other questions about the depths of rhetorical practice itself: How do cultural traditions (musical or otherwise) begin, and how do they then take root? What are the discursive and nondiscursive means for those beginnings? Asking what rhythmic practices have to do with those processes is particularly important to students of sound. Morton's oral and musical history might be best understood as building myth—or even myth-breaking and rebuilding. By 1938, jazz was well on its way to becoming a vital part of the American mythos, and Morton had the challenge of demonstrating not just the ways he should be a part of jazz history but how he belonged alongside its other mythic figures. Before diving into the early 20th-century milieu in New Orleans, I here briefly consider mythos, virtue/value production, and their connections to epideictic rhetoric. The questions mentioned above will have more satisfying answers if we understand virtuosic musical performance's potential for symbolic (re)constitution—for the making of history and/or myth.

In addition to providing a pseudohistorical "reality" from which to build cultural meaning, myth "is always an account of a 'creation'; it relates how something was produced, [how it] began to *be*" (Eliade 6). By extension, as Christopher Johnstone writes, "In its primal meaning *mythos* comprehends the idea of telling a story, of presenting a narrative that enables a people—a tribe, a clan, a culture—to make sense of the mysterious" (16). Further, Bronisław Malinowski explains that myth "expresses, enhances, and codifies belief; it safeguards and enforces morality; it vouches for the efficiency of ritual and contains practical rules for the guidance of men [and women]" (quoted in Johnstone 17). In short, mythos sets the parameters of the values, virtues, and shared ideals within a cultural construct. As I have been exploring in this study through terms like *folkness*, *blues*, and *rhythm*, epideictic rhetorics are more than just rules for living; they set the stage—or establish the time signature—for living, and mythos is one powerful way such work is accomplished. Mythmaking—through ritual, rite, storytelling, folk and blues traditions, and so on—is an important way epideictic values are perpetuated. Epideictic activities, such as those just mentioned, involve the distribution of judgments about community values through the public performance of ritual and rite, which, not incidentally, are often couched in rhythmic language or accompanied by music. If epideictic activates shared ideals and virtues, epideictic rhetoricians are most effective when they embody the ideals in perceptible ways and inhabit a social position of relative power and influence. Shared notions of virtue and value circulate through social agreement on the praiseworthy quality of a virtuosic performance, which, in turn, perpetuates a desire to both emulate the performance and exalt the performer.

Jelly Roll Morton's claims of authenticity were made through careful storytelling and rhapsody, which, in the classical sense, is the stitching together, in rhythmic virtuosity, of value-laden narrative.[5] Virtuosity, the internalization of virtue (external cultural norms learned in the act of the public and private practice or performance of those norms), is eventually habituated, as Debra Hawhee has written, as both a "repeated/repeatable style of living" and a "performative, bodily phenomenon [. . .] produced through observation, imitation and learning" ("Agonism and Aretē" 187). As explained in movement II of this book's introduction, Aristotle calls that embodied excellence *aretē* and draws it together with epideictic rhetoric: *aretē* sets the parameters of epideictic and activates the virtues and vices commonly held within a community or culture, by making them subject to (and the subjects of) performances of praise and blame. Epideictic rhetoric is a performance that both produces and perpetuates codes of value and belief; *aretē* is the skill attendant to that performance. As an art where virtuosic improvisation is paramount to successful performance, jazz is an apropos way of understanding the function of *aretē*, especially when the discussion shifts, as below, to "hot" jazz.

I here advance those claims in the ancient Greek register not to privilege that way of understanding rhetorical activity but because of the ways that they relate to jazz—or any skilled performance, for that matter. But there are clear ancillaries between the Western rhapsodist equipped with *aretē* and the African griot. A hybrid model would make the most sense here. Griots possess the same kind of embodied knowledge as the virtuosic rhapsodist. Though Morton was uncomfortable with his own African American heritage, his connection to and embeddedness within what Adam Banks calls "the depth and complexity in African American oral traditions" provided him with a set of literate tools that would contribute not just to the content of his argument but to the logics of the rhetorical paradigm from which he argued. Using Banks's framing, a griotic treatment of the history and music of early jazz in New Orleans might

> provide a wealth of content reflecting black epistemologies and ontologies, ways of knowing and being in the world that begin with the assumption of black humanity, and provide examples of the wide continuum from access to, participation in, and resistance of broader narratives and structures.

For Morton, and operating under "the premise of black mastery," jazz and storytelling are two of many "forms of literacy that offer relevance . . . [for] the individual performer's and the audience's or community's expectations, and of the importance of both skills and critical consciousness" (32). Though Morton had lost his audience, he was as secure as ever in his skill as a jazz virtuoso. Regaining that audience or at least securing the legacy he felt due depended on finding a conduit amenable to a polyphonic sonic argument.

To crack open the jazz mythos and insert himself into it, Jelly Roll Morton, as rhapsodist-griot, had to make a complex argument. First, he had to make a claim to and demonstrate his knowledge of the "basic codes of value and belief" within jazz culture and society. Those codes were presented for the Library of Congress as a griotic narrative that included rich descriptions of race, space, place, and people, all of which evoke a particular quality of life in the Storyville district of New Orleans (including detailed accounting for the lifestyle of a jazz musician). Second, the process of Jelly Roll's authentication required the performance of specific and embedded jazz values as they existed as part of the matrix of musicianship, mentality, and sociopolitical realities of his day, including performances of racial identity. Those values are communicated not only in Morton's deep repertoire knowledge (well over 40 tunes and melodies are represented in the sessions) but also in his performance of a central jazz value, "hot" playing. Third and most important, Morton had to prove his excellence (his embodied *aretē*), not only through pristine virtuosic jazz performance within that matrix, but also through a careful explanation and conceptualization of those virtuosic elements.

When well performed and positively received, those three elements—rich griotic narrative, virtuosic performance, and technical demonstration—work in concert to constitute the necessary ingredients for rhetorical inception. They gave Morton the tools to revise the creation myth of jazz and insert himself as an "authentic" contributor in the tradition's origins. In the process, they produced a rhetoric of jazz: a set of skills that could be practiced, perfected, and then applied to any tune. As I will demonstrate, Jelly Roll Morton's capacity for virtuosic performance and the quality of his output were the keys to accomplishing his goals with Lomax at the Library of Congress. Further, his task was more complicated than just describing his place and role in jazz's early years in New Orleans or even than demonstrating his command over repertory, his capacity for harmonic sophistication, or the dexterous range of his hands. His proof had to be believable to those that mattered, the gatekeepers of jazz's history. So his argument would be sonic, and his performance had to be hot.

Jelly Roll Morton at the Library of Congress

♫ "Jelly Roll's Background" (https://doi.org/10.3998/mpub.9871097.cmp.20).

(*Jelly Roll Morton plays modulating piano chords while speaking.*)

JELLY ROLL MORTON: Ready?

ALAN LOMAX: Yeah. Uh, Jelly Roll, uh, tell us about yourself. Tell us where you were born, who your folks were, and when, and how?

MORTON: Well, I'll tell you. As I can understand, my folks were in the city of New Orleans long before the Louisiana Purchase. And all my folks came directly from the shores—or not the shores, I mean from France. That's across the world, in the other world. And they landed here in the New World years ago. I remember so far back as my great-grandmother and great-grandfather.

LOMAX: Tell us about what their names were, Jelly.

MORTON: Their names—my great-grandfather's name was Emile Péché. That's a French name. And the grandmother was Mimi Péché. That seems to be all French, and as long as I can remember those folks, they never was able to speak a word in American or English.

LOMAX: Did they own slaves?

MORTON: Uh, well, I don't know. I don't think they had no slaves back there in Louisiana, I don't think so. I don't know, but they never spoke of anything like that. But anyway, my great, my grandmother, her name was Laura. She married a French settler in New Orleans by the name of Henri Monette. That was my grandfather. And [n]either one of them spoke American or English.

Well, my grandmother bore sons named Henri, Gus, Neville, and Nelusco—all French names. And she bore the daughters, Louise and Viola and Margaret. That was the three daughters. Louise, her eldest, her elder daughter, happened to be my mother. Ferd Jelly Roll Morton. Of course, I guess you wonder how the name Morton come in. Why, the name Morton being a English name, it wouldn't sound very much like a French name. But my real name is Ferdinand Lamothe. My mother also married one of the French settlers in New Orleans out of a French family, being a contractor. My father was a brick contractor—bricklayer—making large buildings and so forth and so on.

We always had some kind of a musical instruments in the house, including guitar, drums, piano, trombone, and so forth and so on, harmonica, and Jew's harp. We had lots of them. And everybody always played for their pleasure—whatever the ones that desired to play. We always had ample time that was given us, and periods, to rehearse our lessons, which was given to anyone that was desirous in accepting lessons.

But of course, the families never—the family, I mean—never had an idea that they wanted musicians in the family to make their living. They always had it in their mind that a musician was a tramp, other than the . . . other than the exceptions . . . with the exceptions of the French Opera House players, which they always patronized. They only thought they was the great musicians in the country. In fact, I myself was inspired by going to the French Opera House once. Because the fact of it was I liked to play piano,

> and the piano was known at that time to be an instrument for a lady. So, I had . . . and in my mind that if I played piano, I would be misunderstood.[6]

Jelly Roll Morton's appearance at Alan Lomax's office in the Library of Congress marked a turning point for Lomax in his attitude toward the study of jazz roots. Lomax had been across town to the Jungle Inn, where he heard Morton play. He was compelled, then, when the aging musician—clearly from the old guard of the jazz tradition—came to the library hoping to partner with Lomax, to recast jazz history as a folk phenomenon and wrest it away from the competing voices in jazz's ongoing transformations and from the colonizing forces of the American corporate recording industry. Something about Jelly Roll Morton's audacity was persuasive to Lomax. He recalled Morton's dress, in particular: an aging but sharp hundred-dollar suit; a beautiful hand-painted silk tie with matching shirt, socks, and handkerchief; gold rings and the famous half-carat diamond in his front incisor. Lomax wondered if the man looking the part of an old jazzman from New Orleans sounded like one too (Szwed, "Doctor Jazz" 9).

The Library of Congress sessions that followed their first meeting were not originally planned to be very lengthy. Not until Morton had played a few songs, "Alabama Bound" and "King Porter Stomp," with background information thrown in to explain how they came about, did Lomax realize how resourceful Morton might be. About 20 minutes into their first session, Lomax asked Morton to go back and start from the beginning. From then on, it is clear that Lomax was enthralled by Morton's cool demeanor, his genius at the piano, and his detailed recollection of the music scene in turn-of-the-century New Orleans. Lomax said, "I realized that Jelly was telling me the history of jazz, because jazz was a neighborhood project. Only a few individuals in this small, sleepy town were involved in evoking the music of jazz out of the broad basis of American Negro folk song" (Szwed, *Alan Lomax* 137). Having a keyboard under his fingers allowed Morton to punctuate his history with chords and melodies, giving his stories a multimodal richness not possible in a typical interview. Not only were the Morton sessions unique as musical output, but they were the first recorded oral history in jazz.[7]

By the time of his sessions with Jelly Roll Morton in 1938, Alan Lomax, though only 23 years old, had already emerged as a well-known author, folklorist, and national public figure. He had traveled all over North America, including trips to the Bahamas and an extended recording trip to Haiti with author and folklorist Zora Neale Hurston. A project with Morton fit nicely within the parameters of Lomax's work. While Morton saw the sessions as an opportunity to broaden the reach of his claim as the originator of jazz, Lomax saw Morton as a resource in his ongoing project to record and preserve unique folk traditions. Their different agendas were sometimes in concert and sometimes in competition. In the following analysis of the Morton sessions, it should be remembered that while Lomax's vocal presence on the session recordings waxes and wanes, he is present throughout: questioning, encouraging, prodding, and occasionally (as critics of Lomax's methods have pointed out) supplying Morton with whiskey, which Lomax sometimes used to lower his subjects' inhibitions.[8] To be sure, Morton and Lomax's partnership on the project is marked with the paradoxes of competing rhetorical agendas and is complicated further by the clear asymmetry of both racial and institutional power between them. Yet co-creation occurs amid and through those imbalances. In a sonic rendering of that dialectic (unlike with polished alphabetic biographies), we can listen for ourselves to Lomax's interruptions or hear Morton's voice begin to slur when he has had sufficient drink. Whatever power Lomax wields as gatekeeper of the project is tempered for the listener by the persistence of Morton's musical tale, an eight-hour epic from beginning to end.

In that "epic" designation, I echo historian Philip Pastras, who compares Jelly Roll Morton's narrative style and ethos in the sessions to the mythopoetic ode of an ancient epic poet. Pastras calls Jelly Roll's story an "American odyssey, with its particularly American brand of near misses, and narrow escapes, of Sirens, Circes, and monsters, of far-flung travels and homecomings" (3), fully accompanied by the "verbal one-upmanship" and "braggadocio" essential to Black language practices (16). Much of Morton's tale revolves around his status as a Creole and the various class hierarchies found in New Orleans and Storyville, including the diverse African American community there. In one segment on the first day of recording, Jelly Roll describes the kind of scene where musicians would gather and, especially, the various class mixing among the clientele of the music clubs.

♫ "Miserere" (https://doi.org/10.3998/mpub.9871097.cmp.21; starting at 3:01).

MORTON: I happened to invade that section, one of the sections of the District where the birth of jazz originated.

LOMAX: Where was this and how old were you?

MORTON: At that time, uh, that was the year of nineteen-two. I was about seventeen years old. I happened to go to Villere and Bienville, at that time one of the most famous nightspots after everything was closed. It was only a backroom, where all the greatest pianists frequented after they got off from work. All the pianists got off from work in the sporting houses at around four or after unless they had plenty money involved. And they would go to this Frenchman's (that was the name of the place) saloon, and there would be everything in the line of hilarity there. They would have even millionaires that come to listen to the different great pianists, what would no doubt be their favorites maybe among 'em.

♫ "The Stomping Grounds" (https://doi.org/10.3998/mpub.9871097.cmp.22; 0:00 - 1:08, 2:48 - 3:12).

LOMAX: What did they used to play?

MORTON: Well, they played every type of music. Everyone, no doubt, had a different style.

LOMAX: Were they white and colored both?

MORTON: They had every class—we had Spanish, we had colored, we had white, we had Frenchmens, we had Americans.

LOMAX: Do you remember, uh, specifically, they—Were they Frenchmen who had just come from France, there in those places?

MORTON: Well, we had 'em from all parts of the world. New Orleans was the stomping grounds, we'll say, for all the greatest pianists in the country. Because there were more jobs in that section of the world, in that—for pianists, than any other ten places in the world. The reason for that, they had so many mansions—sporting houses that paid nothing to no pianists. Their salary was a dollar a day in the small places that couldn't afford to pay. The big places guaranteed five dollars a night. If you didn't make five dollars, they would pay you five dollars. But that was never the case, because when you didn't make a hundred dollars, you had a bad night. [. . .]

Well, after four o'clock in the morning, all the girls that could get out of the houses, they were there. There weren't any discrimination of any kind. They all sat at different tables at any place that they felt like sitting. They all mingled together as they wished to, and everyone was just like one big happy family.

A bit later, Morton elaborates on the scene at Frenchman's and other establishments in the district.

♫ "New Orleans was a Free and Easy Place" (https://doi.org/10.3998/mpub.9871097.cmp.23; 0:12–1:23).

(*Jelly Roll Morton plays modulating piano chords while speaking.*)

MORTON: Of course, it was a free and easy place. Everybody got along just the same. And, uh—and that's the way it was. There wasn't no certain neighborhood for nobody to live in, only with the St. Charles Avenue district, which is considered the millionaire district. In fact it was. And that's how it was. Why, everybody just went anyplace that they wanted. Many times you would see some of those St. Charles Avenue bunch right in one of those honky-tonks. They was around—they called theirselves slumming, I guess, but they was there, just the same. Nudging elbows with all the big bums. And I'll go so far to say some of them were even lousy. You would meet many times with some of those fellows that was on the levy such as the inferior longshoremens, the long—what is it?—longshoremens. Is that right? And screwmens. And many of them I would doubt, that uh—very unclean—some of them was even lousy, I believe. I've known many cases where they'd take a louse and throw it on another guy that was dressed up to get him in the same fix that they were in. (*Lomax laughs.*) Oh, it was a funny situation.

At the prompting of Lomax, Morton goes on to describe less "free and easy" times, including a deadly race riot in 1900 and his exploits as a pool shark. He even shares some of the bawdier, sexually explicit tunes that he and others would play in the brothels and honky-tonks that crowded the district, including a raunchy version of the folk classic "Make Me a Pallet on Your Floor" and a song called "Dirty Dozen," the least explicit line of which is also the chorus, "Your mammy don't wear no drawers."

During the turn-of-the-century years Morton describes, New Orleans was a contradiction of progressive and conservative mores and could be both tolerant and violently exclusionary. As he intimates, the city had an open and diverse public society where racial mixing was common, but it also had terrifying and often deadly ethnic, racial, and class conflict. African Americans enjoyed decent schools for their children and were rarely restricted from other public groups, such as labor unions. But they suffered bitterly under corrupt police and government clashes. The city was the stage for multiple riots, Jim Crow segregation, and disenfranchisement under the doctrine "separate but equal," confirmed in *Plessy v. Ferguson* in 1896.

Music, however, was everywhere. On St. Peter Street in the French Quarter, from Jackson Avenue to Congo Square, and inside public parlors and busy churches, one might hear the hollers, shouts, tambourines, and handclaps of parishioners and performers. The sounds of old opera and new ragtime, stride piano, brass bands, string bands, blues bands, and the famous New Orleans funeral processions and parades came together in the coastal city as a great cacophony of sound. Nowhere was the juxtaposition of turbulence and jubilee more pronounced than in the world-famous New Orleans red-light district, Storyville. It was one of the first places where folks like Buddy Bolden, Papa Tio, and Frankie Dunson were playing music that seemed to draw from all the styles just mentioned, music that would not be recorded and named until many years later but that we would certainly recognize today as jazz.

During the early part of the 20th century, Morton, Bolden, and others in New Orleans began to turn up the proverbial temperature in the music scene. Hunched over makeshift Storyville bandstands, those players stitched parts and pieces of the musical culture together in raucous rhapsody, declaring, in so doing, a new and potent reconstruction of musical values. Wherever the music played, those values spread. Foremost among them was the rapid transformation of ragtime into jazz. Gunther Schuller writes that compared to "rigid, conservative ragtime," Morton was distinguished by a vision for jazz that "entailed contrast and variety," a smoother and looser vision than ragtime allowed (143). Morton played in a way that took the best elements of ragtime—its syncopation, unique harmonics, and danceability—and that left behind its more tedious, repetitious aspects. Schuller describes Morton's ability for rhapsodizing the most popular musical elements of the late 19th century in New Orleans—ragtime and blues especially—as "a radical innovation, one that even the early ragtime instrumentalists like Bolden and Bunk Johnson never adopted in quite that way. It was, moreover, an innovation only a composer, thinking in larger structural terms, would make" (144). Those traits, however, would not indelibly link Morton to early jazz history. Positing Morton as "the first theorist, the first intellectual that jazz produced," Schuller observes that "jazz has never been sympathetic to intellectuals" (143).

After an initial burst of innovation and change and by the end of the first decade of the 20th century, the musical climate in New Orleans began to shift. In 1907, Bolden suffered a nervous breakdown and never played there again, and Morton had already been gone for years. He left New Orleans around 1905 to seek his fame and fortune—not as a pianist, at first, but as a pool shark, hustler, and pimp. His hot piano playing would follow him anyway. Soon Morton was playing in many of the swankiest clubs and pubs in greater America, from Los Angeles to Chicago to New York. In those clubs, he began to curate a group of musicians who shared his values and who were in conversation with a music that would not find semiformal acknowledgment as "jazz" until 1915. Morton also did not give such formalities a second thought then, nor would he until many years later.

Morton's problem of dwindling recognition by 1938 had a number of probable causes. Probably foremost among them was the ebb and flow of popular culture. But as with many other art forms at the end of the 1930s, jazz was at the beginning of a cultural and factional shift—one that would escalate to a full-on schism by the middle of the 1940s (Gendron 31). Up until then, jazz had (arguably) experienced three phases: the "traditional" New Orleans jazz of the 1920s, often referred to as "Dixieland"; "swing," the music with which big bands dominated popular sales charts throughout the 1930s; and bebop, the emerging avant-garde movement interested in elevating jazz from popular to art music (32). In 1938, as a part of the aforementioned schism, traditional jazz was experiencing a revival of sorts. As Bernard Gendron writes,

> The seeds for the first jazz war were sown in the late 1930s when a few nightclubs, defying the big band boom, began to feature small jazz combos playing in the abandoned New Orleans style of the 1920s. [. . .] These purists were driven not only by nostalgia but by a revulsion toward the swing music industry, which by shamelessly pandering to the mass markets had in their eyes forsaken the principles of "true" jazz. (32)

A heated rivalry between the "revivalists" and the modernists began to play out in the pages of the jazz journals, such as *Down Beat* and *Metronome*. On the one hand, revivalists were castigated as "moldy figs," their sentimental throwbacks accused of damning the progress of jazz as a legitimate modernist art form. On the other hand, more progressively minded artists and aficionados were lambasted for their apologist connections to the "crass commercialism, faddism, and Eurocentrism" of the swing movement and, later, for their promotion of bebop, which was (in the opinion of some) an inaccessible and undanceable music made for and by elitist snobs (Gendron 32). W. C. Handy is credited with some of the first "blues" recordings, including, in 1914, "St. Louis Blues," a song that would become "one of the most popular songs in American history" (Szwed, "Doctor Jazz" 13). As mentioned earlier in this chapter, though, Handy was not a true "jazzman" by Morton's standards.

Morton likely saw the revivalist movement as his moment. He was a champion of the tradition being revived, but the legitimacy and authenticity of jazz as a cultural phenomenon would be incomplete without his voice. Despite the hubris of his claims as "inventor," Jelly Roll Morton was, without question, a part of the New Orleans scene where jazz was codifying, expanding, and gaining steam for its eventual migration to the broader country and world.

Virtuosic Performance and the Paradox of "Hot" Jazz

Morton sought out Lomax to help him gather and then amplify the substance of his unique backstory. Morton's self-given task—to provide authentic proof of his connection to jazz's inception—was both assisted and complicated by shifting ideas about what counted as "authentic." To paraphrase Miles Orvell's compelling thesis in *The Real Thing: Imitation and Authenticity in American Culture, 1880–1940*, authenticity was an invention; it is one of the tools for (re)composing cultural mythos. Orvell writes that "the culture of authenticity in the early twentieth century [was] one that would restore, through the work of art, a lost sense of 'the real thing'" (155). By the time Morton arrived at the Library of Congress in 1938, his particular brand of authenticity (i.e., his style of jazz piano playing) was just old enough to be considered "real." Through Morton's retelling, it becomes clear that at the time of its inception, jazz may have been too real and too new to be considered safe for broad public consumption.

Though it is not often thought of in such terms, jazz was a powerful new media in the first few decades of its development. Like any new media, jazz's popularity brought with it the same simultaneous exuberance and panic that accompanies most technological innovation. Predating, by at least 20 years, the language Marshall McLuhan would use to describe media affect, jazz's paradoxical impact and affective power in the 1920s and '30s can be found expressed in terms of temperature, as "hot" and then, much later, "cool." As jazz scholar Ronald Radano explains, "African American hot rhythm articulated a pairing of radicalized extremes" (*Lying Up a Nation* 460), and referring to "hot" jazz became a way of naming Black musical performance where hotness, like Blackness, was a racial construct tied into natural, illusory folk authenticity. For many within mainstream (white) culture, the term *hotness* evoked the natural forces of infection—a fever and frenzy so attractive as to be irresistible and so powerful as to defy recovery. Jazz was dangerous. But for jazz musicians, the same term named the excitement of in-the-moment invention and reinvention—the improvisation that made jazz an undeniable innovation from its ragtime and blues roots.

Jelly Roll Morton relied on a demonstration of hot, virtuosic performance as a guiding element in his musical argument at the Library of Congress. Morton first mentions hotness near the start of his very first session with Lomax, in reference to "King Porter Stomp." "Now this tune," he said, "become to be the outstanding favorite of every great hot band throughout the world that had the accomplishments and qualifications of playing it" (Morton, *Jelly Roll Morton* 6). Later in the sessions, he offers a vocal demonstration of how hotness works, using the song "Stars and Stripes Forever" as his example.

♫ "When the Hot Stuff Came In" (https://doi.org/10.3998/mpub.9871097.cmp.24; 0:00–2:51).

LOMAX: When did the hot stuff come in, Jelly?
MORTON: Well, the hot stuff came in nineteen-two. And this—
LOMAX: Yeah, but into the bands?
MORTON: Well, they came in around nineteen-three. They, they came in immediately after the—after nineteen-two, this, uh, the hot idea was arranged. Of course, they had another hot style before. It was, uh, it would say, what you call ragtime. The kind that you start to playing at a certain tempo, then you increase and you increase and you increase. You don't do it deliberately, but you, you increase, due to the fact that there wasn't a perfect tempo set for that, uh, that kind of a music. And—
LOMAX: Yeah, but the tunes that you'd play in those bands, how would they go, now? [. . .]
MORTON: Well, for an instant they, uh, they'd go like this [. . .] Uh, the drums begun: Hrump, hrump, hrump, rump, rump. Then

> the trumpet'd pick it up, you know, they'd be going right along: hrump, rump. Trumpet say: Boo do. And when they say that, the drums'd say: Hrump, rump, hrump, rump, rrrrrr—boom! And then they'd start, see? (*Vocalizes*) Yum, dum, dum, dum. Dum, dum, dum, dum, dum, dum. For an instance we'll say, "Stars and Stripes Forever." They'd play it on this style. (*vocalizes a standard version of "Stars and Stripes Forever"*)
>
> They'd pick up the next strain and play it like this. (*vocalizes a more syncopated, improvised melody of "Stars and Stripes Forever" while tapping his feet*)
>
> You see, they'd be going out then, see? Sometimes they'd start going out a half a strain. I'm telling you, they'd be terrible hot. And everybody—the kids'd be jumping up. And the boys'd—like the drummer—he'd be throwing his sticks up in the air and catching 'em, throwing 'em on the ground, bouncing 'em up there, as they walk, and catching 'em. And he'd better not miss, because the whole bunch'd razz him.

In his rendering of "Stars and Stripes Forever" and in other demonstrations, Morton emphasizes the rhythmic modulations hotness might have on a standard song, focusing on hotness as a skill for that kind of improvisation. But to satisfactorily determine jazz's power as a sonic rhetoric (and thus its use as part of Morton's argument), hotness must be thought of in the hybrid sense mentioned above—as both rhythmic innovation and irresistible infection. The designation of "hotness" (and thus "hot jazz") was made possible in its ability to represent both racist and anti-racist sentiments simultaneously. On one hand, hotness upholds and perpetuates the myth of Black musical essence: "The myth of essence represents a crucial mode of musical coherence that reflects the constituting role of sound in the formation of racial subjects" (Radano, *Lying* 3). Lomax's work, as he understood it at the time, was to perpetuate that myth by collecting authentic (read "essential") Black musical artifacts through a process Radano calls "containment," employing strategies used to "uphold the racial binaries informing the interpretation of black music" (3). Radano argues for unseating the myth of Black music as a stable form, an effort that—with help from even the most revered historians of Black music, such as Amiri Baraka—has forestalled the "consideration of the interracial background from which ideologies of black music developed in the first place" (3). Morton's understanding of that "first place"—a view that, like Radano's argument, ascribes an interracial identity to the history of Black music vis-à-vis the genesis of jazz—is a crucial element of his goals in the Lomax sessions. In that "first place," hotness resounds in a broader, anti-racist key.

Both the essentialist and the expansive inflections of hotness resonate in an interview Alan Lomax recorded in 1949 with the dentist Leonard Bechet. The interview was part of Lomax's research for the book *Mister Jelly Roll: The Fortunes of Jelly Roll Morton, New Orleans Creole and "Inventor of Jazz"* (1950). Bechet was the older brother of the renowned Creole saxophonist and clarinetist Sidney Bechet and had been a trombonist in several bands early in the 20th century. Lomax asked Dr. Bechet to describe that moment in New Orleans history and jazz mythology. Bechet's response indicates the ways in which racial identity and musical style were being conflated.

> You have to play with all varieties of people. Some of the Creole musicians didn't like the idea of mixing up with the—well, the rougher class, and so they never went too far. You see, [Alphonse] Picou—Picou's a very good clarinet, but he ain't hot. That's because he wouldn't mix so much.
>
> You have to play real *hard* when you play for Negroes. You got to *go* some, if you want to avoid their criticism. You got to come up to their mark, you understand? If you do, you get that drive. Bolden had it. Bunk had it. Manuel Perez, the best ragtime Creole trumpet, he didn't have it.
>
> See, these hot people they play like they *killing* themselves, you understand? That's the kind of effort that Louis Armstrong and Freddy Keppard put in there. If you want to hit the high notes those boys hit, brother, you got to *work* for that. (A. Lomax, *Mister Jelly Roll* 98)

According to Bechet, hot playing was best understood as a style—a kind of intensity applied to the music—and was generally produced by the alchemy of a culturally mixed and racially diverse influence. Hot playing modified the standard melody through deconstruction, modification, improvisation, and reconstitution. For Bechet, those modifications were not easy to classify technically: hotness was in the performance, not the definition. Bechet is unwilling to define hotness as anything other than something that the greats either did or did not have. If it was technical, it was not overtly so, but you could feel it. Hot players played hard and were driving and working so hard at being hot that it sounded like it was "killing" them. Also, hotness was a kind of racial gatekeeper. Bechet understands hotness as a quality generally only performed by the best African American players, and one's ability to match that intensity was part of the sociopolitical requirements for successful interaction and collaboration between races.

Bechet's hot take is split: hotness is part of an affective, embodied, sonic Blackness but is also an ability that only the most discerning and virtuosic players—regardless of race—were able to achieve. (The Bechets were Creole, so extending hotness beyond an essential quality of Blackness would have been important to him in his description.) Hotness stands in, then, as an early notch on the thermostat of jazz's complex and racialized creation myth—as an aural epideictic designator of a certain kind of shared praiseworthy virtuosity. If you were a hot player (or knew how to recognize what hot was), you were keyed into a certain standard of excellence manifest as valuable in an emergent community. Hotness was also born of and betrays the racist urge to classify, codify, and designate racial existence and to understand the racial performance of the other (and of Blackness in particular) as both fevered infection and utterly irresistible.

Morton's argument relies on hotness in all of its sonic complexities and intoned, sometimes explicitly, as both racist and nonracist rhetorics. Born into a middle-class French-European family of African descent (as implied in an audio clip quoted earlier) and part of a racial group generally designated as "Creole of color," Morton guarded his racial identity with both pride and prejudice. While he credits many of his African American colleagues as sharing in his authorship of jazz, he is often quick to point out their otherness. During the sessions, Morton comments on the ugliness of the darker African Americans with whom he associated and makes offhand remarks about their "thick lips" or even their dirtiness. The performance of race was important to Morton. By 1904, the lighter-skinned Creoles in New Orleans had been part of a long, complicated, increasingly bitter struggle for social status in an expanding Black and/or White racial public sphere. As jazz historian Burton Peretti remarks, "Creoles of color [. . .], caught between a growing 'American Negro' population and increasingly intolerant whites, developed an intense caste consciousness in these years" (with "downtown creoles" looking down their noses at "uptown Negros"), and that view was reinforced by the starkly racialized social arrangement (24–25). In his book *Jazz Cultures* (2002), David Akes writes,

> Resuscitating Creole identity [helps] to challenge today's too neatly circumscribed racial categories. And, just as important, it upsets many prevalent notions of New Orleans jazz—and, by extension, all

> jazz—as "folk music" and its participants as "natural," if somewhat backward, folk heroes, notions that persist in many ways to this day, though mostly in subtle and unacknowledged guises. (14–15)

My agreement with Akes stops short of his demonization of folk music. If anything, jazz's early Creole contributions complicate and thus enrich our sense of jazz's folkness. Jazz's folk are multiethnic and multiracial, and if jazz is the most American of American music, America itself is born from the interplay and intermixing of many ethnicities and their traditions, not from a monoculture and especially not from racially binary structures. An alternative mythos of jazz, then, might highlight its capacity to knit together the history of struggle between many competing classist and racial ideologies, in all their many contradictions, symphonically. Morton's frequent references to the relationship between African American and Creole American musicians in New Orleans around the turn of the 20th century as sometimes symbiotic, sometimes not, indicates that the sessions with Lomax were important to Morton in forwarding Creole-ness as one of the "essential" elements of jazz's genesis. Morton's sonic rhetorics are evidence of the ways an active participant within that sociocultural context embodied that struggle. His rhetorics redraw the politics and struggle of ethnic hybridity and revise the more cut-and-dried imaginary from which the racial divide derives its power.

"Jelly Roll Blues" and "Tiger Rag"

Morton's authenticating argument relied (if not always explicitly) on the hybrid sonic notion of hotness, and I think his most successful evidence is his capacity for hot performance. An explicit "hot" moment in the sessions comes in Morton's introduction to his song "Chicago Blues," which was renamed "Jelly Roll Blues." He explains how the name change came about and how he himself came to be known as Jelly Roll. Interesting beyond the details of the story (which are amusing considering the way he dances around the use of the term *jelly roll* as a sexual euphemism) is Morton's initial claim that the "hot tune" was known as one of his originals by all of the "musicians, publishers" and other "members of the music world" of its day. Morton's reliance on a kind of hearsay evidence is outstripped almost immediately by his own virtuosic playing. Hot performance is always more powerful than talking about hotness.

♫ "How Jelly Roll Got His Name" (https://doi.org/10.3998/mpub.9871097.cmp.25).

(*Jelly Roll Morton plays modulating piano chords while speaking.*)

MORTON: I'm going to try to play the "Jelly Roll Blues" for you. One of the numbers that's supposed to have had more originality to it than any other hot tune or blues in America, according to, uh, musicians, publishers, and so forth and so on—members of the music world.

I didn't name the "Jelly Roll Blues" the "Jelly Roll Blues." It was named by the people of the city of Chicago. How I happened to get the name myself thrown on me as an alias was due to the fact, in the show business, with one of my old partners, a blackface comedian and the first eccentric dancer in the United States—Sammie Russell, who was later known as Barlow, the teammate of Sandy Burns. One night, while working ad lib on the stage doing comedy, Sam said to me, "You don't know who you talking to." I told him I didn't care, and we had a little argument. I finally asked him who was he. And he stated to me, he was Sweet Papa Cream Puff, right out of the bakery shop. That seemed to produce a great big laugh.

While I was standing there mugging, as you call it, the thought came to me that I'd better say something about the bakery shop. I said to him, he didn't know who he was talking to. He finally wanted to get acquainted, so he asked me who was I. And I stated to him, I was Sweet Papa Jelly Roll with the stovepipes in my hips, and all the women in town was dying to turn my damper down.

LOMAX: What you mean by saying you had stovepipes in your hips?

MORTON: Well, stovepipes—I don't know—it was one of these kind of a things, you know, was very warm—hot hips. So, the people automatically named it. But my original title for this tune was the "Chicago Blues." I'll now try to see if we can do a little bit of it.

(*Morton plays "Original Jelly Roll Blues" and then continues speaking*)

I remember, I—how the folks used to say when I used to play, to get around to chitin suppers after work hours and play these things—why, they said, "Boy, bring me some more o' those chitins," see? (*laughs*)

Earlier in the sessions, Morton is a little more explicit about his jazz methods. Using the song "Tiger Rag," he demonstrates how a song might come to be transformed into jazz. His argument in that case is not unlike the one he used for "Stars and Stripes Forever" but is much more specific. Adding nuance to his claims as its inventor, Morton asserts that jazz is not necessarily a genre or type of music separate from other genres but, rather, something more accurately defined as a style that "you can apply to any type tune . . . depend[ing] on your ability for transformation" (Morton 36).

Like many of the songs Morton played for the Library of Congress archive, the origins and authorship of the song "Tiger Rag" are contested, partly because Morton often failed to copyright his material. In an era when artists rarely saw royalties for their published work, Morton did not see the sense in selling a song to a publisher for $15 or $20 when he could often make more than $100 a day playing in the busy clubs and "sporting houses" of the city (Morton 7). His oversight of future prospects would prove problematic for Morton. The "Tiger Rag" copyright, for example, was owned by the Original Dixieland Jass Band, who recorded and published it in 1917. Morton asserts that "Tiger Rag" was his composition, written early in the first decade of the 20th century. The 1917 Jass Band recording sold a million copies and would become one of the most recognizable jazz standards of all time: Duke Ellington, Louis Armstrong, and Benny Goodman—and, later, even Frank Sinatra—made it a part of their repertoire. Yet "Tiger Rag" and a host of other standards that Morton might have composed or arranged and that would tie him inextricably to the early history of jazz brought the pianist neither enduring fame nor fortune.

All too aware of that history, Morton demonstrated his claim to authorship of "Tiger Rag" in a unique way, appealing not to documentary history or memory but to his "ability for transformation" (36) of "an old quadrille" (31) on which the song was based. The quadrille was a historic form of music dating to 18th-century France and composed to accompany a multithemed, multitempoed French dance for couples. As Morton imagines it, a quadrille would have several "strains," including, in the case he was making, a waltz strain and a strain drawing on the Polish mazurka (which Morton calls the "mazooka"). To show his ability to transform a song using the quadrille's modulated forms as a model, Morton performs his transformation to "Tiger Rag" for Lomax, explicitly naming each modulation as he goes and connecting the process to the origins of jazz.

♫ "Oh! Didn't He Ramble" (https://doi.org/10.3998/mpub.9871097.cmp.26; 2:40–end).

MORTON: Now jazz started in New Orleans. And this, uh, "Tiger Rag" happened to be transformed from an old quadrille that was in many different tempos. And I'll, no doubt, give you an idea how it went. This was the introduction, meaning that everyone was supposed to get their partners. (*Morton plays introduction.*) "Get your partners! Everybody, get your partners!" And people would be rushing around the hall getting their partners. And maybe—have maybe five minutes lapsed between that time—and, of course, they'd start it over again and that was the first part of it.

(*replays introduction*)

And the next strain would be a waltz strain, I believe.

(*plays waltz*)

That would be the waltz strain.

♫ "Tiger Rag" (https://doi.org/10.3998/mpub.9871097.cmp.27; 0:00–6:24).

MORTON: Also, they'll have another strain that comes right belong, uh, right beside it. (*plays*) The mazooka time! (*plays*)

Of course, that was that third strain. And, of course, they had another strain and that was in a different tempo.

(*plays in two-four time*)

LOMAX: What kind of a time . . .
MORTON: (*speaking over playing*) That's a two-four time. (*plays*)
Of course they had another one.
LOMAX: That makes five.
MORTON: Yeah.

(*plays fifth strain*)

Now I will show you how it was transformed. It happened to be transformed by your performer at this particular time. "Tiger Rag," for your approval.

LOMAX: Who named it the "Tiger Rag"?

MORTON: I also named it. Came from the way that I played it by making the "tiger" on my elbow. And I also named it. A—a person said once, "It sounds like a tiger hollerin'." I said, "Fine." To myself, I said, "That's the name." So, I'll play it for you.

(*plays "Tiger Rag"*)

It was many years before the Dixieland had ever started when I played the "Tiger Rag." Of course, we named it "Tiger Rag" but we had a lot of other numbers . . . (*recording ends*)

Morton's biographer John Szwed points out that ex-enslaved peoples interviewed for a WPA project said that the "dances most often remembered from slavery days were contra dances (or 'contredanses'), square dances, the cotillion, the waltz, and the quadrille" (Morton, *Jelly Roll Morton* 37). The quadrille form exemplifies Morton's contention that jazz used ideas drawn from operas, symphonies, and overtures: "There is nothing finer than jazz music . . . because it comes from everything of the finest class music" (36). So did the quadrille. Jazz historian Thornton Hagert writes that quadrilles were made up of music from "bits of popular songs or snatches from opera arias" (41). Borrowing, improvising, and stitching together was the norm for jazz as Morton theorizes it, but the musical curator would need a set of practiced skills to apply to those tunes in order to bring the disparate parts and melodies into a single stylized whole.

After Morton plays the fifth strain of the quadrille, the strain carrying the melody he claims "Tiger Rag" is drawn from, he enacts his jazz transformation. The transformation is marked mainly by Morton's flourishes and a slight uptick in the tempo of the piece. The underlying melody is still there, but the song takes on a different character, with extensions and exaggerations of the melody here, improvisations there, and movement between riffs and figures, each of which represented forms that, according to Morton, might be applied to any tune, from any tradition, dependent on the virtuosity of the players in the band. Morton thus supports his claim that jazz is a style applicable to any type of tune.

Using his music and technique as evidence, Morton definitively declares that he made the "Tiger Rag" transformation "many years before the [Original] Dixieland [Jass Band] had ever started" (Morton, *Jelly Roll Morton* 32). His argument rests mainly on the melody he constructs in the fifth strain of the unnamed "old" quadrille. If Morton is indeed the author of "Tiger Rag," it makes sense that that the quadrille's fifth strain would bare resemblance to the song developed from it. If he is not the author, the fifth strain would have to be backward engineered into a pared version. Morton was capable of both efforts, so the implicit argument has more to do with his technique and style than with some kind of indisputable proof. Even so, the part of the song that Morton describes as "making the tiger on my elbow" provides one more piece of possible evidence for his authorship. He is referring to a section in the song where each first beat in the measure is played in the low notes on the piano with his left arm and elbow. The effect is not unlike the sound of a large cat growling or grunting. That stylistic flourish is a bit of a trademark for Morton but also appears in nearly every version of the song that followed when it was picked up as a jazz standard.

It is left to us to decide whether the more persuasive arguments are those that rely on empirical historical evidence—such as those made against the Jass Band and those made for the originality of "Jelly Roll Blues"—or the performed sonic arguments Morton makes at various times throughout the sessions, such as his demonstration of transformation as it relates to the origins of the "Tiger Rag." Though he will (somewhat confusingly) continue to argue both sides of the creation/transformation coin, my contention is that Morton is most persuasive in the more conservative assertion that jazz was not something one could invent. As Szwed posits, "[Morton] never truly claimed to have invented jazz, only to have transformed music into jazz" ("Doctor Jazz" 33). The recording of Morton's transformation of "Tiger Rag" offers persuasive evidence for that claim. He is interested, as we have heard, in claiming a few early jazz compositions as his own, but he is more persistent in his efforts to show how a tune would or should be played in the jazz vernacular, including performing the elements within the song that tie it to turn-of-the-20th-century New Orleans. We might more precisely say, then, that Jelly Roll Morton claimed to have invented a process that could transform any song into jazz.

(Re)constituting the Jazz Mythos: Elements of Virtuosity

Soon after the "Tiger Rag" demonstration, Morton fleshes out his transformation process—his rhetoric of jazz—in greater detail. In an era where jazz musicians and bands were a dime a dozen, Morton must have heard his share of terrible attempts at jazz playing. He is especially critical in matters of tempo and volume. Critiquing playing too loud is understandable, but (as we have heard) Morton himself used tempo as a marker for defining jazz transformations. Additionally, high-tempo playing was the paragon of swing-era jazz. Louis Armstrong's orchestras were known for their breakneck speeds. Morton admired Armstrong but was critical of the ways that tempo was placed before style during the various evolutions of jazz that occurred up until the Lomax sessions. Playing fast was a parlor trick of many ragtime pianists, and it was easier to fake good musicianship when details were fudged because of speed. In Morton's estimation, speed did not necessarily add up to "jazz," but a collection of virtuosic skills and intuitive affectations did.

♫ "Slow Swing & Sweet Jazz Music" (https://doi.org/10.3998/mpub.9871097.cmp.28; 0:17–4:16).

MORTON: The fact of it is, every musician in America had the wrong understanding about, uh, jazz music. Uh, somehow or another it got into the dictionary that jazz was considered a lot of blatant noise and discordant tones, that is, something that would be even harmful to the ears. [. . .] Jazz music is based on strictly music. You have the finest ideas from the greatest operas, symphonies, and overtures in jazz music. There's nothing finer than jazz music, because it comes from everything of the finest class music. [. . .] Jazz music is to be played sweet, soft, plenty rhythm. When you have your plenty rhythm with your plenty swing, it becomes beautiful. To start with, you can't make crescendos and diminuendos when one is playing triple forte. You've got to be able to come down in order to go up. If a glass of water is full, you can't fill it any more. But if you have a half a glass you have an opportunity to put more water in it. And jazz music is based on the same principles. (*begins to play*)

MORTON: I will play a little number now, of the slower type, to give you an idea of the slower type of jazz music. Which you can apply to any type tune. That depends upon your ability for transformation. (*plays "sweet jazz music"*) There you've got sweet jazz music.

LOMAX: What's the name of it?

MORTON: (*speaking over* playing) I don't—I don't have any name for it. Just a number that I—just thought I'd play awhile here, just to give a

> person a good idea. *(plays a few passages in double time)* That's also one of my riffs in, what you call riffs in, uh, jazz you know, in the slower tunes. I've seen this blundered up so many times that it's given me the heart failure. No, I haven't got a drum. That's my foot, if you happen to, to think of something I, I can say. *(laughs) (recording ends)*

Morton's demonstration modulates the song into double time and then utilizes the moment to demonstrate one of the elements he had tried to explain to Lomax earlier, the riff: "A riff is what you would call a foundation, as, like—you would walk on. Something that's standard" (Morton, *Jelly Roll Morton* 35). A jazz tune might modulate through several "standard" riffs. As Morton demonstrates a riff, it becomes clear that he is speaking of a sort of musical trope or figure—a way of "jazzing up" the melody—that can be applied to a section of a tune. Like a rhetorical trope or figure, riffs are standardized in a way that makes them like tools. They can be moved from tune to tune, and when applied, they enhance a melody.

For Jelly Roll Morton, jazz was a flavor, a seasoning "tinge." Later in the sessions, he refers to an important jazz element that, for him, advances his thesis that New Orleans was the "cradle" of jazz. Before playing the song "New Orleans Blues," Morton encourages the listener to pay attention to what he calls the "Spanish tinge." He argues that "New Orleans Blues" was transformed into a "playable composition" in about 1902 and that "[a] ll the black bands in the city of New Orleans" played it (Morton *Jelly Roll Morton* 104).

> *(Morton plays "New Orleans Blues.")*

> MORTON: Uh, this was one of the early tunes . . . *(recorder paused; microphone repositioned)* That's the type of tune, was no doubt one of the earliest blues that was created as a composition, a playable composition, in the city of New Orleans. This tune was wrote about nineteen-two. All the black bands in the city of New Orleans played these tunes—that's this tune, I mean. Of course, you may notice the Spanish tinge in it. This has so much to do with the typical jazz idea. If one can't manage a way to put the tinges of Spanish in these tunes, they'll never be able to get the right season, I may call it, for jazz music. [. . .]

♫ "The Spanish Tinge" (https://doi.org/10.3998/mpub.9871097.cmp.29; 0:00–0:57, 2:40–end).

> Of course you got to have these little tinges of Spanish in it, uh, in order to play real good jazz. Jazz has a foundation that must be very prominent, especially with the bass sections, in order to give a great background. Plus, what's called "riffs" today, which was known as "figures." But figures has, hasn't always been in the dance bands. I'll give you an idea what, uh, the idea of Spanish there is in the blues. (*Morton plays short demonstration of "New Orleans Blues."*)
>
> [. . .]
>
> As, as I before said, maybe you may be able to, uh, notice the Spanish tinge. But you must have a powerful background. For an instance, those days they used "La Paloma." Was one of the great Spanish tunes. You know, New Orleans was inhabited with maybe every race on the face of the globe. And of course we had Spanish people there—plenty of 'em—and plenty French people. Of course, I'll—I may demonstrate a little bit of "La Paloma" to show you that the tinge is really in there.
>
> LOMAX: Take it easy.
>
> (*Morton plays "La Paloma."*)
>
> MORTON: (*speaking over* playing) That would be the common time, which it gives you the same thing in the—. I hope this is quite clear to you, see? Only one is a blues, but differentiating, in these things, it comes from the right hand. You play the left hand just the same, but of course, blues you—you get the syncopation in there. (*demonstrates syncopation*) It gives it, uh, a entirely different color. It really changes the color from red to blue. And maybe you can notice this powerful bass hand?

By acknowledging jazz's "tinges," Morton "was calling attention to what some call the habanera, and others call the tango bass line" (Szwed, "Doctor Jazz" 33). There is some controversy around the place of those elements in jazz music, as some critics saw them as merely a passing fad. But as Szwed argues in reference to Morton's acknowledgment of such tinges, "Those who ignored him erected a false evolutionary perspective that emphasized jazz as a radical break from the musical past, and by excluding the whole range of folk, ritual, and foreign musics from jazz history, all of the music of the United States was grossly oversimplified" (33). There were many names, including those mentioned above, for the tinged way of playing. Some called tunes played in that style "slow drags" or "sashays." Often differentiated from a straightforward four-four European rhythm, those beat patterns would have syncopation or different emphases in their eight-beat cycles. Polymetric rhythms such as syncopation and rhythms found in blues, ragtime, and jazz are distinctly non-Western.

Gunther Schuller writes that "jazz inflection and syncopation did not come from Europe, because there is no precedent for them in European 'art music'" (14). So Morton's designation of his polyrhythmic playing as Spanish was a misnomer, "since this rhythm figure does not appear to be specifically Spanish or even Latin" (Szwed, "Doctor Jazz" 33). Instead, that type of playing is a characteristic of much of sub-Saharan African music and could be found in Brazil, Jamaica, Haiti, and other traditions that had come to influence African American musical traditions, especially in New Orleans. Morton recognizes that rhythmic flavor in jazz because it had circulated within African American music for decades. You could hear it in the offbeat accents and syncopations of ragtime and early jazz and in the rhythms of rural Black religious songs and early blues. Whereas "riffs" were generally musical in nature, the "tinge" was a rhythmic trope (though it often had the accompanying "habanera bass line"). Those rhythms were and still are "at the heart of the famous New Orleans 'second line' beat, a pattern so widely shared by New Orleans musicians that it constitutes the center of that city's party and parade tradition" (33). They also wind their way in and out of early rock and roll.

The "Spanish tinge" falls in among the other aspects of Jelly Roll Morton's rich repertoire of performed virtuosic evidence, which combine to demonstrate both his cognizance of the primordial elements essential to the jazz sound and his deep knowledge of jazz's cultural value system—from "hotness," to "transformation," to riffing and beyond. Morton's rhythmic rhetoric is a demonstration that mythos and virtuosity persist in their resilience as griotic/epideictic tools for the building of cultural systems of value and virtue.

Within embedded networks of historicized rhetoricity, music has power. The more recent emergence of hip-hop culture and music (including the virtuosic acts of disc jockeying, dancing, and MC rapping) is as well-disposed to sonic rhetorical analysis as the 1930s preoccupation with notions of cultural authenticity. In both cases (and in any number of others), depth of musical knowledge and virtuosic performance have power to both synthesize and re-present traditional cultural norms, to create new mythos, and, in so doing, to revise and reconstitute values for the next generation. The substance of virtuosic performance—what it sounds like and which valued elements are performed—is always embedded within and contingent to the historical moment and its milieu. Understanding those historical contexts vis-à-vis sensory evidences (in the present chapter's case, Jelly Roll Morton's sonic rhetorics) provides an opportunity to interface directly with history's contradictions and paradoxes. In this chapter, hotness has been my primary touchpoint for demonstrating a sonic historiography embedded in and through its contradictions. Black music's place in the United States has generally been one of both fear and celebration. Hotness encapsulates those two notions.

It is no wonder that hot jazz was so affecting and so popular in the 1910s and '20s, an "era of epidemic diseases," when Black music was considered infectious and when the "fear of racial transmission through sound" was both terrifying and exciting. Radano refers to "rhythmacized blackness" as a "key causal element in the constitution of modernity" and calls "hot rhythm . . . a sonic articulation of what we are" (263). In that context, Jelly Roll Morton's hot performance is particularly poignant. As a Creole of color living in the midst of the *Plessy v. Ferguson* legislation, he resisted and defied racial hierarchies just as the racial divide was receiving renewed political and cultural power. As a griot, rhapsodist, innovator, and composer, he stitched together African and European musical tropes, and that process of recombination became a blueprint for jazz method. Through the virtuosity and combustibility of his "hot" performance, Jelly Roll Morton revised the mythos of jazz history and inserted himself into it as not only a participant but one of its prophets.

INTERLUDE III

Popular Front Education

For Alan Lomax, 1939 was a watershed year. His reputation as curator at the Library of Congress had grown, as had his influence in New York, where he attended Columbia University for a year to work on (but eventually abandon) a master's degree in anthropology. In New York, Lomax busied himself with a variety of projects, some self-directed and others assigned by the library. With his library credential, he was brought on as a consultant for the recording divisions of the Radio Corporation of America (RCA) and Columbia Records. Lomax's keen knowledge of American music roots was useful to the company, for settling copyright disputes about song origins that might otherwise take several months of correspondence and costly litigation to solve. Alan's access to the commercial archives opened his eyes to the value of what were often known as "race" and "hillbilly" records. His preconceived notions about commercial recordings began to diminish, as he found that the commercial phonograph archives of RCA and Columbia contained music very much like that he and his father had collected during their Southern trips in 1933 and 1934 (Szwed, *Alan Lomax*).

Lomax began a systematic search through those archives, recruiting his sister, Bess Lomax, and his New York friend Pete Seeger to help him find quality recordings. His goal was to "develop a discography of the best American commercial recordings and organize them by artist, biographical information, title, geographical location and type of music, 'so that the basis would be laid for a really intelligent study of American taste'" (Szwed, *Alan Lomax* 142). In a letter, Lomax said,

> My opinion is that the commercial recording companies have done a broader and more interesting job of recording American folk music than the folklorists and that every single item of recorded American rural, race, and popular material that they have in their current lists and plan to release in the future should be in our files. (A. Lomax, "Letters, 1939–1940" 130)

That comment was no small concession for a man who had spent the better part of a decade as a folklorist out in the field. (Szwed, *Alan Lomax* 143). Lomax was surprised by the diversity of the recordings, including several that exchanged or modulated stereotypical ballad tropes common in much of folk music for protest songs recorded "without the constraints or censorship of commercial interests" (143). Perhaps Lomax's experience as a field recorder and archivist gave him a unique ability to see archives anywhere, and he was among the first to take commercially recorded music seriously as important to history.

Lomax's growing notoriety around the country, particularly in New York and Washington, made opportunities to utilize his knowledge of folksong more and more common. But that expanding fame and influence also began to make him a target. Like many others working toward a more socially conscious understanding of art and culture, Lomax became a subject of suspicion for those orchestrating the nascent Red Scare that would begin in earnest in the United States after World War II. Occasionally, Lomax confronted both of those realities simultaneously. An example is his 1939 invitation to perform at a special concert at the White House. Eleanor Roosevelt was the organizer for the event, which was being held as part of a visit from King George VI and Queen Elizabeth of England. The First Lady asked composer and musicologist Charles Seeger to produce the concert, and when Seeger could not find any real cowboys who could sing the traditional Western songs he wanted at the performance, he asked Alan to perform. Lomax agreed and took his preparation for the concert very seriously. He never considered himself a professional musician, and though he was asked to perform publicly more and more often, it always made him uncomfortable. His discomfort was compounded by being asked to perform not just for the president and First Lady but for the king and queen of England (Szwed, *Alan Lomax* 148).

Lomax's reluctance was tempered by a sense of greater mission. "When the evening arrived," Lomax's biographer reports, "Alan was thinking about all those singers who had asked him to let them send a message to the president or Mrs. Roosevelt, messages he sometimes recorded, sometimes wrote out as letters for them. It was how he saw himself on his best days, as the people's messenger" (Szwed, *Alan Lomax* 149). But Lomax's ideological view of himself was in stark contrast with the way that he was treated once he arrived at the White House for the concert. He later recounted that men in suits kept bumping into him. At first, he thought they were just clumsy, but after it kept happening, he figured out that they were secret service agents taking covert opportunities to frisk him: "They told me later that some woman who said she was my aunt had warned the FBI that her crazy nephew was going to blow up the building" (149).

Though the woman (who was not Lomax's aunt) knew something about Lomax's history, most of her claims were outlandish and inconsequential. She knew that Lomax had been arrested while at Harvard, for his involvement in a political demonstration organized by a radical leftist organization. The woman claimed that Lomax "had lived with a Russian-born Communist," a "Jewess," during that time and that his current wife was a Communist (Szwed, *Alan Lomax* 150). She also claimed to have overheard a wedding conversation in which Alan confessed support of the Communist Party to his father. Lomax pushed ahead with his part in the program that night at the White House, but even Eleanor Roosevelt would remember that while he was onstage, Alan looked "so frightened he could hardly sing," and she "hoped fervently that he would not reach for his handkerchief during the performance" (Roosevelt 191). The FBI's investigation of Lomax would continue for the next 30 years (Szwed, *Alan Lomax* 150).

"Unless I Go Red"

Alan Lomax was not a Communist, but he was sympathetic to some of the Communist Party's platforms and ideals. Indeed, Lomax was part of a growing number of citizens in the United States who identified with some ideals on the radical left but who did not profess a primary allegiance. He had thought—or at least joked—about joining the party. In a 1932 letter to his father, he goadingly wrote that "unless I go red, I should like to look at the folk-songs of the country along with you" (Szwed, *Alan Lomax* 33). Alan chose music over Marxism as his primary occupation. Communism in the United States, then and now, has been fetishized. Lomax was subject to that fetishizing vis-à-vis government leaders like J. Edgar Hoover, who had launched the investigation that led to Lomax's White House shakedown. Communist fever would reach a particularly shrill pitch after World

War II, and the later blacklisting campaign under the influence of Senator Joseph McCarthy would actually drive Lomax overseas for a time. Michael Denning, a cultural historian and expert on the political and cultural climate of the 1930s, argues that many contemporary historians have been influenced by the fetishized view of Communism when considering its place in the American landscape in the first half of the 20th century. The variety of competing social and political ideologies, movements, and beliefs are often collapsed too easily and codified into the single idea of Communism, though the Communist Party was only one of many circulating systems of belief organized by a much looser framework often designated as the "Popular Front." Denning suggests that the "heart of the Popular Front as a social movement lay among those who were non-Communist socialists and independent leftists, working with Communists and with liberals, but marking out a culture that was neither a Party nor a liberal New Deal culture" (5). Such independent leftists—among them Alan Lomax, Orson Welles, and Kenneth Burke—worked with but not for the Communist Party.

David Roediger calls those participating on the periphery of the Communist Party "fellow travelers," (quoted in Denning 5), but as Denning points out, the numbers of those on the periphery of the party were far greater than those within it. Contributors to the Popular Front movement included union members, nonparty sympathizers, and others who, while not explicitly Communists, were influenced by (and supportive of) some, but not all, Communist activities. Denning's work on Popular Front ideals is crucial to understanding Lomax and cultural workers of the time. Denning shows that the Popular Front was part of a larger cultural shift during the era, a cultural front that promoted, for the first time, a diverse American populous. The Popular Front was made up of the "new America," the "depression generation," which was "the most working-class cohort in American history," was ethnically diverse, and, as such, had created "the multi-racial, multi-ethnic metropolises of modernism" (8). As both an artistic and literary movement and an increasingly public and economic one, that modernism might be understood as a vast merging of disparate narratives and a rhapsodic forging of a new "we" in the constitutional "We the People." That forging included a "paradoxical synthesis of competing nationalisms—pride in ethnic heritage and identity combined with an assertive Americanism—that might be called 'ethnic Americanism'" (9). "Under the sign of the 'people,'" Denning argues,

> this Popular Front culture sought to forge ethnic and racial alliances, mediating between Anglo American culture, the culture of the ethnic workers, and African American culture, in part by reclaiming the figure of "America" itself, imagining an Americanism that would provide a usable past for ethnic workers, who were [generally] thought of as foreigners. (9)

Modernism's new multiplicities of thought, ethnicity, political ideology, and artistic taste stand in paradox to the emerging concept of the "mass," promoted through mass production, mass consumption, mass media, and mass culture. Modernism might be understood in terms of those paradoxes and the tensions between the functionalist utilitarianism of Fordism's assembly-line production model, the experimental art of the avant-garde, new progressive moral standards, and their accompanying class, gender, and even age struggles for prominence. "Thus," Denning concludes,

> modernism came to be the expression of the dreams, discontents, and cultural contradictions of the disaffected young people of the predominantly Anglo bourgeoisie as they came to grips with the changes in the corporate economy and the changes of proper sexuality and gender roles, with the new imperialism, with the "foreign hordes" of immigrant workers. (28)

Popular Front Radio in a Climate of "Uplift and Sell"

At the center of the modernist cultural milieu was the radio, a medium with the power to project, promote, and proliferate all of modernism's multiplicities. Radio's potential for reaching a mass audience appealed to corporate advertisers and Popular Front adherents alike. Those two groups would find themselves in an odd partnership during the 1930s, along with a third bedfellow, the US government. Regulating legislation (or threat of legislation) acted as a buffer between competing corporate and Popular Front ideals and resulted in programs developed along a variety of trajectories. Programs like the hugely popular serial *Amos 'n' Andy* were designed (often by the advertisers themselves) to have a mass appeal but played alongside such programs as the experimental *Mercury Theater on the Air*, which was produced by a troupe of Popular Front writers and actors led by Orson Welles. On the day before Halloween in 1938, the *Mercury*

Theater on the Air broadcast Welles's *War of the Worlds*, famously fooling many thousands of listeners into thinking that the country was experiencing an invasion from Mars. Welles's reflection on that event is telling of the ways that radio was being challenged by noncorporate producers looking to balance the playing field.

> We were fed up with the way in which everything that came over this magic box, the radio, was being swallowed. [Radio in the 1930s] was a voice of authority. Too much so. [. . .] It was time for someone to take some of the starch . . . out of some of that authority: hence my broadcast. (quote in Lenthall 4)

The existence of programs like *Mercury Theater on the Air* testifies to the way that Popular Front influence, buoyed by some governmental support, was able to wrest a small amount of power from growing corporate influence. Popular Front programs were rare and existed as part of a compromise—for what was called "sustaining" noncommercial programming—that came about as a result of the creation of the Communications Act of 1934, which created the Federal Communications Commission (FCC). That small gap created a large enough opening to allow for a variety of programming—not only experimental work like what Welles was producing, but also (and especially) educational programming, including the development of long-term programs like the Colombia Broadcasting System's (CBS) popular *American School of the Air*.

The 1934 Communications Act came at the conclusion of many years of debate and litigation. Broadcasters wanted more freedom to monetize the air, and in the end, that freedom was largely granted. There was, however, an expectation—an implicit sense of responsibility carried by broadcasters—to be "the best possible custodians" of a dual mission within broadcasting, to both "uplift and sell" (Hilmes 188). As Michele Hilmes explains, "[C]onditions in the regulation of the broadcast industry made a visible commitment to public service and educational programming highly advisable" (140). In the early 1930s, in both anticipation of and response to the Communications Act, both NBC and CBS instituted educational and so-called cultural programming. With an aim to "uplift," cultural programming supplemented the regular schedule of news programs, soap operas, and dramatic and comedic serials. Broadcasters introduced programs that dramatized history or explored and explained classical music, as well as programming aimed at making public policy and politics more legible to the average citizen. President Roosevelt's broadcasted fireside chats are one of the most famous examples of radio's power to strengthen (and propagandize) national ideals in the Popular Front era. As Robert McChesney explains,

> The commercial broadcasters had to convince the public and public officials that they were firmly committed to high-grade cultural and educational programming . . . establishing a commitment to cultural programming was seen as being of fundamental importance in keeping increased government regulation or even radical reform at bay. Any and all network programs along these lines were heavily publicized by the networks. (115)

The sacrifices of such programs were also noted. In 1934, for example, CBS president William Paley reported that only 30 percent of CBS programming was supported by advertising and that the cost of the remaining 70 percent "was defrayed by revenues from this 30 per cent" (3).

One way broadcasters explicitly took up the mission to "uplift" was through producing programs specifically for the classroom. The power of radio as an educational tool was widely promoted. For example, in "The Radio Influences of Speech," one of many articles about radio that the *Quarterly Journal of Speech* published during the Popular Front era, L. B. Tyson writes, "It is a well-known fact that radio has become one of the greatest educational mediums in the world today. It is one of the most powerful factors in moulding public opinion. Every word that is uttered over the radio has its effect upon some person's mind" (221).[1] A variety of opinions emerged to promote strategies for making the best of that power. In a 1945 text titled *Teaching through Radio*, prominent Cleveland educator and broadcaster William B. Levenson chronicles his experience and expertise in educational radio. In that book's first chapter, a section titled "How Can Radio Help?" lists the virtues of radio education. The following highlights from that list serve as a useful litany for understanding the pedagogical conceptions of radio at the time:

- Radio is timely: "Radio presents and interprets the event while it is still current and before it becomes history, whereas textbooks and even magazines cannot do that." (6)
- Radio can give pupils a sense of participation: "When a child hears an 'actuality' program, such as a presidential inauguration or the

opening session of Congress, he has a feeling of participation in the event and history becomes a living and vibrant experience." (7)

- Radio can be an emotional force in the creation of desirable attitudes: in other words, radio can be a useful teaching method to aid in the accumulation of facts, "but in the whole process of democratic living, attitudes, not facts, are paramount." (8)
- Radio can be used to develop discrimination.

In modern vernacular, that radio might help develop "discrimination" is a bit disconcerting. As Levenson explains, however, by "discrimination," he means the "development of good taste and the ability to make intelligent choices." (8). In Levenson's view, radio helps develop critical thinking based on a well-developed palate of "good" art, drama, literature, and music. His list includes several other virtues: "Radio can add authority" (in specialized areas, beyond that of the teacher), "Radio can integrate the learner's experience," "Radio can challenge dogmatic teaching," "Radio conquers space," "Radio can help in continuous curriculum revision," "Radio can 'up-grade' teaching skills," and "Radio can interpret the schools to the community" (9–17). Despite those virtues, Levenson promises (in all caps) that "RADIO CANNOT REPLACE TEACHERS" (19). We hear similar refrains in contemporary commentary on technology's power and place in the classroom.

By the time Levenson's text was published, educational programming on the radio was at least a decade old, and his observations reflect a broadcaster's long experience teaching with the medium. Particularly striking, then, is his section on the shaping of attitudes. Levenson's description of radio's epideictic power differentiates between the rote memorization of information, on the one hand, and education's power to transform the learner's values, on the other.

> The conveyance of information is a comparatively simple phase of teaching. Far more difficult is the development of desirable attitudes [. . .] Emotional drives have a powerful influence. Here is where radio can be of great help to the teacher, for radio has learned to use drama and music, two potent forces for creating emotional impact. (8)

Levenson understood the rhetorical power of both dramatic and musical oral performance and recommends them, without reservation, for use in sonic educational contexts.

The list Levenson offers reveals a particular historical moment in both education and communication (and media). His observations resonate with others made subsequently about television and, later, the Internet. Levenson's views of radio as "timely" and "participatory" and his description of radio's power to shape attitudes, taste, and culture foreshadow Marshall McLuhan's theories of radio and other media, which would emerge, a few decades later, in McLuhan's *Gutenberg Galaxy* (1962) and *Understanding Media* (1964). Levenson's pedagogy—steeped in philosophies of civic mindfulness and engaged participation—was also the result of what media theorist Daniel J. Czitrom (1982) calls the "progressive sensibilities" of pragmatist thinkers, theorists, and teachers. John Dewey was particularly fascinated with the speed, power, and efficiency of media technology and with the "nearly mystical qualities" that communication technology had for encouraging and enhancing sharing and participation (108).

The influence of Dewey's educational philosophies could be seen in the various "schools of the air" across the country, including Columbia's. Dewey's educational influence was broad, but he had interest in "the political and social implications of modern communication" (including radio), particularly "the durable tradition in American thought that has ascribed spiritual meaning to new communications technologies" (Czitrom 108). That "spiritual meaning" might be ascribed to the idea of communion, or, more specifically, to radio's power to make common and, by extension, to make society. In *Democracy and Education* (1915), Dewey writes,

> Society not only continues to exist *by* transmission, *by* communication but it may fairly be said to exist *in* transmission, *in* communication. There is more than a verbal tie between the words common, community, and communication. Men live in virtue of the things they have in common; and communication is the way in which they come to possess things in common. (5)

The idea of common people having a common experience and sharing common ground through ritual, aesthetics, and modern communication demonstrates the power and potential Dewey saw in the mediated arts. Dewey believed that art was the "paramount expression of communication as shared ritual" (Czitrom 109), and in an often-quoted line from his 1934 book *Art as Experience*, Dewey wrote that artistic expression offered "the only media of complete and unhindered communication between man and man" (109).

Important here, however, is that Dewey saw in those ideals a potential for what might be understood as an artful democracy—a reconceiving of education that served community by promoting what was "common" and not insisting on the primacy of the individual. For Dewey and as Czitrom argues, democratic theory that placed the individual at its center "was obsolete, or at least in dire need of repair."

> For the machine age had "enormously expanded, multiplied, intensified, and complicated the scope of the indirect consequences" of conjoint behavior, forming "such immense and consolidated unions of action, on an interpersonal rather than a community basis, that the resultant public cannot identify and distinguish itself." There was too much public, a public too diffused and scattered. (Dewey quoted in Czitrom 111)

That argument implies that a diffused and disconnected public needs common artifacts, not as a means of producing same thinking, but as a starting point—a common rhetoric of understanding—before the tangle of democratic difference emerges. They need folkness.

Nathan Crick, a rhetoric scholar and Dewey expert, expands on those notions, reminding us that the "commonness" of art (rhetoric itself being an art) was central to Dewey's conception of a new radical democracy with a sophistic bent: "Dewey put great faith in the emancipatory potential of aesthetic experience, but his attitude toward art—as a mode of production—was wholly continuous with the Greek tradition that linked it not just to sculpture and painting, but also to industry, knowledge, and economy" (5). Crick invites us to take seriously the critique that sophistic rhetoric "makes the weaker argument appear stronger," by embracing that principle as the kernel of radical democracy's potential. Sophistic rhetoric's power to disrupt hierarchies—institutions built on the "stronger argument"—in order first to notice, then to begin to understand, and finally to identify with the minority view (with its so-called weaker arguments) is part of rhetoric's promise. As Crick writes,

> to make a minority view into one accepted by the majority, one must seize the opportunity to envision new possibilities by making full use of the playfulness of language to break the engrained habits of thought of one's audience through aesthetic performance that simultaneously critiques, advocates, and creates. (12)

Folk music meets those qualifications almost perfectly. It is quintessentially an exercise in playful language use, and when the songs were offered from a minority point of view, the resulting music had power not only to offer a new perspective but to break "engrained habits" and begin forging new ones.

The next chapter, on educational radio, focuses on a program produced for the masses and featuring folk music culled for its ability to communicate commonness, or the power of the "weaker argument." Remarkable about the program Alan Lomax was asked to host in CBS's radio suite *American School of the Air* was that African American life was selected and broadcast as part of what was common to life in the United States. While, like all of the Lomaxes' products, the sonic rhetorics of that radio program were not without their problems and paradoxes, they might certainly be heard, in the Dewian sense mentioned above, as a starting place, a locus of possible understanding.

CHAPTER 4

Folksong on the Radio

The Sounds of Broadcast Democracy on Columbia's American School of the Air

Radio was such an effective documentary medium, a central medium in the 1930s, because it inextricably joined the other two methods of persuasion, direct and vicarious. The listener witnessed firsthand, yet through another's eyes. The relation of listener and speaker was paradoxical, and like all paradoxes unstable and unresolvable. The listener never could get from the speaker just the information he wanted as he wanted it, because to believe entirely he needed it firsthand. The speaker never could give the information he wanted as he wanted to.

—William Stott, *Documentary Expression* 9

Radio, more than any other agency, possessed the power not only to assert actively the unifying power of simultaneous experience but to communicate meanings about the nature of that unifying experience. Radio not only responded to the dominant social tensions of its era but, by addressing its audience's situation directly in music, comedy, and narrative drama, made those tensions the subject of its constructed symbolic universe.

—Michele Hilmes, *Radio Voices: American Broadcasting, 1922–1952* 11–12

Resounding Radio

♫ *(COLUMBIA TRUMPET FANFARE)*

NILES WELCH: Columbia Music Presents: Folk Music of America.

(orchestra plays theme music)

WELCH: There are only two important kinds of work songs in the United States, the sea shanties which Captain Robinson sang for us some weeks ago and the work songs of the American Negro. Both serve the same purpose to make a hard job easier and pleasanter through the melody and particularly the rhythm of music. They are the natural expression of natively musical people to whom singing is as much a part of their lives as eating and drinking.[1]

Folk Music of America was a program in the radio series *American School of the Air*, produced by the Columbia Broadcasting System (CBS). The episode of *Folk Music of America* quoted above was titled "Negro Work Songs." It was hosted by Alan Lomax and aired on February 20, 1940, The program's general aim was education—teaching America's school-age children about the people of America through a study of their folk music. "Negro Work Songs" was an effort toward reeducation, a resounding of African American identity in a country still accustomed to caricatured representations of Blackness in print, on the stage, and, now, on the radio. Given the general cultural upheaval experienced in the United States during the 1930s, such reeducation was occurring everywhere. In much the same spirit as Jelly Roll Morton, who resounded jazz history through virtuosic performance, thousands of skilled and even virtuosic individuals and agencies were seeking to influence the sound and shape of a renewed America. The new America was being fashioned not just to survive the crisis at hand but to be reborn, phoenix-like, in the wake of it. Such refashionings were abundant, occurring within a milieu of competing political, cultural, and corporate ideologies, with various leaders and movements seeking to repair, assuage, or take advantage of the pervasive uncertainty brought about through the ongoing Depression. In an effort to establish a new, distinctly American culture (one unmoored from European cultural ideals), artists and intellectuals worked to reconstitute or undermine old notions of cultural and artistic authority. Their effort, which was anything but unified, led to a burgeoning of cultural, intellectual, political, and artistic production.

A critical undercurrent guiding those tectonic shifts was the unprecedented rise of leftist political and ideological influence. Such a move constituted a distinct paradigmatic shift in the United States, where "the left had little influence on the cultures" up until the 1930s (Denning 3). During the Depression, political minds were changing due to a number of contributing factors, including (most prominently) widespread economic uncertainty and the rise of organizations and programs to guide Americans to a more secure financial footing. Unions and union collectives like the Congress of Industrial Organizations began to find prominence in order to make what jobs existed more secure. Under Franklin Delano Roosevelt's influence (and not without significant suspicion and opposition), government programs in the form of New Deal legislation like the Works Progress Administration attempted to demonstrate how progressive government worked by putting citizens across the country to work.

Educational reform was an important but often overlooked component of the paradigmatic shift. In the 1930s, influential ideas from philosopher John Dewey and others began to find practical application in school districts interested in promoting activity-based, student-centered learning activities focused not only on the standard "reading, writing, and arithmetic" but also on guiding students toward good citizenship. According to Dewey, schools provided an opportunity for academic learning but might also be models for character building and, by extension, civic democracy, as "education must be an active endeavor that connects classroom students to the 'real' world" (Bianchi 89). In *Education and Democracy*, Dewey argued for the importance of cultivating a citizenry steeped in the habits of artful living, a philosophic ideal where participation in the material and cultural arts was an integral part of the good life. Dewey believed that an education invested in promoting democracy would find success by emphasizing the cultivation of a distinct set of democratic values, which would shape attitudes toward culture, experience, and history.

This chapter delves into the implications of that educational movement and the public pedagogies it inspired, particularly the idea that one must experience democracy in order to know how to practice it. I examine one corner of that effort, educational radio, where producers were interested in exploring what the democratic experience should sound like. I argue that *American School of the Air*, especially Lomax's contributions, sonically encapsulated the ferment at the intersection of leftist idealism, educational reform, and commercialism and exemplifies how mass media contributed to the reconstitution of what it meant to be an American at the time.

Accompanying and accelerating the pedagogical trends of the 1930s and early '40s was an increased movement toward a "mass" American culture, brought about through the unifying power and increasing ubiquity of mainstream media. The rise and mass circulation of print culture in the 18th century began that movement, which was continued by the invention of telegraphy in the mid-19th century and by later technologies in telephone and film. But the invention and popularization of radio would have a profound and markedly different effect on how the people of the United States understood themselves in relationship to one another. As William Stott observed, "Radio was the ideal medium for putting the audience in another man's shoes. Unlike the written word, it offered a sense of intimate participation, the immediacy of the human voice and of spot-coverage" (90). Given its mass distribution, radio's capacity for faux intimacy—and for mass appeal—was remarkable. Indeed, as Sterne explains, "Broadcast had to incorporate the form of interpersonal talk into an utterly impersonal medium" (*Sound Studies Reader* 325). Not incidentally, higher education responded to that new radio culture, as speech departments in the 1930s and '40s took it on themselves to develop and offer courses on speaking on the radio. Radio labs were built, and students were trained in a variety of techniques for broadcast speaking, especially in what was often called "radio speech." Sterne notes that as a result of those and other efforts toward professionalizing radio speech and performance, "audiences could have intense affective relationships with radio personalities, even though the broadcast was strictly impersonal in orientation" (325).

Those new imagined relationships between listener and speaker and among the thousands of disparate-yet-together audience members (the so-called masses) challenged conventional notions of public and democratic interaction, particularly for those tied to the ideal of a town meeting in the public square (with its attendant face-to-face dialectic and debate) for citizen interaction and community building. David Kennedy argues that radio "catalyzed the homogenization of American popular culture" and "assaulted the insularity of local communities," changing their shape and scope forever and promising to "revolutionize politics." He further laments,

> Radio provided a means to concentrate and exercise power from the top, to bypass and shrink the influence of leaders and institutions that had previously mediated between individuals and local communities on the one side and the national political parties and the national government on the other. . . . The radio created a political environment unimaginably distinct from the give-and-take of the town meeting, which Thomas Jefferson had praised as "the best school of political liberty the world ever saw." (229)

Kennedy's thoughts express a common anxiety of mass media's effect on democracy and citizen engagement. Anxieties notwithstanding, the leaders of the various cultural movements of the interwar period—be they political, commercial, or cultural—would do their best to capitalize on radio's mass appeal, its potential for mass influence, and, by extension, its power for shaping public opinion. The sound of the radio in the 1930s and early '40s—its music, news, politics, drama, and comedy—is representative of any number of compromises and conquests between those various groups and their sometimes-competing, sometimes-conspiring interests.

This chapter addresses those interests and their attendant movements—from leftist idealism to broadcast capitalism—to get a sense for how various attempts toward "mass influence" were motivated, theorized, and deployed in sonic registers. Put another way, this chapter explores several significant rhetorics of radio broadcasting in the 1930s. Explicit in this exploration is an accounting for the various sonic rhetorics and the powers seeking to control them, including the effects (and affects) of broadcasting's widening dissemination and, conversely, its various (indeed, "mass") receptions.

My primary concern here is to explain how, in the midst of that milieu, Alan Lomax came to be the host of a nationally broadcasted children's radio program about folk music and why such a show is significant given both the larger commercial broadcasting trends at the time and also as the terminus of Lomax's archival work during the decade. I trace Lomax's career in the years leading up to the war, with attention to his contribution to CBS's popular educational radio series *American School of the Air* (*ASA*). Lomax was the host of two consecutive daytime *ASA* shows, *Folk Music of America* (1939–40) and *Wellsprings of Music* (1940). The development and success of those programs is evidence of radio's impact and educational potential given a vast (and often captive) broadcast audience and invites some important questions about radio's rhetorical power. How, for example, did Lomax's archive of folksongs for the Library of Congress come to be seen as "educational," and what exactly was the intended educational outcome of their use? What happens when songs and vernacular voices recorded in prisons, hollers, roadsides, bars, living rooms, and any number of other "field" locations become part of "mass" communication and, thus, popular culture? These questions are best explored in and answered through a careful listening of the "Negro Work Songs" episode of *Folk Music of America*, where Alan Lomax chooses to present American culture as African American culture.

Radio's New Communities

When radio became part of the national mainstream in the late 1920s and early '30s, its communicative power was not better or more effective than print was or had been, but it was different. "Listening to the radio," observes media historian and communication scholar Susan J. Douglas, "was like being a child again, having stories read to you and being expected to have—and use—a vivid imagination" (4). Douglas emphasizes the power of imagination in constructing an authentic self in a diverse world:

> Unlike other major technologies—automobiles, airplanes, or trains—that move us from one place to another, radio has worked most powerfully inside our heads, helping us create internal maps of the world and our place in it, urging us to construct communities to which we do, or do not, belong. (5)

The impulse to understand radio in terms of the imaginations it evokes is a guiding theoretical principle of one of communication's most noted scholars of the radio, Michele Hilmes. In *Radio Voices: American Broadcasting, 1922–1952* (1997), Hilmes sites Benedict Anderson's influential theory of "imagined communities" as central to understanding both radio's "unifying power of simultaneous experience" and what that unifying experience means for listeners (11). Simultaneity of experience distinguished radio from mass print media, which, as Anderson explored, had been revolutionary in its ability to draw together audiences who could, by reading the same newspaper, imagine themselves as part of a larger grouping of engaged everyday citizens (B. Anderson 35).

Radio's simultaneity of experience enhanced the experience of belonging to the print-based imagined communities Anderson theorized and linked it with other common mediated experiences. Like print, radio was

> a system of productive relations driven by that hallmark of twentieth-century capitalism, advertising; a technology of communications significantly different from print, yet even more capable of negotiating not only the linguistic but the ethnic and cultural diversity brought about by the transformations of the modern age; and like film, a machine for the circulation of narratives and representations that rehearse and justify the structures of order underlying national identity. (Hilmes 12)

Radio promoted an even more focused experience of unity, connection, and communication "in its purest sense" (Hilmes 13). Citing an article by Stanley Frost that appeared in a 1922 issue of *Colliers*, Hilmes asserts, "Radio would unite a far-flung and disparate nation, doing 'more than any other agency in spreading mutual understanding to all sections of the country, to unifying our thoughts, ideals, and purposes, to making us a strong and well-knit people'" (13). Not only would radio's capacity to bridge huge physical distances begin to produce, for better or worse, a "homogenization of the American mind," but it would also "bring the public into remote private spaces" and, in so doing, introduce the United States, more broadly, to itself (Hilmes 13–14).[2] In that sense, the new imagined community of the radio produced an audience becoming more and more alike but also more and more aware of its many differences and of the many others who also inhabited the country.

That new connectedness with the other held, in Hilmes's words, both a "threat and a promise": "In a society built on structured segmentation and social division as much as on its rhetoric of democratic equality," she writes, "connectedness posed a danger to the preservation of those physical and geographic divisions supporting social distinctions" (15). Included within those distinctions were divisions relating to race and ethnicity. On the one hand, some early programs, like the wildly popular *Amos 'n' Andy* (which combined a minstrel show and vaudeville comedic stylings) maintained and even trafficked in the racial stereotypes of earlier generations. On the other hand, "race music," a genre developed by commercial record companies to be sold to Black customers, was now accessible on the radio to anyone who chose to dial it in, including a growing (and eventually booming) white suburban audience, "threatening a cultural miscegenation that made self-appointed moral guardians apoplectic" (Douglas 18). Indeed, according to Susan Douglas, radio's position as a "passageway between white and black culture [. . .] simultaneously reinforced and profoundly destabilized white supremacy and racial segregation in the United States" (18). Listening to the radio could be an act of both acquiescence and rebellion.

Radio's unique impact on Western culture during the 1930s and '40s, its capacity for communication in so many modes, its potential for creating and sustaining new communities of the air, and its quick rise to cultural centrality ushered in what Jonathan Sterne terms a "new sonic culture." As Sterne explains, radio "provided its listeners [with] a 'new mental world' and a 'new type of auditory background for life' structured by new modalities of listening and interaction" (*Sound Studies Reader* 325). Given those modes, it is not difficult to understand the multiplicities and even conflicting debates around radio. Individual radio listeners were both isolated and "coupled" intimately with the sounds of the airwaves. Families who gathered around dinner tables and in living rooms replaced conversing with passively listening to evening dramas or situation comedies. Yet thousands of those "passive" listeners—some unable (or unwilling) to tell the difference between fact and fictional representation—sent letters to actors or characters on the shows they liked (Douglas 134). Radio's keen ambivalences as "both passive and active" and at once "participating and withdrawing" would, according to Sterne, make it a harbinger of (and amplifier for) post-structuralism, postmodernism, feminism, and other theories built in and through uncertainty and contradiction (325). Not incidentally, drawing on foundational work by McLuhan, Hilmes, Douglas, and others, Sterne identifies radio studies' potential for interrogating collectivity as one of the possible origins for modern sound studies.

Collectivity was an integral part of radio's contradictory nature, as its "collectives" were not the publics of the "sphere" of the Habermasian bourgeois coffeehouse, nor could they be characterized in quite the same way as the collective "public" of participants in newspaper print culture. As Sterne points out and as is apparent in the above discussion, "the problem of radio's collectivity"—the way it accounts for "relationships among concepts of audience, public, polity, and nation"—should be central in studies of radio (*Sound Studies Reader* 325).

Airing Authenticity: Alan Lomax on the Radio

By 1935, over two-thirds of American homes had a radio (Russo 155). Broadcasting had matured beyond its experimental and novelty phases of the first two decades of the century and into the realm of everyday experience. Recognized as an important "new media," radio's possibilities began to inspire innovation from citizen, artist, politician, and theoretician alike, each anxious to take advantage of radio's powers of collectivity and coupling. The ubiquity of radio in the 1930s presented the United States, now a country steeped in the ideals and industrialism of Henry Ford, with new opportunities for participating in both commercial mass production and consumption. Beyond cars or cornflakes, Americans were recipients of the conveyer-belt presentation of mass culture. Fueled by a steady stream of commercial advertising, regulated by the newly organized Federal Communications Commission (FCC), and directed at captive audiences across the country, the sound of radio broadcasts became a locus for debate for influential citizens across the country, from business executives to public intellectuals and from artists to radical politicians.

At the center of that debate was concern about radio's and broadcasters' potential for influence—about broadcasting's epideictic power as a disseminator of cultural, political, and consumer values. Some feared that radio would create a monoculture and, in so doing, preempt the democratic process. Others believed the opposite—that political ideas could travel much farther by radio and that radio's many channels and programs gave listeners freedom to access information and content in new and exciting ways.[3] Those opinions, which came in response to radio's increasingly central place in American lives and to its potential for shaping lifestyle, inevitably produced intense debates about the power structures governing radio's production and content. CBS's *American School of the Air* might be understood as a compromise between various "collectivities"—corporate, governmental, an educational. Alan Lomax's programs on that series would introduce a listening audience—millions of them schoolchildren—to programming and content that he believed to be unique. "It was the first time America had ever heard itself," he would later say, "and it went into all the schools" (quoted in Eisenschitz 52). But that programming should also be understood as the product of a number of competing interests.

Whether it was the "first time" Americans heard traditional music from "other" American traditions can be debated. Music—including folk music—was a common subject in educational programming and could be heard on other radio programs with educational content, in the sciences, history, and the arts. For example, the not-yet-famous broadcaster Edward R. Murrow was collecting and recording folksongs in Europe for a similar *ASA* program in 1938, and American folksongs were used prominently in music-focused programs several years before Lomax's program aired. But most of the nation's children and educators had likely not encountered the variety of musical American folklife introduced to them through Lomax's programs for *American School of the Air*, especially when those programs featured the voices of African American musicians.

The diversity and depth of Lomax's content and knowledge, obtained from his experiences in the field and as an archivist, brought *American School of the Air* programming a sonic authenticity fetishized during the period when it aired. Lomax's ethos granted him wide popular acceptance. He was the "real deal," and so was his program. It helped that he had at his disposal a growing network of friends and acquaintances like Lead Belly, Woody Guthrie, and Pete Seeger, who (like himself) had begun performing archival material publicly and were willing to contribute to the radio programs. While it may seem odd that the programs presented only reappropriations of the field recordings, producers (including Lomax) likely would not have even considered using the actual recordings for on-air programming. Playing recorded music on the radio (let alone grainy field recordings) would not be a common radio practice until the mid-1940s (M. Fisher 11). FCC regulations (and often the recording artists themselves) favored the use of live music on the air. For Lomax, the songs were much more interesting and important than the material recordings. For contemporary listeners, however, there is a particularly authentic American irony in noting that songs recorded in the Black prison yard were being silently repurposed by professional musicians in order to be made more accessible to the audiences inhabiting the country's white suburban classrooms.

"Columbia presents . . . *Folk Music of America*"

When CBS executive Davidson Taylor offered Alan Lomax the opportunity to develop a 25-episode series of programs for *American School of the Air*, Lomax was reticent. He was no fan of radio, believing it to be a "waste of time" or, worse, "a tool with the potential for fascistic manipulation" (Szwed, *Alan Lomax* 152). Lomax's criticism of the radio did not stop short of scatological: "I thought this was a joke. I didn't know that anybody could be seriously interested in working on the radio, a pile of crap" (Eisenschitz 52). Lomax's friend Nick Ray, a Popular Front writer and director, would help convince Lomax of radio's potential for social commentary and change, partly by encouraging him to listen to the radio documentaries of Norman Corwin. Lomax said he "did a flip" after that and, with the help of good scriptwriting and well-developed drama, "realized that radio was a great art of the time" (52).

American School of the Air was developed in partnership between CBS and the Board of Education of New York City. While the *ASA* had hosted many different kinds of educational programming over the years, Lomax's program was to be a singularly unique endeavor. "It would be the most costly production radio had ever attempted," Szwed writes, "with four scriptwriters, ten actors, five producers, three commentators, a fifty-piece symphony orchestra, singers, educational directors, engineers, and announcers" (*Alan Lomax* 152). Szwed reports that in addition to those tuning in at home, *Folk Music of America* would reach 120,000 classrooms, roughly 3.5 million student listeners (153), and that by its second season, when the target audience was broadened and the program name was changed to *Wellsprings of Music*, an estimated 15 million listeners tuned in, schoolchildren and adults alike (165).[4] "Each week," notes Szwed, "[Lomax] would present a new musical or social theme: British ballads in America, the gold rush, love songs, lumberjacks, railroads, sailors, the American Negro, the blues" (153). The shows proceeded with Lomax introducing each song with a brief historical vignette or anecdote about his travels, after which he or a guest would perform a series of related songs on or around the topic. The music would often be supplemented by a bit of drama, acted out by the visiting guest singers. Each episode also featured a special orchestral reimagining of one or two of the folk tunes presented. Popular Front composers (among others) were recruited and paid $400 for their work. Many participated, among them Aaron Copland, Ruth Crawford Seeger, Charles Seeger, Roy Harris, Henry Brant, Ross Lee Finney, William Grant Still, Nathaniel Dett, and Ferde Grofe. As Szwed explains, that scenario, where the raw material for art was supplied by the "folk" and was then repurposed and refined by a "serious" artist and presented to the public via popular media, was, "in the eyes of the high modernists of the times," the way "culture was supposed to operate" (153).

Still, Lomax was uneasy with the process. He was worried that the radio program would be a way of pandering or selling folk music to an audience who did not really appreciate it. The move to transform folk music into "high art" did not sit right with him either. Lomax was initially unimpressed by Aaron Copland, whose uninspired rendering of "John Henry" left Lomax wondering if the composer even understood the power and beauty of folk music. Copland would later catch the spirit of folk transference in his masterful repurposing of the Library of Congress's recording of the fiddle tune "Bonaparte's Retreat" (played for the library's archives by William H. Stepp), which would become the central theme of Copland's "Hoe-Down" in his well-known ballet *Rodeo*. ♫

Despite his reservations, Lomax's programs on *American School of the Air* were precisely what the Library of Congress hoped for in terms of publicity for the archival material. The library was thrilled with the possibility that "the music it had recorded and collected would be the means of introducing all of America to its many parts and regions, while at the same time communicating the government's interest in the vernacular arts of the country" (Szwed, *Alan Lomax* 153). The actual production process of the sessions tempered that vision for the music of the archive. Alan complained that producers of the radio program did not seem interested in the quality of the folk performances, especially his own. His lack of confidence in his own abilities as a performer was only assuaged in a negotiation to hire other, more professional musicians. Ironically, that action, which would introduce the nation to the talents of Woody Guthrie, Pete Seeger, Josh White, and Burl Ives (among others), would further undermine Lomax's desire to bring vernacular voices to the nation. Instead, Lomax settled for an "authentic-enough" approach. He believed that the professional musicians performing folk music on the program could do so in a way that represented the folk ethos most accurately and that could be accessible to the students on the other side of the radio broadcast. The one regular performer who had legitimate ties to a so-called authentic folk history was Lead Belly, but producers were concerned that his thick Southern accent was too difficult to understand for the broadcast audience. Lead Belly is featured in "Negro Work Songs," but later in the season, when producers recommended a replacement for his spoken parts, Woody Guthrie was incensed at his friend's mistreatment and quit the program (Szwed, *Alan Lomax* 167).

Even with reservations, bumps, and departures, *Folk Music of America* was quite successful, so much so that the National Association of Music Education (NAME) began including folk music in recommended curricula for public schools. NAME even awarded one episode (which featured Guthrie) as Best Music Education Program (Szwed, *Alan Lomax* 165). In *Pix*, the publication CBS used for press releases, Lomax was quoted as saying that the purpose of his program was "to show that America has an authentic music lore which should be as important and exciting to students as the works of great masters" (Szwed, *Alan Lomax* 155).

Such quips notwithstanding, tensions between the competing ideologies of Lomax, the CBS producers, and the participating musicians that performed on the shows remained off-air. The programs themselves produced an illusion of fluidity between the folk singers, the host, and the composers creating pieces "inspired by" recorded folk music. Students and teachers were encouraged to participate within that interrelationship. Lomax and CBS prepared teaching materials to supplement the programs, with lesson plans and assignments in a printed manual. For the episode on February 20, 1940, the teaching material includes an introductory description of the episode, a list of featured songs, and the following "activities":

1. Try making a work song in connection with some activity with which you are familiar that involves a regular repeated series of observations.
2. Find out what work songs have been or are sung in your community and study how and when they are sung.

3. Learn "Tie-Tamping Chant."
   (*The American School of the Air Teacher's Manual and Classroom Guide for 1939–40*)

Students were invited to further the folk process by making up their own verses to the aired folksongs. They were also encouraged to submit folksongs that they knew to CBS. Dozens of letters with such submissions survive in the American Folklife Center at the Library of Congress.

African American Music on the Radio

In a letter written to a colleague in late August 1939, Alan Lomax described his program on *American School of the Air* as "aimed at stimulating the interest of children in . . . very simple and straightforward presentations of American folk music and folklore" (A. Lomax, "Letters, 1939–1940" 139). *Folk Music of America* relied on a very simple formula. Each episode began with a short introduction from *ASA* announcer Niles Welch, who would give some context and description for the episode before segueing into Lomax's prepared content. Lomax introduced the week's topic in greater detail before moving to a prepared dialogue with guest musicians. The dialogues, each of them scripted and rehearsed for dramatic impact, further contextualized the music by inserting it into a performed narrative. Listeners could then be transported to the deck of a fishing vessel in Nantucket Sound in an episode on sea shanties, into a Tennessee holler to dance along to a fiddle tune, or out to the playground in an episode on children's game songs.

As noted above, the performers included Lomax's friends and associates, among them Pete Seeger, Woody Guthrie, and Lead Belly. With Lomax's help, CBS also recruited the Golden Gate Quartet, a well-known African American singing troupe, as well as blues guitarist Josh White and singer Burl Ives, who (with Seeger, Guthrie, and Lead Belly) would become key contributors to the various narratives and dramatics worked into the program.[5] *Folk Music of America* was 30 minutes long (like all *American School of the Air* programs) and aired on CBS at 9:15 a.m. (Bryson 19). Explicit pedagogical content in the programs was usually minimal, with Lomax or his guests pausing only occasionally to give specific instruction for the student audience. The instructions generally came from the program's announcer Niles Welch at the beginning or near the end of the program.

The following analysis of "Negro Work Songs" shows how the program might be understood as part of the larger tapestry of sociohistorical movements and ideologies explored in the previous discussion. The episode appeared as part of a three-part series on the "songs of the Negro." I have chosen the "Negro Work Songs" episode because it draws directly on field recordings collected by Alan Lomax and his father, John, during their 1933 trips to Southern African American prisons. As noted earlier, the adaptation of those field recordings on the radio was precisely the kind of use that the Library of Congress had in mind for the archival music. The bulk of the rest of this chapter examines the episode and works to determine the various rhetorics at play on Lomax's program. As I have been foregrounding, *American School of the Air* was the product of any number of competing interests, and Lomax's programs, especially those that take up African American history as an educational topic, only intensify that dissonance. Listening carefully to that portion of the Lomax archive is an opportunity to hear, for better and worse, how those interests are distilled into a consumable public product: radio folkness.

"Work Songs of the American Negro"

In the opening of the episode of *Folk Music of America* that aired on February 20, 1940, Welch's introduction of that week's theme, African American work songs, continues after the lines already quoted at the beginning of this chapter.

> ♫ WELCH: Today, for our *American School of the Air* program on Negro Work Songs, Alan Lomax has as his guests the Golden Gate Quartet of Charlotte, North Carolina and the famous Negro singer Huddie Ledbetter. In Negro work gangs throughout the South, each laborer is given a nickname by his comrades and Huddie's nickname of "Lead Belly" has become familiar to lovers of folk music all over the country.
>
> Now in today's broadcast we're going to take you on a trip from Virginia down through South Carolina, Alabama, and Mississippi and then up through Tennessee, Arkansas and Texas following a gang of Negro laborers at their jobs of road-building, cutting timber, hoeing in the fields, and piling up the levees along the muddy rivers of the South. And there are two songs we want you to join Lead Belly in singing on the choruses. The first is "Stewball," and your part to remember goes like this:

LEAD BELLY: (*singing*) You bet on Stewball and you might win, win, win. Bet on Stewball and you might win.

WELCH: Then, the last song on today's program is "The Grey Goose" and we want you to sing with the quartet on all the refrains. Lead Belly sings:

LEAD BELLY: (*singing*) One Sunday Morning

WELCH: And you sing:

QUARTET: (*singing*) Lawd, Lawd, Lawd!

LEAD BELLY: Creature went a hunting.

QUARTET: Lawd, Lawd, Lawd!

LEADBELLY: Carry along his shotgun.

QUARTET: Lawd, Lawd, Lawd!

LEADBELLY: Along came a grey goose.

QUARTET: Lawd, Lawd, Lawd!

WELCH: Alright now? Now when we come to them, don't forget to sing out on the choruses of "Stewball" and the refrain "Lawd, Lawd, Lawd" after each phrase of "The Grey Goose." And here is Alan Lomax our folk song expert from the Library of Congress.

In this segment, Welch introduces the program, the participants, and the theme of the episode. He also gives the listening audience a participatory task—to sing along during two of the songs.

Welch's introduction gives us a sense for the program's general pedagogical and rhetorical underpinnings. Students of *Folk Music of America* are to be introduced to a particular facet of "folk life" and then invited to participate in that experience sonically. In that way, student listeners are able to have a breadth of proxy experiences: as seamen, lumberjacks, cowboys, balladeers, callers of square dances, and—as presented here—African American laborers. Each subject is, no doubt, a vernacular trope, and the songs reflect a codification of the people and traditional practices represented. "Negro Work Songs" is one of three episodes focusing on African American vernacular tradition, with accompanying episodes on railroad work songs and gospel music. Listening to that part of the Lomax archive is an opportunity to determine the extent to which Lomax was able to use his knowledge and experience to push past caricature and into more educational renderings of African American life.

"Negro Work Songs" proceeds with Alan's opening remarks, which exemplify the pedagogical approach of the program.

♫ ALAN LOMAX: Africa is the continent of work songs. Early explorers always reported that their porters sang as they carried loads through the jungles or paddled their dugout canoes up the rivers. The natives sing while they are grinding grain, the blacksmith while he hammers his iron, the farmer as he clears his land. These people, brought to this continent as laborers, naturally kept singing as they worked. Their employers soon found out that the Negroes did more work when they were singing.

It can be difficult to listen to that depiction with ears from the 21st century and not hear its blatant misrepresentations. With help from Lomax's opening monologue, schoolroom listeners were entreated to imagine an African monoculture of singing workers who, once under the "employ" of their American captors, continued singing, "naturally." However, the larger theme of Lomax's opening paragraph speaks to the possibility of a more progressive purpose than the mere propagation of racist African American stereotypes. For example, the depiction of a world where Africans were industrious and productive before being "brought to this continent as laborers" runs counter to narratives, still in circulation in the early 20th century, that justified their enslavement. (Even Lomax's narrative, though, may substitute an old argument for African enslavement with a new one: that Black Africans are a hardworking but dependent race and require the "guidance" of masters.) The depiction of African Americans on Lomax's program would have been competing directly with concurrent popular broadcasts like *Amos 'n' Andy*, a program that, as noted earlier, trafficked in the racist comedic stylings of the blackface minstrel show. The 1940s would also see a number of other popular renditions of African American life with infamous distortions, as in, for example, Disney's *Dumbo* (1941) and *Song of the South* (1946).

Lomax and the other writers of *Folk Music of America* had 30 minutes to communicate something about African American folklife that moved beyond popular stereotypes. The replacing of old tropes with new, slightly less racist ones is difficult to champion as a productive method of social progress, but it may be the most important legacy of that program. Though there is much to criticize in Lomax's production, the critique is leavened when the program is contextualized within a larger time frame of racial progress in the United States. Generationally speaking, the seeds sown in the radio programs may have contributed productively toward shaping the ideas and beliefs of the listening students. Children listening in the late 1930s and early '40s grew to become adults working, voting, and raising children of their own a generation later, when civil rights moved from a radical ideal to the popular movement of the 1960s.

To its credit, the *Folk Music of America* episode on African American work songs eventually acknowledges that the singers working for American "employers" were actually enslaved people and that their singing was an accompaniment to the grueling nature of their work.

> ♫ LOMAX: Singing seemed to enable them to endure unbelievably long hours under the hot sun of the South. Sometimes a greatly talented singing leader was employed to do nothing else but sing so that the work would go faster—a sort of musical speed-up system.
>
> After the Civil War, the slaves were turned out into the world to shift for themselves. They cleared the land of the South; they built the roads, piled up the levees along the muddy rivers of the South, laid the railroads, picked the cotton. They wandered, these workers, looking for better times, better jobs, better bosses, better food, prettier girls. They had the blues and they sang them away on the job. Virginia down to North Carolina, Georgia on down to Texas, they were throwin' those hammers. Listen to them down in Virginia breaking rock.

Lomax here argues that African American labor was integral to the redevelopment of the South and that work songs were part of the tools used in that rebuilding, not merely incidental to it. When the Golden Gate Quartet and Lead Belly, acting in roles as laborers, then take up the dialogue and introduce the first song of the program, "Take This Hammer," they are, in effect, reenacting that labor for the audience. The working men sing "Take this hammer / carry it to the captain / tell him I'm gone," explicitly expressing their discomfort and dissatisfaction, as the song pushes the work along with a rhythmic "Ha!" and "Yow!" to represent hammer strikes.

> ♫ WORKER: Come on up here, little buddy, with sumpin to ease my troubled mind so I can throw this hammer.
>
> LEAD BELLY: Some of these days I'm going to ask one of you boys, "Take this hammer and give it *back* to the captain." Grab your hammers and let's go.
>
> WORKER: On it!

LEAD BELLY: (*singing*) Take this hammer
QUARTET: Ha!
LEAD BELLY: Carry it to the captain
QUARTET: Yow!
ALL: (*singing*) Take this hammer (ha!) and carry it to the captain (ha!) take this hammer (ha!) and carry it to the captain (ha!) and tell him I'm gone (ha!) and tell him I'm gone (ha!)
LEAD BELLY: If he asks you
QUARTET: Yow!
LEAD BELLY: Was I runnin'
QUARTET: Ha!
ALL: If he ask you (ha!), was I runnin' (yow!), if he asks you (ha!) was I runnin' (ha!) tell him I was flyin' (ha!)
WORKER: (*speaking*) Lord, ain't gonna be here long!
ALL: Tell him I was flyin' (yow!)
WORKER: (*speaking*) Lord when I stay too long in one place, I gits hankty. I gotta move on up. My home ain't here no how. It's further on down the line.

Here and throughout the episode, the performance presents a Southern dialect in African American Vernacular English (AAVE), which Lomax had become accustomed to writing out as part of his several publications. Interestingly, the formally trained men of the Golden Gate Quartet had to be coached by Lead Belly on how to sing prison songs and speak in that dialect (Szwed, *Alan Lomax* 163). Guided by experience and also Lead Belly's presence, Lomax's insistence on a carefully rendered Southern AAVE dialect (rather than the cartoonish "darkie" dialect popular in print and radio) are indicative of the kind of shift that he was seeking to promote related to African American vernacular experience in the national imagination. That shift might be understood as part of the effort to move the proverbial needle on racial attitudes, even if that move was slight (or even negligible, given its source)—from the easygoing or easily confounded simpleton caricature of minstrelsy and *Amos 'n' Andy* to a more nuanced sonic depiction of the underpaid, overworked, and undervalued African American labor force. In any case, it is a notable example of the way radio programs might contribute to the shift in "attitude" proposed by Levenson (8, discussed in interlude III) and activated by Lomax through his program. "The result," Lomax would later write, "was *not* complete authenticity, but I believe the nearest thing to it that could be achieved away from the prison farms themselves" (Lomax quoted in Szwed, *Alan Lomax* 163).

In the episode's next segment, the work changes from hammering to saw work, but the theme of progressive messaging about past injustices couched within a dubious racialized context continues. Lead Belly sings the stanzas of a song that the Library of Congress titled "Almost Done" but that Lead Belly later recorded as "Ain't Gonna Ring Dem Yallow Woman's Do' Bells." Sung to the rhythm of pulling a saw back and forth through lumber, the song's questionable content and title also offer a stunning depiction of an incarcerated or otherwise imprisoned African American man.

♫ WORKER 1: (*speaking*) Say, what are we gonna do with all this wood now we got it laying around?
WORKER 2: What we gonna do? We gotta git round with these ol' cross-cut saws.
WORKER 3: Four foot long.
WORKER 1: One real man on each end.
WORKER 2: Listen to that ol' saw a-talkin'
WORKER 3: Spittin' dus'!
WORKER 1: Call them yallow women, little buddy, to run down here and help us out.
LEAD BELLY: (*sings while the others make a rhythmic "che che che" sound in the background simulating the sound of a saw.*)
On a Monday, I was arrested
a Tuesday I was locked up in jail
On a Wednesday, my trial was attested
On a Thursday, nobody wouldn't go my bail
ALL: (*singing*) Yes, I'm all almost done
Yes, I'm all almost done
Yes, I'm all almost done
An' I ain't gonna ring them yallow women's do' bells
LEAD BELLY: Take these stripes, stripes from 'round my shoulder
Take these chains, chains from 'round my leg
Lawd, these stripes, stripes they sho' don't worry me
But these chains, chains 'bout to kill me dead
ALL: Yes, I'm all almost done
Yes, I'm all almost done
Yes, I'm all almost done
An' I ain't gonna ring them yallow women's do' bells

It is difficult to imagine how that song's depiction of human suffering at the hands of an unsympathetic (implicitly white) justice system would play in a classroom. The several mixed messages it sends about racial prejudice, including what seems to be an appeal to empathy for the incarcerated alongside a reference to the implied transgression of cavorting with a lighter-skinned African American woman ("yallow" is an abbreviated form of the offensive designator "high yellow"), may have been confusing to children and teachers listening over the air. Or the song may have been taken in stride, its central message as again pointing to the injustice experienced by African Americans. From the perspective of those working on the production of the program, a song such as "Ain't Gonna Ring" may have been chosen due to its depiction of a different kind of work (sawing).

The work songs introduced in the first part of the episode are remarkable beyond their expressed message or even their particular controversies. Both "Take This Hammer" and "Ain't Gonna Ring" brought the rhythmic sound of African American labor into the classroom. The program invited students to move from mere spectators (or auditioners, as the case may be) to embodied, engaged workers, at least by proxy. That participation had both material and phenomenological implications: the realities of African American folklife (abstracted and diluted as it was on the radio program) could be sensed in both student bodies and minds.

The episode also introduces audiences to songs such as "Stewball" and "Rock Island Line," which would go on to have lasting popularity. While those songs present a less-explicit emphasis on African American suffering, they were first recorded by the Lomaxes during the Southern prison visits and are good examples of work songs about less-heavy subjects. Both also may have offered entry points for further classroom conversation. "Stewball," for example, is a song appropriated from an Irish song about a popular racehorse named "Skewball." It was recorded by the Lomaxes in 1933 in a Mississippi state penitentiary and is featured as a hoeing song on *Folk Music of America*. Notably, "Stewball" also receives an orchestral rendering in the episode, and given the three versions of the song (Irish, African American, and orchestral), a classroom discussion about what constitutes an "American" song would be fruitful.

♫ WORKER 1: (*speaking*) Hey Buddy, didn't I hear you singing about some kind of horse called Stewball here the other day?

WORKER 2 [LEAD BELLY]: It's a whole song about Stewball and the part that everybody join in, it go like this: (*singing*) "Bet on Stewball and you might win, win, win; you bet on Stewball and you might win."

QUARTET: Oh!—(*singing*) "Bet on Stewball and you might win, win, win; you bet on Stewball and you might win."

WORKER 3: (*speaking*) Ok, fella, let's get on this Stewball here while we beat down these Mississippi weeds with these hoes. Whatcha say, huh?

WORKER 2: Come on, let's everybody sing about Stewball! (*singing in call-and-response with the caller* [Lead Belly] *singing the first line and the group responding with "uh-huh" and also joining in on the choruses*)

Way out in (uh-huh)
California (uh-huh)
Where Stewball (uh-huh)
Was born, was born
All the jockeys (uh-huh)
In the country (uh-huh)
Say he blew there (uh-huh)
In a storm, in a storm.

CHORUS: Well, bet on Stewball, you might win, win, win
Bet on Stewball and you might win
Was a big day (uh-huh)
In Dallas (uh-huh)
Don't you wish you (uh-huh)
Was there, was there
You could be yo' (uh-huh)
Las' dollar (uh-huh)
On that i'on (uh-huh)
Grey mare, grey mare

CHORUS: Well, bet on Stewball, you might win, win, win
Bet on Stewball and you might win
When the horses (uh-huh)
Was saddled (uh-huh)
An' the word was (uh-huh)
Given "go," given "go"
All the horses (uh-huh)
They shot off (uh-huh)
Like an arrow (uh-huh)
From a bow, from a bow

CHORUS: Well, bet on Stewball, you might win, win, win
Bet on Stewball and you might win
Ol' Stewball (uh-huh)
Was a race horse (uh-huh)
Ol' Molly (uh-huh)

Was too, was too
Ol' Stewball (uh-huh)
Run ol' Molly (uh-huh)
Right out of (uh-huh)
Her shoe, her shoe
CHORUS: Well, bet on Stewball, you might win, win, win
Bet on Stewball and you might win
De ol' folks (uh-huh)
Dey hollerd (uh-huh)
An' de young folks (uh-huh)
Dey bawl, dey bawl
An' de lil chillum (uh-huh)
Des look-a-look (uh-huh)
At de noble (uh-huh)
Stewball, Stewball
CHORUS: Well, bet on Stewball, you might win, win, win
Bet on Stewball and you might win

I am speculating, of course, about what classroom discussions took place around those songs. There may have been very little discussion at all. The rendering of "Stewball" into the more "serious" music of the orchestra reveals the questionable nature of one of the major pedagogical premises of *Folk Music of America*: that folk music is legitimized only through its transformation into the higher art form of symphonic orchestration.[6] We can surmise that somewhere within the discussions and compromises that led to the production of *American School of the Air*, the producers determined that music's educational value was diminished without the inclusion of music in that more sophisticated form. That point is undermined, however, by the difficulty of making real connections between "Stewball" and the piece inspired by it, "A Negro Work Song" by William L. Dawson, an African American composer and director of music at Tuskegee Institute. As Welch relates during that segment of the program, "A Negro Work Song" is not an exact reinterpretation of "Stewball" but, rather, follows the "spirit of the original work song."

♫ WELCH: Now today's CBS Commission work for the Columbia Concert Orchestra is based on this song about Ol' Stewball. It is by another of America's leading Negro composers, William L. Dawson, Director of Music at Tuskegee Institute and conductor of the famous Tuskegee Institute Choir.

> Mr. Dawson calls his composition "A Negro Work Song"; and in keeping with the free rhythmic and melodic style of the Negro singers themselves, he has followed the spirit of the original work song rather than the exact form in which we have heard it.
>
> The theme of Mr. Dawson's work is announced at the very beginning. It is based on the chorus of "Stewball" and it starts with the solo trumpet, like this:

(*Trumpet plays.*)

WELCH: The theme then continues in the woodwinds . . . played by the flute, oboe, clarinet, bassoon and horn, like this:

(*Woodwinds play.*)

WELCH: Then, after a dramatic middle section in which the solo cello stands out, a variant of the opening then returns once more in the trumpet. After this the original theme is taken up by the woodwinds and then passes to the strings for a full-bodied finish in the whole orchestra.

Dawson's piece is beautiful, but even with Welch's coaching, it can be difficult to hear its connection to "Stewball" or any other song from the program.

♫ WELCH: Here is the piece in full: "A Negro Work Song," by William L. Dawson:

(*Dawson's instrumental piece for orchestra plays.*)

WELCH: (*spoken*) That was "A Negro Work Song" the CBS commissioned piece by William L. Dawson based on the chorus of a folk song "Stewball."

Informative while listening to Dawson's piece is a lengthy critique from a critic and staunch proponent of "serious music," Theodor Adorno, writing about a different but contemporary program to *American School of the Air*, the National Broadcasting Company's *Music Appreciation Hour* (1939–1940). Adorno was not a fan of the pedagogical approach of the program, for a number of reasons that he elucidates over 50 pages in his article "Analytical Study of the NBC 'Music Appreciation Hour.'" He addresses the ways that radio programs try but ultimately fail to properly demonstrate thematic connections between "higher" and (by association) "lower" art.

> The pupils should be made to feel, although in different terms, that a theme is a sort of "statement" which obtains its meaning only within a functional unity and not as a thing in itself. If this character of the theme were demonstrated by analysis of a folk tune, and if the similarity between the musical structure of the folk tune and the developed musical form were made clear, one could easily show the difference between them as well. That is, one could demonstrate that the unity of the folk tune is an "immediate" unity, a unity in which the parts do not dissociate themselves from one another, whereas the unity of serious music is an articulated unity consisting in the function of parts marked by contrast or, at least, by difference . . . The Music Appreciation Hour, however, as soon as higher art forms are involved, insists only upon the articulation and overlooks the functional unity. In this way the articulation ceases to be an articulation at all and becomes a disintegration of the work: the elements of articulation actually degenerate into mere atoms. (332–333)

Though Adorno comes at the problem from the opposite ideological position as my own, I tend to agree with his analysis of how instruction in classical music appreciation breaks down in the radio forum. Unless the shared themes between the folk music and its symphonic reinterpretation are exceptionally conspicuous, students have very little incentive to make the connections desired as part of the pedagogical program. In other episodes of *Folk Music of America*, those thematic connections are less abstract, but students listening to "Negro Work Songs" might have struggled to understand the point of the orchestral exercise.

Fortunately, the episode does not dwell for long on the orchestral segment and moves next to one of the most exciting parts of the program, the performance of "Rock Island Line." As I mentioned in this book's introduction, that railroad song would eventually become a huge hit in the United States. As its later popularity shows, it is the most memorable song featured on the "Negro Work Songs" program. The song introduces the railroad line as the end point and distributor for lumber cut by day laborers and/or prisoners, as a "mighty good road" and the "road to ride." "Rock Island Line" serves as an example of genre mixing. Most obviously, it is an introduction to railroad songs (Lomax would devote a whole future episode to others), but it contains lyrics you might expect in a gospel tune: "Jesus died to save our sins, glory to God we gonna meet him again." It is also a game song: "A, B, C, double X Y Z, cat's in the copper, but they don't see me." The accompanying teaching manual encourages teachers to invite their students to add lyrics—refrains or new verses—to the program's featured songs. With its open genre potential, "Rock Island Line" would have been a perfect song for student experimentation.

♫ GOLDEN GATE QUARTET: (*singing*)
Oh, the Rock Island Line is a mighty good road
Oh, Rock Island Line it's the road to ride
Oh, Rock Island Line it's a mighty good road
If you wants to ride, you got to ride it like you find it
Get your ticket at the station on the Rock Island Line
LEAD BELLY: Jesus died to save our sins,
WORKER 1: Glory to God, we're going to meet him again!
QUARTET: Oh, the Rock Island Line is a mighty good road
Oh, Rock Island Line it's the road to ride
Oh, Rock Island Line it's a mighty good road
If you wants to ride, you got to ride it like you find it
Get your ticket at the station on the Rock Island Line
LEAD BELLY: A-B-C double X-Y-Z,
WORKER 2: Cat's in the copper but they don't see me.
GOLDEN GATE QUARTET: Oh, the Rock Island Line is a mighty good road
Oh, Rock Island Line it's the road to ride
Oh, Rock Island Line it's a mighty good road
If you wants to ride, you got to ride it like you find it
Get your ticket at the station on the Rock Island Line
LEAD BELLY: I may be right and I may be wrong
WORKER 3: Lord you're going to miss me when I'm gone
QUARTET: Oh, the Rock Island Line is a mighty good road
Oh, Rock Island Line it's the road to ride
Oh, Rock Island Line it's a mighty good road
If you wants to ride, you got to ride it like you find it
Get your ticket at the station on the Rock Island Line
Oh, the Rock Island Line is a mighty good road
Oh, Rock Island Line it's the road to ride

Oh, Rock Island Line it's a mighty good road
If you wants to ride, you got to ride it like you find it
Get your ticket at the station on the Rock Island Line

(*Worker 2 vocalizes a horn sound.*)

After concluding "Rock Island Line," a member of the Golden Gate Quartet offers a short monologue that moves back to a more somber tone and describes the loneliness and unrelenting nature of work in the fields. The monologue reflects on the song "Ol' Hannah" (or "Go Down, Old Hannah," as my analysis in chapter 2 references the song).

♫ WORKER 1: (*speaking*) When a man's on the road, you can't depend on nobody. You can have you a buddy, but you got to watch your buddy. That's what make these ol' roads so lonesome. Don't have nobody but yo'se'f to depend on. Yet an' still, wherever ya go, traveling from east to west and from west to east and travelin' through Georgia and through Alabama, and walkin' tired in Louisiana, and throwin' your pick in Tennessee, you're gonna fin' one friend to meet you every mornin' when you rise. I mean, Ol' Hannah. I mean the sun. (*Other men begin humming.*) Old Hanna just a beamin' and a boilin' up there all day long. Look like she stops long 'bout three o'clock. Look like she just stops up there an' punishes you. Now, down in Texas where they really works a man, where they drive a man, where mens is tough men from billy-goat town, they be out in the fields and they beg Old Hannah, they say "Hannah please go down. Git off there Ol' Hannah." Lets get out there and pick this cotton, boys.

ALL: (*singing*) Go down ol' Hannah; and don't you rise no mo'
If you rise in the mornin', bring judgement day
the sun was shinin' an' the men was flyin'
And the cap'n was holl'in'; the men almost dyin'
Go down ol' Hannah, please don't you rise no mo'
If you rise in the mornin', set the world on fire
Go down ol' Hannah, please don't you rise no mo'
If you rise in the mornin', set the world on fire

The song depicts "ol' Hannah," the sun, as the only reliable companion but a nuisance "boilin'" and "beamin'" all day to "just stop an' punish you" at about three o'clock. Such sentiment is also expressed in unbroadcasted lyrics recorded by the Lomaxes: "Go down, old Hannah. Won't you rise no more?" (quoted in chapter 2). The treatment of loneliness in "Go Down, Old Hannah" is juxtaposed with the final and perhaps most poignant segment of the work songs episode, an exposition of the song "Grey Goose" and a recollection of the "ol' slav'y days." In those days (paraphrasing the script), slaves woke at four in the morning and worked until eight or nine at night. That work, be it plowing, hauling corn, chopping cotton, driving cows, or feeding pigs, was backbreaking.

♫ WORKER 1: (*spoken*) Boy, it's a hard world.
WORKER 2: You gotta be a hard man to make it.
WORKER 1: Yeah, you gotta have iron jaws too.
WORKER 3: Now, take back in the olden times, you get up at four o'clock in the mornin' an' you gotta go till eight or nine o'clock at night.
WORKER 4: Yeah. Some be plowin', some be choppin' cotton, some be haulin' corn
WORKER 2: Forty head to milk, 'fo' day in the mornin'
WORKER 1: Some callin' pigs
WORKER 4: 'Fo' day in the mornin' till you can't see at night. You had to go back in them ol' slav'y days.
WORKER 3: If anybody asked you anything, you better not say about it.
WORKER 1: Yeah, you had to say it low an' easy. You had to make a joke about it—ha—boy, you had to laugh about it.
WORKER 1: Now, you know, people back in the olden time made up a song about this.
They made up a song about themselves and they sung it about an ol' grey goose. 'Twas the Ol' Grey Goose that you couldn't stop. You know what? They shot that grey goose an' picked him for six weeks
WORKER 2: Ah, that didn't stop him.
WORKER 1: Nah! Then they cooked him for six weeks.
WORKER 2: And that didn't stop him!
WORKER 1: Then they took the ol' grey goose and they cut him and they threw him to the hogs, and they even put him up against the circular saw.
WORKER 2: an' that ol' grey goose still laughin' at 'em.
WORKER 3: uh, and they still (*unintelligible*)

WORKER 4: Well, I declare, how did all that happen, fella?

LEADBELLY: well let's git to hoein' here an' I'll tell you just exactly how it happened:

LEADBELLY: (*singing*) One Sunday morning.

QUARTET: (*singing*) Lawd, Lawd, Lawd!

(*The Golden Gate Quartet sings the callback above after each line.*)

LEADBELLY: Preacher when a huntin' (Lawd, Lawd, Lawd!)
Carried 'long a shotgun (Lawd, Lawd, Lawd!)
Long come a grey goose (Lawd, Lawd, Lawd!)
Gun wen' off boo-loom (Lawd, Lawd, Lawd!)
and down come the grey goose (Lawd, Lawd, Lawd!)
He was six weeks a-fallin' (Lawd, Lawd, Lawd!)
They was six weeks a-haulin' (Lawd, Lawd, Lawd!)
My wife an' yo' wife (Lawd, Lawd, Lawd!)
well, give a featherpickin' (Lawd, Lawd, Lawd!)
They was six weeks a pickin' (Lawd, Lawd, Lawd!)
they put him on to par-boil (Lawd, Lawd, Lawd!)
They put him on the table (Lawd, Lawd, Lawd!)
and the fork wouldn't stick him (Lawd, Lawd, Lawd!)
An' the knife wouldn' cut him (Lawd, Lawd, Lawd!)
and they throwed him in the hog-pen (Lawd, Lawd, Lawd!)
And the hog couldn' eat him (Lawd, Lawd, Lawd!)
and it broke the hog's teeth out (Lawd, Lawd, Lawd!)
And they took him to the saw mill (Lawd, Lawd, Lawd!)
but he broke the saw's teeth out (Lawd, Lawd, Lawd!)
The last time I seed him (Lawd, Lawd, Lawd!)
he was flyin' cross the ocean (Lawd, Lawd, Lawd!)
With a long string of goslings (Lawd, Lawd, Lawd!)
They all went quack-quack (Lawd, Lawd, Lawd!)

WORKER 1: That was a tough goose!

NILES WELCH: Thank you Alan Lomax, the Golden Gate Quartet and Huddie Ledbetter.

"Grey Goose" is a comic song about an invincible magical bird. Saw blades break, hog teeth crack, guns explode, and no knife is sharp enough to kill the goose. Children are to sing along with the refrain, "Lawd, Lawd, Lawd," even as they root for the goose to escape its next dangerous captor. The Grey Goose is a metaphor for the unbreakable persistence of people enduring slave life. By extension, it is a powerful symbol of both hidden power and hope, even in the worst of circumstances. Not unlike portrayals of other popular trickster characters in African American (and more broadly, African) literature and folk traditions, such as the Br'er Rabbit stories, the symbology of the Grey Goose invites listeners to consider both the injustice and absurdity of African American captivity. Kathleen Glenister Roberts writes that while there is ongoing debate around the purpose and precise nature of meaning attached to Br'er Rabbit and other folk heroes often connected to African and African American identity, "one thing is certain. . . . Tricksters propel, without hesitation, the right of the individual to question inequalities in society." Like Br'er Rabbit, she explains, the Grey Goose's seeming invincibility "captures the audience's imagination because [it] never closes off the option of freedom; [it] espouses the rhetoric of possibility and perhaps even inspires it in his listeners" (176). It is impossible to know whether students made those connections as they sang the refrain of "Grey Goose" ("Lawd, Lawd, Lawd!"), but the rhetoric of possibility for future empathy, understanding, and care intoned and enjoined in the words of that shared short chorus may have been an important first: a call with a million-voiced response.

Identifying Commonality, Listening to Difference

In the introduction to his 1937 book, *Attitudes toward History*, Kenneth Burke introduces the notion of "identification" that would go on to become central to his thinking, if not his most famous contribution to rhetorical theory. Interestingly, he does so within the context of epic poetry. "The epic is designed," argues Burke,

> under primitive conditions, to make men "at home in" those conditions. It "accepts" the rigors of war (the basis of the tribe's success) by magnifying the role of the warlike hero. Such magnification serves two purposes: It lends dignity to the necessities of existence, "advertising" courage and individual sacrifice for group advantage—and it enables the humble man to share the worth of the hero by the process of "identification." The hero, real or legendary, thus risks himself and dies that others may be *vicariously* heroic. . . . The process of identification [. . .] dignifies any sense of persecution that may possess the individual, who may also feel himself marked for disaster. This sense of a flaw serves happily to promote an openness to realistic admonition—the invitation to seek the flaw in oneself promotes in the end the attitude of *resignation*. (44–45)

Burke's emerging definition of identification as a meditation on the usefulness of poetic ideals and heroic figures resonates well with how songs like "Grey Goose" or "Take This Hammer" might work to help reconstitute public opinion. The promotion of African American figures and symbols as subjects for heroic emulation—as folk metaphors for courage, perseverance, and hard work in the face of nearly impossible obstacles—might resign listeners of *Folk Music of America* to a reconstituted belief about African Americans as a larger group. In other words, exposure to and identification with the poetic materials of folk life can lead to new attitudes toward the real lives of those they represent, and thus new attitudes toward history.

Of course, Burke's theory develops beyond identification as a tool for interpreting poetry, toward a more complete reexamination of rhetoric's power for encouraging understanding, cooperation, unification, and the "acting-together" possible when people experience mutual "consubstantiality."[7] All of those capabilities, Burke admits, are ideals, as division is the default human condition. Identification retains its folksy earnestness, he argues, "precisely because there is division. Identification is compensatory to division. If men were not apart from one another, there would be no need for the rhetorician to proclaim their unity" (*Rhetoric of Motives* 22). Symbolic discourse, best expressed by Burke through analysis of poetic masterpieces, is useful in its power to create a "common substance of meaning" in the face of constant divisiveness—"[t]he Wrangle of the Market Place, the flurries and flare-ups of the Human Barnyard, the Give and Take" and, ultimately, "the War" (*Rhetoric of Motives* 23). For Burke and in the argument I have sought to make in this chapter and throughout this book, the promise of rhetoric is its potential for the co-creation of something "common," and the promise of sonic rhetorics—folksongs like "Grey Goose"—is their ability to broaden the bandwidth of the commonalities we might be unified around. In 1940, an ability to hear commonness resonating in and through African American folk music on the radio had revolutionary implications for status-quo America. Finding oneself in common with another (especially an "other") is a first but significant step towards more profound anti-racist revolutions (turn, turn, turn). Being first "in common" casts our inevitable divisions within a different rhetorical frame. It prepares us to listen further.

In her monograph *Rhetorical Listening: Identification, Gender, Whiteness* (2005), Krista Ratcliffe draws the notion of identification and the problem of race relations together with the challenge to listen. Rhetorical listening, as Ratcliffe defines it, is a "stance of openness" that advances the pursuit of understanding as part of the ongoing negotiation of difference (1). As a regimen to be employed during moments of "cross-cultural conduct" (17), rhetorical listening might be understood as identification in action. Particularly concerned with learning to "hear people's intersecting identifications with gender and race" (17), Ratcliffe recommends avoiding the impulse to displace listening—to not hear or ignore difference. That recommendation resonates well with Nathan Crick's argument that "the unique function of rhetoric in a democracy is to express and advance minority viewpoints in exigent circumstances such that they have the opportunity to transform public opinion" (12). Ratcliffe would have us make a greater effort to become accustomed to listening to those expressions—especially if we find ourselves within the majority or experiencing what she calls "troubled identifications"—"those identifications troubled by history, uneven power dynamics, and ignorance" (47). The present book has been a similar plea for more careful listening.

Race relations in the 1930s were certainly a mesh of troubled identifications. Rhetorical listening, Ratcliffe teaches, neither collapses difference nor seeks to ignore the substance of what is troubling about differences. According to Ratcliffe, employing listening as a rhetoric of attentive care brings more audibility to the troubling aspects of disidentification (injustices, inequality, and power and privilege differentials) and opens up new possibilities for understanding and discourse, though with no guarantees (66, 68). For her, rhetorical listening is about humbly learning to recognize "interdependency among subjects" and, out of that interdependency, building new avenues for accountability (73). Rhetorical listening, then, brings a profound ethics to Burke's notion of identification and Dewey's radical democracy, reminding us what is at stake when we seek to teach about and work through differences. Working through difference requires abundant care.

A pedagogy that included listening to the radio program *Folk Music of America* on *American School of the Air* was attuned for careful rhetorical listening. Tuning in to the program was an opportunity for identification that did not ask anyone for votes, money, or immediate societal change. Episodes like "Negro Work Songs" invited students and other listeners to contemplate the experience of the other, to imagine a community different from their own, and, if possible, to identify aspects of that experience worth deeper consideration. *Folk Music of America* was about learning to listen carefully to difference and, if so inclined, to sing along.

Conclusion

Hearing the Lomax Archive

Alan Lomax's work for the Library of Congress would extend briefly into the 1940s, but soon after the United States joined the war effort in 1941, Lomax found himself being investigated by the FBI, under suspicion, once again, for Communist activities. He denied affiliation, but when Lomax's boss and supporter Archibald MacLeish was reappointed from the Library of Congress to a new position in the Office of War Information (OWI), Lomax resigned his position as "assistant in charge" at the Archive of Folk Song. Soon after, the FBI cleared his name of any suspicion, and he went back to work for MacLeish at the OWI, building programs that would improve wartime morale and promote a common nationalism among the enlisted. As enthusiastic about his work as ever, Lomax even joined the army in 1944, serving in stateside training camps before being discharged in 1946.

After his official association with the US government ended, Lomax's efforts as a folklorist and an educator persisted. He spent several more years doing fieldwork in the US and teaching people, via radio, to listen to and appreciate the traditional music of the Americas. He won a Guggenheim Fellowship in 1947 to aid him in that work. Eventually, however, Red Scare pressure mounted again, and Lomax was blacklisted along with many of his friends, including Pete Seeger, Orson Welles, and Aaron Copland. Lomax left the country in September 1950 and spent much of the next decade overseas. While in Europe, he continued his work as a folklorist and made thousands of recordings and films that would become national treasures for a number of countries.

Lomax returned to the United States in 1959 and continued his work for almost four more decades, developing new theories and methods for understanding vernacular traditions, as well as new technologies to promote and champion them. In 1983, Lomax founded the Association for Cultural Equity on the Fine Arts Campus of New York City's Hunter College. Cultural equity, he argued, was "the right of every culture to have equal time on the air and equal time in the classroom" (Pareles). That philosophy motivated Lomax's work until his death, on July 19, 2002, soon after which the *New York Times* published a tribute that summed up Lomax's method: "He did whatever was necessary to preserve traditional music and take it to a wider audience . . . Bob Dylan once described him as a 'missionary'" (Pareles). Dylan's descriptor is fitting and poignant. Perhaps more than anything else, Alan Lomax was a folk music evangelist.

As with any evangelical movement, we might wonder about the impact and legacy of the Lomaxes. In this book, I have sought to both celebrate and complicate that legacy, particularly when it comes to the Lomaxes' ideas about race. Their work—which I have framed using a sonic rhetorical historiographic methodology—contributed to ideas and ideals that both complicated previous racial tropes and helped to codify new ones in the national imagination. In their edited collection *Music and the Racial Imagination* (2000), Ronald M. Radano and Philip V. Bohlman comment on the ambivalent legacy of Lomax and his contemporary folklorists and scholars.

> One must certainly commend the early figures of a discipline in their progressive commitment to a bolder kind of musical scholarship than that which characterized commentaries of non-European music before. They sought to chart an ambitious, democratic vision that expressed as much new sympathy for realms of difference as it reflected an imperial self-confidence after America's world victory. It is certainly not our intention to denigrate their mission, but only to observe how their scholarship reinforced as it reflected ideologies pervasive in an academy still dominated by white, male privilege. In these positions toward race, we can now recognize, from a distance, the extent to which they carried the denial of race forward. (23)

Ironically, the "denial" spoken of by Radano and Bohlman was often accomplished, as I have argued throughout the present book, in the Lomaxes' attempts at racial celebration. The beauty of Black folk music for Alan and especially John Lomax was tied to its ability to be representative

Figure 4. Alan Lomax playing guitar onstage at the Mountain Music Festival, Asheville, North Carolina, 1938

of a kind of essence, but—importantly—that essence had to be accessible and perceptible to a broader (white) public. The Lomaxes listened for the qualities that communicated that dubious sonic rhetoric of essence, and as listeners for the country, they made decisions about what a broader listening audience might be able to hear. In the present context, I am using the words *hear* and *listen* in a multivalent way that includes both sensory reception and the ability to decipher meaning—a signal through the noise. My approach throughout *Listening to the Lomax Archive* has been to push beyond the typified receptions of the folklife archive that the Lomaxes provided—to, as I say in the introduction—"listen carefully both to what is there but also to the noise that music organizes, obfuscates, and silences."

This book has been an exercise in "careful listening," particularly to representations of race in the Lomax archive. That listening has been broad and deep, encompassing multiple locations, from the African American prison farm, to the streets and clubs of Old New Orleans, to the broadcasts of Popular Front radio. When practiced as a methodology for sonic rhetorical historiography, careful listening reveals history and its people, places, and problems as a symphony, sometimes beautiful and harmonious and sometimes dissonant and cacophonous. Or, careful listening reveals history as a folksong: John Gibson's "Levee Camp Holler," a sinful song sung under duress by a country incarcerated by its own injustices; Jelly Roll Morton's "Tiger Rag," composed at the intersections of place, race, class, and time, reverberant with their unresolvable ambivalences, but performed with a virtuosity powerful enough to forge new myths; and the rendition of "Grey Goose" sung by Lead Belly and the Golden Gate Quartet, joyful and mischievous in its presentation of how systematic racial oppression creates an indefatigable people, unwilling to relent on their march toward equity, despite a near constant stream of violence and tyranny. History is those and other folk songs in the archive that are waiting to be resounded and broadcast to a new generation of listeners.

Listening without Hearing

Radano and Bohlman's critique that Alan Lomax's methodologies during and after his tenure at the Library of Congress "denied" race is another way of articulating the process of deciphering signal through noise, including the failure to do so. Sonic rhetorics are dense—rife with meaning—and reception occurs on a spectrum, rich for some and virtually meaningless to others. One person's noise is another's signal. To paraphrase a biblical phrase, those with "ears to hear" are best positioned for meaningful reception (Matthew 11:15). Lomax's "denial" is another way of saying that he listened and understood race in a particular way but could not hear it in many other and perhaps the most crucial ways. Both John and Alan assumed that folkness sounded the same regardless of subject position. The value and virtue assumptions they made about the African American folk music in their collection reflected their own ideas about folk authenticity more often than ideas of the people they recorded. They thought they could hear Black folkness in the songs they collected, but in many ways, they listened but could not hear.

We may be tempted to judge that reality harshly, but we might ask ourselves what evades our own listening and what further work, change, and effort is required in order for us to hear. More than 80 years after the collection of the Lomax archive, we are confronted with our own society's continual hearing failures. The sad circumstances surrounding the Black Lives Matter movement offer an example in recent memory. Black Lives Matter (or #BlackLivesMatter) is the activist response to repeated occurrences of deadly violence perpetrated against African Americans, often at the hands of police. On February 26, 2012, 17-year-old Trayvon Martin was shot and killed by neighborhood watch volunteer George Zimmerman in Sanford, Florida. More violence followed, including Eric Garner's death at the hands of Daniel Pantaleo, an officer of the New York Police Department, on Staten Island in July 2014. Then, on August 5, John Crawford was killed by police in a Walmart in Ohio after being seen holding a toy gun that was on sale at the store. Four days later, on August 9, 2014, Michael Brown was shot and killed by police officer Darren Wilson in Ferguson, Missouri; Brown was unarmed. (In the short months between the submission and revision of this chapter for publication, Breonna Taylor, George Floyd, and many others were added to this wretched list.)

Ferguson—a suburb of St. Louis—is only a few hours south of Champaign, Illinois, where, as a graduate student at the University of Illinois, I was working on the initial drafts of this book at the time of Brown's shooting. I remember the irony and anguish I experienced when writing about racial "progress" in 1930s America while Black men in what felt like my backyard were shot and killed by officers of the law. By the end of that year, Cleveland's 12-year-old Tamir Rice was also shot and killed by police. In the wake of that violence, the phrase and social media hashtag #BlackLivesMatter emerged and gained rapid popularity. The hashtag first appeared as a way of expressing sorrow, exasperation, and public support to the families of those who experienced the unimaginable losses of life and future mentioned above. Then #BlackLivesMatter became an organizing rally cry—an act of solidarity as protests were organized around the country in response to those horrific acts as they persisted even beyond the events listed above.

Soon, however, another phrase began to circulate: All Lives Matter. The #AllLivesMatter movement (and later, to an extent, #BlueLivesMatter) represent well a collective inability to hear. #AllLivesMatter is another example of racial denial. The extent to which such denial is or is not unconscious is open for debate, but even a generous read of the situation would make the #AllLivesMatter response akin to a kind of tone deafness, an inability to identify with and tune in to the anti-racist objectives of #BlackLivesMatter. Feminist scholars of rhetoric have used similar language to describe the challenge of navigating difference. In drawing to conclusion here, I turn again to Krista Ratcliffe's book-length treatment of rhetorical listening. In her exploration (and critique) of Kenneth Burke's theory of identification, Ratcliffe describes the ways that "cultural discourses become embodied in people" according to their "particular experiences and identifications" (52–53). Such embodiments may preclude or prevent identification—the finding of common ground, or ability to hear—between individuals. Ratcliffe refers to the lack of overlap or ability to connect as "non-identification"—a gap or margin between shared experience, often due to disparities of equity. #AllLivesMatter is an example of non-identification, a place where, as Ratcliffe explains, "two concepts are metonymically juxtaposed—that is, where concepts of the negative and of identification are associated but not overlapping" (72). In the case of #AllLivesMatter and #BlackLivesMatter, the associated ideal is around the notion of lives and how they matter. The disconnect comes from what the word *lives* is being used to metonymically represent. #AllLivesMatter proponents seem unable to hear—to identify with—the need for an emphasis on Black lives.

Such a lack of hearing is sometimes described in visual language when folks say that they "don't see race," a statement meant to communicate a lack of racism by a willful ignoring of it. From that perspective, statements like those made in 2016 by Donald Trump, then Republican presidential nominee, are disappointing, if unsurprising. Trump told the Associated Press, "A lot of people feel that [the phrase Black Lives Matter] is inherently racist. It is a divisive term because all lives matter. It's a very, very divisive term" (Daly and Colvin). Calling #BlackLivesMatter racist when it is an organization created to promote awareness of and activism against racism is an especially frustrating example of non-identification.

What is to be done about such embodied incongruities? Ratcliffe imagines the hyphen in the term *non-identification* as having some answers to that question. The hyphen represents the "margin between," a place wherein people may consciously choose to position themselves to listen rhetorically. That "margin between" does not transcend ideology; it does, however, provide a place of reflection, a place that invites people to admit that gaps exist. According to Ratcliffe, admissions of gaps may take such forms as "I don't know you," "I don't know what I don't know about you," or even "I don't know that I don't know that you exist"—whether that "you" is a person, place, thing, or idea (72–73). "What's important in the process of non-identification," she continues, "is that people recognize the partiality of our visions and listen for that-which-can-not-be-seen, even if it cannot yet be heard" (73). Of course, that process of recognition is never a given, and even when attempts are made, they are not always successful. Ratcliffe reminds us that understanding

> the concept of non-identification and engaging in rhetorical listening across gaps is important to the field of rhetoric studies because it maps a place, a possibility, for consciously asserting our agency to engage in cross-cultural rhetorical exchanges across both commonalities and differences. Such a performance of rhetorical listening makes hearing a possibility; in turn, hearing provides a ground for action motivated by accountability. (73)

In a decade marked by a kind of hopelessness around issues of race and accountability in the United States, Ratcliffe's phrase about the possibility of hearing across and through our gaps and non-identifications provides a modicum of hope.

Despite the critiques I have leveled against the Lomaxes, I hear the sounds of hope resonating throughout the Lomax archive. It provides any number of places to begin practicing the kind of listening through and to the problems and gaps inherent to non-identification. The Lomaxes and others of their ilk are best understood not as demons to be cast out but as symbolic representations of ourselves in our attempts and failures to listen and hear across difference. Hindsight provides the advantage of recognizing particularly egregious examples of their failings, but we would do well to remember that our own actions might one day be subject to the same scrutiny. Despite John and Alan's inadequacies and frequently frustrating inability to hear, they were out in the world listening as hard as they could. Much of what has become the most popular and powerful parts of the

Lomax archive are based on the results of that listening, imperfect as it was. Alan's radio program is one early example, but the public has long listened to the Lomax archive through hundreds of popular physical media releases over the years. Those releases only scratch the surface of the Lomax archive, which is full of songs and sounds that were never celebrated by the Lomaxes or their predecessors and that were never released commercially to the public. Thousands of songs, oral histories, and other sonic ephemera in the archive have had very little or no audience, and much of the archive is now more accessible than ever.

Sin-Killer Griffin's Sermon

The final examples I discuss here from the Lomax archive involve a sermon attributed to the Reverend "Sin-Killer" Griffin, an African American chaplain employed by the Texas penitentiary system. The sermon was recorded in April 1934, as part of the Lomaxes' prison trips discussed in chapter 2. John Lomax wrote in his autobiography, *Adventures of a Ballad Hunter*, that Griffin "looked the part" of a prison chaplain: the reverend had "grizzly grey hair and mutton chop whiskers" and wore a "Prince Albert coat which almost touched his shoe tops"; he was "dignified" and "most impressive" and possessed a "deep and sonorous voice" (221). Griffin is known to the world from two tracks released by the Library of Congress, the song "Wasn't That a Mighty Storm" and a speech Griffin titled "The Man of Calvary," an excerpt from an Easter sermon. "Wasn't That a Mighty Storm" has been covered over the years by many popular recording artists, but Library of Congress catalogers appear to have misattributed Griffin as the singer of the Lomaxes' archived version. The voice singing the song does not match the voice of the sermonizer, and John Lomax's recounting has Griffin taking the podium after a few songs (including "Wasn't That a Mighty Storm"), a prayer, and a solemn distribution of the Lord's Supper (bread crumbs and grapefruit juice substituting for wine), each led by someone else.

The portion of the sermon released under the title "The Man of Calvary" might be described as a speech that veers into a rhythmic and mostly monotonic reverie, more sung than spoken. Griffin's nasal voice is powerful and persistent and rises occasionally to a lifted note, expressed as "Oh!" Griffin's audience is responsive, and encouragements from the audience are frequently audible. The recording is clear and mostly untroubled by static or other aural blips. Griffin is quite audible, and his words are easily understood. Lomax transcribes a majority of "The Man of Calvary" in *Adventures of a Ballad Hunter*. I here offer a short excerpt with Lomax's transcription (which I have edited, slightly, to better match the recording).

♫ SIN-KILLER GRIFFIN: (*preaching*) Roman soldiers come riding in full
speed on their horses,
And splunged Him in the side,
We seen blood and water come out.
Oh!—Oh, God A'mighty placed it in the minds of the people
Why the water is for baptism.
And the blood is for cleansin'.
I don't care how mean you've been,
God A'mighty's blood'll cleanse you from all sin.
I seen my dear friends, the time moved on,
Great God looked down,
He began to look at the temple.
Jesus said to tear down the temple,
And in three days I'll rise up again in all sight.
They didn't know what he was talkin' about—
Jesus was talkin' about His temple body.
I seen while He was hangin', the mounting began to tremble
On which Jesus was hangin' on;
The blood was dropping on the mounting, holy blood
dropping on,
my dear friend,
Corrupted the mounting;
I seen about that time while the blood was dropping down,
One drop after another,
I seen the sun that Jesus made in creation;
The sun rose, my dear friend,
And it recognized Jesus hanging on the cross.
Just as soon as the sun recognized its Maker,
Why it closed itself inside glory[?] and went down,
Oh—went down in mournin'. (J. Lomax, *Adventures* 225)

"The Man of Calvary" has been released by the Library of Congress several times over the years. It is about five minutes in length. John Lomax writes that Sin-Killer's sermon lasted for two hours but that "Alan had been able to catch only segments" of it, because "[e]very seven minutes a disc must be turned, every fourteen minutes a new one had to be inserted" ("Sin-Killer's Sermon" 182). When I initially came across the clip that I share below, I assumed it was another part of Griffin's sermon. All of the archival reference material indicates as much. At the beginning of the recording, the archivist names the Archive of Folk Song (AFS) number, "AFS 186 a-side," which was how and where the recording was cataloged and stored by the library. That number corresponded correctly with the number on the digital file I received from the library, and I used it to find the scanned catalog card. The card identifies the content of the recording as a "sermon with singing" by Sin-Killer Griffin. Given the AFS number, the card identifying Griffin as the voice on the tape, John Lomax's description of the length of the speech, and the fact that Alan and John only got parts of the longer speech, there would seem to be no doubt about the content of the recording.

When listened to against the "The Man of Calvary" recording, however, I am not so sure. As with the earlier example involving "Wasn't That a Might Storm," the two voices—Griffin's and the one on the "Sermon with Singing" recording—sound quite different. So do the recordings. It is very difficult to understand the content of "Sermon with Singing." That difficulty—my difficulty—is more remarkable and instructive than the fact that Griffin may be misidentified. "Sermon with Singing" has many distinct differences from "The Man of Calvary." The quality of the recording is lower overall and sounds slightly sped up. The recorded voice competes with the static and scratches that play over it. As in "The Man of Calvary," the preacher sings as much as he speaks, with other voices rising in response. But instead of Sin-Killer's deep nasal intonation and distinct enunciation, "Sermon with Singing" features the higher tones of a tenor (which may be the result of the sped-up recording).

Unable to understand much of the speech, I can catch only bits and pieces. The topic of the sermon is different from "The Man of Calvary." Instead of giving a typical Easter sermon, the speaker begins by preaching about the meeting between Jesus and Nicodemus from the third chapter of the New Testament book of John. The speaker frequently repeats the phrase "You must be born again!" At various moments on the recording, he mentions several famous figures, among them Alexander the Great, Abraham Lincoln, and George Washington. Beyond those details and for most of the recording's 10 minutes, the speaker/singer's words, which are delivered with a strong Southern accent in African American Vernacular English, are indecipherable to me. A persistent rhythmic tapping that begins in the first half of the recording becomes louder and louder as the sermon persists. The combination of these various sonic layers leaves me confounded. Even when I listen as intently as I know how, I find much of the sermon impossible to discern. Indeed, I listen and I cannot yet hear.

For "Sermon with Singing," this book's final offering from the Lomax archive, I have not included a transcription for the recording in the printed text, because, at this moment, I lack the ability to do so adequately.[1] I have described it above as well as I can. With work, persistence, and the patience of others, I hope my own abilities and capacity to hear through and despite difference improve. I am committed to that process for this short piece and also to the larger project of careful listening, which is to say anti-racist listening. It is likely that some listeners to "Sermon with Singing" will have capacities beyond mine to hear and understand what is being said and sung. To those with ears to hear, let them hear. ♫

Appendix

List of Audio Resources

Resources are listed here in order of their appearance in each chapter. Citations include Library of Congress catalog information (where applicable), including American Folklife Center (AFC) and Archive of Folk Song (AFS) designations.

Preface

"Home on the Range," banjo performance by Dakota Waddell, *YouTube*, May 26, 2015. https://www.youtube.com/watch?v=JeRAOCEdfQk

"Turn, Turn, Turn," sung by Pete Seeger and Tao Rodríguez-Seeger, recorded by WFUV radio, Newport Folk Festival, August 1, 2009, distributed by NPR. https://www.npr.org/2009/08/01/111337844/pete-and-tao-seeger-and-friends-saturday-night-singalong-newport-folk-festival-2

Introduction

"Rock Island Line," sung by Kelly Pace and a group of prisoners, recorded by John A. Lomax, 1934, AFS 248 A1.

"In the Pines" ("Black Girl"), sung by Huddie (Lead Belly) Ledbetter, on *Folkways: The Original Vision; Songs of Woody Guthrie and Lead Belly* (New York: Folkways Records, 1989). Compact disc.

"Grey Goose," sung by James Baker (Iron Head), recorded by John A. Lomax, Central State Farm, Sugar Land, TX, December 1933, AFS 00207.

Chapter 1

"Governor Pat Neff," sung by Huddie (Lead Belly) Ledbetter with guitar, recorded by John A. Lomax, Wilton, CT, February 1934, AFS 00053.

Chapter 2

"Levee Camp Holler," sung by John Gibson (Black Samson), recorded by John A. Lomax, Tennessee state penitentiary, Nashville, TN, August 1933, AFS 00179 B03.

"The Angels Drooped Their Wings and Gone on to Heaven," sung by a "group of Negro convicts," recorded by John A. Lomax, Tennessee state penitentiary, Nashville, TN, August 1933, AFS 00179 B02.

"Good God A'mighty," sung by a "group of Negro convicts" and featuring the sound of axes cutting, recorded by John A. and Alan Lomax, state penitentiary, Huntsville, TX, November 1934, AFS 00179 B03.

"Run Nigger Run," sung by Mose Platt (Clear Rock), recorded by John A. and Alan Lomax, Central State Farm, Sugar Land, TX, December 1933, AFS 00196 A01.

"Ol' Rattler," sung by Mose Platt (Clear Rock), recorded by John A. and Alan Lomax, Central State Farm, Sugar Land, TX, April 1934, AFS 00208 B01.

"Shorty George," sung by James Baker (Iron Head), recorded by John A. Lomax, Central State Farm, Sugar Land, TX, February 1934, AFS 00202 A02.

"Go Down, Hannah," sung by James Baker (Iron Head), Will Crosby, R. D. Allen, and Mose Platt (Clear Rock), recorded by John A. and Alan Lomax, Central State Farm, Sugar Land, TX, December 1933, AFS 00195 A02.

Chapter 3

"Wolverine Blues," played by Ferdinand (Jelly Roll) Morton on piano, Washington, D. C., by Alan Lomax, June, July, August, 1938. AFS 1675 B, AFS 1676 A.

"Jungle Blues," played by Ferdinand (Jelly Roll) Morton on piano, recorded by Alan Lomax, Washington, D. C., June, July, August, 1938. AFS 1673 B.

"King Porter Stomp," played by Ferdinand (Jelly Roll) Morton on piano, Washington, D. C., recorded by Alan Lomax, June, July, August, 1938. AFS 1674 A.

"Jelly Roll's Background," on "Monologue on his ancestry, early life and first music lessons," spoken by Ferdinand (Jelly Roll) Morton on piano, Washington, D. C., by Alan Lomax, June, July, August, 1938. AFS 1640 A.

"Miserere" on "Monologue on his ancestry, early life, and first music lessons," spoken by Ferdinand (Jelly Roll) Morton on, recorded by Alan Lomax, Washington, D. C, June, July, August, 1938. AFS 1641 A.

"The Stomping Grounds" on "Monologue on his ancestry, early life, and first music lessons," spoken by Ferdinand (Jelly Roll) Morton, recorded by Alan Lomax, Washington, D. C., June, July, August, 1938. AFS 1641 B.

"New Orleans Was a Free and Easy Place" on "Monologue on New Orleans honky-tonks," spoken by Ferdinand (Jelly Roll) Morton, recorded by Alan Lomax, Washington, D. C., June, July, August, 1938. AFS 1644 A.

"When the Hot Stuff Came In" on "New Orleans street bands," spoken by Ferdinand (Jelly Roll) Morton, Washington, D. C., by Alan Lomax, December, 1938. AFS 2487 A.

"How Jelly Roll Got His Name" on "Monologue on Jelly Roll blues and the origin of his nickname," spoken by Ferdinand (Jelly Roll) Morton, recorded by Alan Lomax, Washington, D. C., June, July, August, 1938. AFS 1659 B.

"Oh! Didn't He Ramble" on "Monologue on New Orleans funeral customs and the beginnings of jazz," played by Ferdinand (Jelly Roll) Morton on piano, Washington, D. C., recorded by Alan Lomax, June, July, August, 1938. AFS 1648 B.

"Tiger Rag" on "Monologue on beginnings of jazz," sung and spoken by Ferdinand (Jelly Roll) Morton on piano, Washington, D. C., recorded by Alan Lomax, June, July, August, 1938. AFS 1649 A & B.

"Slow Swing and 'Sweet Jazz Music'" on "Monologue on 'breaks' and 'riffs' in jazz, on swing, and on his theories of jazz," spoken by Ferdinand (Jelly Roll) Morton with piano, recorded by Alan

Lomax, Washington, D. C., June, July, August, 1938. AFS 1651 B.

"The Spanish Tinge" on "Dialogue on jazz and blues," spoken by Ferdinand (Jelly Roll) Morton with piano, recorded by Alan Lomax, Washington, D. C., June, July, August, 1938. AFS 1682 A.

Chapter 4

"Negro Work Songs," opening, from "Negro Work Songs," an episode of *Folk Songs of America* on *The American School of the Air* (New York: Columbia Broadcasting System) (the full episode hereinafter referenced as "Negro Work Songs"), AFC 1939/002: AFS 13,497A.

"Bonaparte's Retreat," played by W. M. Stepp on fiddle, recorded by Alan and Elizabeth Lomax, Salyersville, KY, October 1937, AFS 01568 A02.

"Negro Work Songs," Welch's introduction, from "Negro Work Songs," AFC 1939/002: AFS 13,497A.

"Negro Work Songs," Lomax's introduction, part 1, from "Negro Work Songs," AFC 1939/002: AFS 13,497A.

"Negro Work Songs," Lomax's introduction, part 2, from "Negro Work Songs," AFC 1939/002: AFS 13,497A.

"Take This Hammer," sung by Huddie (Lead Belly) Ledbetter and the Golden Gate Quartet, from "Negro Work Songs," AFC 1939/002: AFS 13,497A.

"Almost Done," sung by Huddie (Lead Belly) Ledbetter and the Golden Gate Quartet, from "Negro Work Songs," AFC 1939/002: AFS 13,497A.

"Stewball," sung by Huddie (Lead Belly) Ledbetter and the Golden Gate Quartet, from "Negro Work Songs," AFC 1939/002: AFS 13,497A.

"A Negro Work Song," introduction, from "Negro Work Songs," AFC 1939/002: AFS 13,496B.

"A Negro Work Song," composed by William L. Dawson, from "Negro Work Songs," AFC 1939/002: AFS 13,496B.

"Rock Island Line," sung by Huddie (Lead Belly) Ledbetter and the Golden Gate Quartet, from "Negro Work Songs," AFC 1939/002: AFS 13,496B.

"Go Down, Old Hannah," sung by Huddie (Lead Belly) Ledbetter and the Golden Gate Quartet, from "Negro Work Songs," AFC 1939/002: AFS 13,496B

"Grey Goose," sung by Huddie (Lead Belly) Ledbetter and the Golden Gate Quartet, from "Negro Work Songs," AFC 1939/002: AFS 13,496B.

Conclusion

"The Man of Calvary (Easter Service)," sung and spoken by Sin-Killer Griffin, recorded by John A. Lomax, Darrington State Farm, Sandy Point, TX, April 1934, AFS 00186 A&B.

"Sermon with Singing," sung and spoken by Sin-Killer Griffin, recorded by John A. Lomax, Darrington State Farm, Sandy Point, TX, April 1934, AFS 00186 A&B.

Notes

Introduction

1. Translation by Poulakos (341).

2. Wade spoke of such things in his talk "The Wanderings of 'Rock Island Line' and 'Coal Creek March,'" presented at the University of Illinois Sousa Archives and Center for American Music on October 31, 2013.

3. The study of folklore has its own history and discipline, stretching back to the late 19th century. In a useful synopsis titled "An Introduction to Folklore Studies," folklorist Jeana Jorgensen notes that "folklore studies thrives at a number of universities, sometimes as independent departments or programs, and sometimes under the title of another department (comparative studies, literary studies, and anthropology are common ones)." As an introduction to the field, Jorgenson recommends *International Folkloristics: Classic Contributions by the Founders of Folklore* (1999), edited by Alan Dundes, and Lynee McNeill's *Folklore Rules: A Fun, Quick, and Useful Introduction to the Field of Academic Folklore Studies* (2013).

4. Here and often throughout this study, I use the term *American* as a convenient shorthand for the United States of America, recognizing that neither *America* nor *North America* are US-exclusive terms.

5. In "Rhetorical Folkness: Reanimating Walter J. Ong in the Pursuit of Digital Humanity" (2018), I expound on Seeger's notion of "folkness," arguing that it "points to a more or less universal idea about the ways that humans build systems of value and public memory together in vernacular, or everyday, discursive spaces" (69).

6. See Mary E. Hocks and Michelle Comstock's "Composing for Sound: Sonic Rhetoric as Resonance" (2017); Jonathan W. Stone, "Listening to the Sonic Archive: Rhetoric, Representation, and Race in the Lomax Prison Recordings" (2015); Erin Anderson, "Toward a Resonant Material Vocality for Digital Composition" (2014).

7. For a useful genealogy of those movements within rhetorical studies, see Greg Goodale's *Sonic Persuasion* (2011).

8. For excellent examples of work in visual rhetoric, see Cara Finnegan's *Pic-*

turing Poverty: Print Culture and FSA Photographs (2003) and *Making Photography Matter: A Viewer's History from the Civil War to the Great Depression* (2015), Christa J. Olson's *Constitutive Visions: Indigeneity and Commonplaces of National Identity in Republican Ecuador* (2013), and Laurie Gries's *Still Life with Rhetoric: A New Materialist Approach for Visual Rhetorics* (2015).

9. For examples of how scholarship on rhetorical history has perpetuated the false binaries mentioned, see Eric Havelock's *Preface to Plato* (1963) and *The Muse Learns to Write: Reflections on Orality and Literacy from Antiquity to Present* (1986). Walter J. Ong is frequently cited as one of several prominent scholars to build theory around ethnocentric historical inaccuracies in what has come to be known as the "great divide" theory of literacy, which implies that writing and literacy represent the domestication of a "savage," oral mind. Brian V. Street is the most celebrated critic of that thinking, to which he devotes a whole chapter , "A Critical Look at Walter Ong and the 'Great Divide,'" in his book *Social Literacies: Critical Approaches to Literacy in Development, Ethnography and Education* (1995).

10. Over the last 20 years, multimodal theory has had a profound impact on writing studies. Starting, perhaps, with Gunther Kress and Theo Van Leeuwen's *Multimodal Discourse: The Modes and Media of Contemporary Communication* (2001), there have been numerous influential works, including, to name a few, Anne F. Wysocki and Dennis A. Lynch's *Compose, Design, Advocate: A Rhetoric for Integrating the Written, Visual, and Oral* (2006), Cynthia Selfe's collection *Multimodal Composition: Resources for Teachers* (2007), Joddy Murray's *Non-discursive Rhetoric: Image and Affect in Multimodal Composition* (2009), Jodi Shipka's *Toward a Composition Made Whole* (2011), Tracey Bowen and Carl Whithaus's collection *Multimodal Literacies and Emerging Genres* (2013), and Kristin L. Arola, Jennifer Sheppard, and Cheryl E. Ball's *Writer/Designer: A Guide to Making Multimodal Projects* (2014).

Thomas Rickert's influential *Ambient Rhetoric* (2013) also bears mentioning here, though he intentionally avoids the term "multimodal" in the articulation of his theory of rhetorical ambience. "Multimodality," he writes, "indicates various, discrete modes that are then combined" whereas ambience acknowledges "the idea that such 'modes' derive from an a priori ambient situation in which they are interactively combined (142–143). For Rickert, *multimodality* names an artificial separation of phenomena that are only conceptually distinct. While I do not disagree with this assessment, I stop short of Rickert's reservations for the theoretical utility of multimodality, especially given its prominence and legibility in the field. Even so, my work with sonic rhetorics and folkness is indebted to *Ambient Rhetoric* and especially Rickert's insights on music (see chapters 3 and 4).

11. In *Resounding the Rhetorical*, Hawk makes a useful distinction between the terms *re-sound* and *resound*. Having covered both terms, I will collapse that distinction going forward.

12. See, for example, Gregory Clark's *Civic Jazz: American Music and Kenneth Burke on the Art of Getting Along* (2015).

13. Beyond those I have already cited, recent book and article publications indicative of the growing body of work in and around sonic rhetorics include (but are not limited to) Eric Detweiler's "Sounding Out the Progymnasmata," Kati Fargo Ahern's "Understanding Spaces Sonically, Soundscaping Evaluations of

Place," Crystal VanKooten's "The Music, The Movement, The Mix: Listening for Sonic and Multimodal Invention," and Michelle Comstock and Mary E. Hocks's, "The Sounds of Climate Change: Sonic Rhetoric in the Anthropocene, the Age of Human Impact."

14. A prime example of the development of contemporary rhetoric from classical Greek roots is Chaïm Perelman and Lucie Olbrechts-Tyteca's 1973 text *The New Rhetoric*, in which the authors move systematically through classical (generally Aristotelean) rhetorical concepts, offering contemporary updates. For example, they argue that the importance of the epideictic genre was underplayed and that it is actually "central to the art of persuasion," its purpose being to "increase the intensity of adherence to values held in common by the audience and the speaker" (47–50).

15. Besides Foss and Griffin's "Beyond Persuasion: A Proposal for Invitational Rhetoric" (1995), the list of transformative feminist scholarship is long and growing. For work in historiography alone, see Jacqueline Jones Royster and Gesa E. Kirsch's *Feminist Rhetorical Practices* (2012); Eileen E. Schell and K. J. Rawson's collection *Rhetorica in Motion: Feminist Rhetorical Methods and Methodologies* (2010); the 2002 special issue of *Rhetoric Society Quarterly* titled "Feminist Historiography in Rhetoric," edited by Patricia Bizzell; Jacqueline Jones Royster's classic *Traces of a Stream* (2002); and Cheryl Glenn's *Rhetoric Retold: Regendering the Tradition from Antiquity Through the Renaissance* (1997). Additionally, see my "Resounding History: A Rhetoric of Sonic Historiography (in Two Parts)," in the collection *Tuning into Soundwriting* (2021), edited by Kyle D. Steadman, Courtney S. Danforth, and Michael J. Farris. That chapter's analysis of musician Vera Hall's contributions to the Lomax archive draws exclusively on feminist rhetoricians and historiographers. "Resounding History" is meant as a preemptive corrective to the present volume, in which women's archival voices are conspicuously absent.

16. See Romeo Garcia and Damian Baca's *Rhetorics Elsewhere and Otherwise: Contested Modernities, Decolonial Visions*.

17. Protagoras was a prominent Greek Sophist in 485 BCE. For a careful accounting of both the historical and the literary Protagoras, see Michael Gagarin and Paul Woodruff's *Early Greek Political Thought from Homer to the Sophists*. The book also contains Gagarin and Woodruff's translations of a number of pre-Socratic texts, including the passages from Protagoras that I cite in this chapter (see pp. 173–189).

18. *Aretē* is a cognate of *agathos* (good). As David Payne writes, "The standards for judging one to be *agathos* were not enunciated or objective criteria, they were values held tacitly and uniformly in society. The tradition of Greek ethics is grounded in this early concept of a unified and 'instinctive' good" (191).

19. In the *Protagoras*, soundness of mind is part of a trivium that includes two other ideals, justice and piety. Soundness of mind is epitomized by the virtues of moderation, sensibility, self-control, prudence, and so on. *Aretē* does not just hearken to a single-dimensional configuration of "virtue" but indexes a tradition of typified "wise" living ideals. It is the stuff of ethics and morals.

20. Quotations of Aristotle's *Rhetoric* are from George Kennedy's 2007 translation.

21. In addition to the works in comparative rhetoric mentioned earlier in the chapter, see George Kennedy's *Comparative Rhetoric* (1998) and Sue Hum and Arabella Lyon's "Recent Advances in Comparative Rhetoric," in the *SAGE Handbook of Rhetorical Studies* (2009).

22. Throughout this book, I capitalize the word *Black* when it is used to reference the race of African Americans, and I do not hyphenate the phrase African American, even when it is used as a modifying compound adjective. Those choices reflect recent updates to style guides and make a rhetorical statement about the importance of both. There are places where my usage is juxtaposed with a referent's alternative usage. I have not, of course, updated the reference to reflect the current style manual. In fact, the presence of both styles is a reminder of the ongoing (and up-to-the-minute) efforts to examine race and adjust rhetorics of representation.

23. Relevant journal issues include a 2006 *Computers and Composition* special issue edited by Cheryl Ball and Byron Hawk, titled "Sound in/as a Compositional Space," and Joshua Gunn, Greg Goodale, Mirko M. Hall, and Rosa A. Eberly's "Auscultating Again: Rhetoric and Sound Studies" produced for the *Rhetoric Society Quarterly* (2013), as well as several edited digital collections: Byron Hawk and Thomas Rickert's "Music/Writing/Culture" at *Enculturation* (1999), "Writing with Sound" at *Currents for Electronic Literacy* (2011), and Jon Stone and Steph Ceraso's "Sonic Rhetorics" at *Harlot of the Arts* (2013).

24. See Courtney Danforth, Kyle Stedman, and Michael Ferris's edited collection *Soundwriting Pedagogies* (2018).

Interlude I

1. See "Timelines of the Great Depression," http://www.hyperhistory.com/online_n2/connections_n2/great_depression.html

2. In a 1904 letter to his wife, Bess, John Lomax mentions his excitement related to the music he heard among Black students during "inspection trips to the state college for blacks at Prairie View" (Porterfield 168). In 1907, John proposed a book on "Negro songs," which was rejected in favor of a project that would eventually become *Cowboy Songs and Other Frontier Ballads* (Porterfield 167). In 1910, John had already collected at least 100 examples of what he called "mating ballads" and was anxious to find a potential publisher for Negro music in its "native form" (Porterfield 167).

3. Burke's reticence to address race and his preference for the symphony over folk music both find a rare exception in his 1933 review of Hall Johnson's play *Run, Little Chillun!*, which was later published in his *The Philosophy of Literary Form* (1941). The review, titled "The Negro's Pattern of Life" is a revealing look at Burke's changing attitudes on race in American intellectual society. In the essay, Burke contrasts the prevailing "child symbol Negro" common to the blackface minstrel show with Johnson's depiction of "the power side of the Negro" (*Philosophy* 386). Black power is a "Negro-symbol with which the theater-going public is not theatrically at home" (386). The play is set in a Black Southern town and Hall Johnson infuses it with spirituals, the music the region was best known for. Burke identifies the spirituals in the play as "folk-music" and recognizes the dilemma they

might present for African Americans in the audience engaged in combatting the racial equity issues at hand. He writes,

> Already the "advance guard" of Negroes are teaching their suffering people to "organize" in ways more suited to these nasty times—and I am sure there is much in *Run, Little Chillun!* which they must consider with distrust, attempting to stamp it out of their people: it survives there in its purity, only by reason to the poet's consciousness, which keeps him close to the roots of his folk-music (391).

Put another way, Burke recognizes in the play (which he admires) its paradoxical sonic rhetorics—its folkness. This insight, however, is weakened by Burke's inability to hear African American voices outside of a hyperbolic and objectifying range. For Burke, the voices in the play are best compared to the non-human orchestra: "They do not vary merely as ordinary tenor, soprano, bass, but as viola, 'cello, flute and horn" (388).

4. For insights on Enlightenment rhetoric as well as its shifting into the 18th and 19th centuries, see Ong's *Ramus, Method, and the Decay of Dialogue* (1958) and Conley's *Rhetoric in the European Tradition* (1990).

Chapter 1

1. Porterfield spells Huddie Ledbetter's nickname as a single word, "Leadbelly," as do many other sources, including later commercial releases of his music. I prefer the two-word rendering because that is how Ledbetter signed his name. It is also the way his name appears on his tombstone (http://www.findagrave.com/cgi-bin/fg.cgi?page=gr&GRid=6121635, retrieved August 3, 2019).

2. Lomax includes a footnote to the story, stating simply, "General Manager Hymes has since written to me that Lead Belly's Pardon was due to his 'good time'" (Lomax, Lomax, and Herzog 36). Lomax still uses the word *pardon*, however, which, as I explain in the following discussion in text, does not appear to reflect the reason for his release.

3. Summing up historiography in one or two lines of text threatens to obscure its long tradition and wide-ranging disciplinarity. My gateway to that tradition has been Hayden White, whose books *Metahistory: The Historical Imagination in Nineteenth-Century Europe* (1973) and *Tropics of Discourse: Essays in Cultural Criticism* (1985) present historiography in the rhetorical frame I use here: as a composed and ideological narrative and thus an argument about the past.

4. In 1998, David Zarefsky broke historically interested rhetorical studies into four "senses": "the history of rhetoric, the rhetoric of history, historical studies of rhetorical practice, and rhetorical studies of historical events" (26). While over 20 years old, his essay and others collected in the volume *Doing Rhetorical History: Concepts and Cases* provide a thorough treatment of each of those senses and still offer a useful foundation to the subject.

5. In recent years, studies that bring the concerns of writing to rhetoric have experienced a relative historiographical boom in published literature. For a use-

ful entry point to that work, see Jaqueline Jones Royster's now-classic *Traces of a Stream: Literacy and Social Change among African American Women* (2000) See also Jaqueline Jones Royster and Gesa Kirsch, *Feminist Rhetorical Practices: New Horizons for Rhetoric, Composition, and Literacy Studies* (2012); Ellen Cushman's "Wampum, Sequoyan, and Story: Decolonizing the Digital Archive," Pamela VanHaitsma's "Digital LGBTQ Archives as Sites of Public Memory and Pedagogy," and Christine Mason Sutherland's "Feminist Historiography: Research Methods in Rhetoric."

6. See, for example, Susan Jarratt's *Rereading the Sophists* (1991) and Collin Brooke's *Lingua Fracta: Towards a Rhetoric of New Media* (2009).

7. The essays in Michelle Ballif's edited collection *Theorizing Histories of Rhetoric* (2013) respond to a complex, ongoing and often heated conversation in rhetorical studies over the last 30 years, which has examined what it means to write histories of rhetoric. Ballif entreats us to join that conversation and to focus on establishing new theories of historiography by asking "difficult questions about the purposes and methodologies of writing histories of rhetoric" (2). As Ballif notes in her introduction, the most important threads in the conversations of the 1980s and '90s were centered on the problems of revising who and what we imagined as the central figures of rhetorical history. Victor Vitanza's *Writing Histories of Rhetoric* (1994) was an attempt to both recognize and theorize our "obligation to search for the 'third men' and 'third women'—for that which has been 'systematically excluded'" from the history of rhetoric (Ballif, *Theorizing Histories* 3, quoting Vitanza 181). Exclusion is "symptomatic of the logic of the dialectic: *the* epistemic motor of Western thought which establishes some *positive* ('The Good,' 'The True,' 'The Beautiful') through a *negation* of the Other and an *exclusion* of all that can't be synthesized" (Ballif, "Victor J. Vitanza" 338).

8. In "Rhetorical Folkness: Reanimating Walter J. Ong in the Pursuit of Digital Humanity," in Duke University Press's *Digital Sound Studies* (2018), I acknowledge and respond in depth to Sterne's "audiovisual litany" and critique of Ong.

9. See also Miles Orvell's *The Real Thing: Imitation and Authenticity in American Culture, 1880–1940* (1989).

10. The Archive of American Folk Song the Lomaxes contributed to was created in 1926 and housed in the Library of Congress's Music Division. In 1976, and as part of The American Folklife Preservation Act (or Public Law 94-201), the American Folklife Center was created and the Archive of American Folk Music became the Archive of Folk Culture.

11. Others doing the same work as the Lomaxes at the same time were more discerning of the ethics involved in folksong collection. Lawrence Gellert, a writer for *New Masses*, publicly critiqued the Lomaxes' methods. In an article titled "Entertain Your Crowd," published in *New Masses* on November 20, 1934, Gellert condemns John Lomax as "embod[ying] a slavemaster attitude intact," claiming that Lomax's work "failed to get at the heart of contemporary Negro folk lore"(19). Condemning Lomax's work in the prisons, Gellert wrote, "I'd wager that many a work-tired Negro in dirty bedraggled stripes was yanked off a rock-pile by bribed plug ugly guards and ordered to 'sing for the gentleman" (19). Gellert, who was also interested in African American folksong, believed that the Lomaxes' project and product reinforced damaging tropes about African Americans and that the Lomaxes were

collecting the wrong songs. Speaking of the *American Folk Songs* collection, Gellert writes, "[Lomax] has included not one single song which reflects unmistakably the contemporary environment and could not just as well have been collected, ten, twenty, or even fifty years back" (19).

12. The Beastie Boys line referenced—"'Cause I be dropping the new science and I be kicking the new ka-nowledge, An MC to a degree that you can't get in college"—is from the song "The New Science" (from the album *Paul's Boutique*). In his article "The Making of Ka-Knowledge: Digital Aurality," Jeff Rice riffs on the Beastie Boys' notion of "ka-knowledge" and "dropping science," connecting it to invention, rhetoric, and digital writing.

Chapter 2

1. The Lomaxes' coauthored *American Ballads and Folk Songs* presents a number of the recordings from the prison trip (along with dozens more collected from other sources), which were carefully transcribed and published as simple sheet music with lyrics and the occasional short description. Such publications were once relatively common and followed a similar production formula, in which a professionally trained musician worked painstakingly with a vernacular musician to transcribe a tune that would then be re-presented visually as sheet music within the published text. *American Ballads* was among the first folk collections to be compiled using recordings (instead of live performance) as the source material. Selections from the Lomax collection were re-presented in various stage performances by a number of musicians over the course of a decade, performed live on the radio, and released on LP phonographs in the early 1940s by the Library of Congress. The field recordings would eventually change how American vernacular music could be experienced, studied, and emulated by an expanding audience of both scholars and citizens. The voices of convicts, farmers, preachers, and many others could at last be heard.

2. In 2012, West Virginia University Press released "Levee Camp Holler" on *Jail House Bound*, a collection of songs culled from the Lomaxes' 1933 prison trip. The liner notes observe correctly that John Lomax often "altered the sequence of stanzas, changed words, or even compiled a version from several sources" for *American Ballads and Folk Songs*. Lomax justified his changes from the standpoint of a curator. His goal was neither the capture of a single performance nor a statement about a particular performer (even when one is implied) but a comprehensive understanding of a song's variety.

3. According to folklorist Patrick B. Mullen, John Lomax's Southern paternalism made the "idea that the white man was the hope of freedom for the black convict" resonant within his worldview. In contrast, the growing leftist sentiment among the rising educated generation shaped Alan's ideals and contributed to his sense of "pity and desire to help" the African American men and women he began to meet during his first field recording trip. Mullen observes that both Lomaxes "had their whiteness reinforced by contact with blackness and their own sense of freedom intensified by the lack of freedom of the prisoners they were recording" (84).

4. As mentioned in the previous chapter, the concept of identification on which Burke was working in the 1930s did not come to full fruition until *A Rhetoric of Motives* was published in 1950. Burke there dances around a firm definition of identification, most often describing it in concert with its opposite—division: "Identification is affirmed with earnestness precisely because there is division. Identification is compensatory to division. If men were not apart from one another, there would be no need for the rhetorician to proclaim their unity" (22). Later in the same text, Burke contextualizes identification in relation to rhetoric's typified purpose, persuasion: "You persuade a man insofar as you talk his language by speech, gesture, tonality, order, image, attitude, idea, *identifying* your ways with his" (55).

5. In *The Sound Studies Reader* (2012), Jonathan Sterne curates a productive list of scholarship on the voice as the subject relates to the nascent field of sound studies. Among those whose work is important to the discussion of voice are Ferdinand de Saussure, whose *Course in General Linguistics* situates the voice "as a fundamental modality of social enunciation"; Marshall McLuhan and Walter Ong, who "based an entire psychological theory of orality around ideas of the voice as presence"; and Jacques Derrida, who critiques the positions of the others as a misguided "metaphysics of presence" (491–492). Sterne's own positioning on voice is resonant with Derrida, and Sterne's collection draws together several other works that complicate and expand on traditional conceptions of voice.

6. See Birnbaum's *Before Elvis: The Prehistory of Rock 'n' Roll* (2013) for a short but thorough history of the song "Run Nigger Run" (84–85), versions of which date back to 1851. Though its origins are unknown, it was sung by both enslavers and enslaved individuals, as well as in blackface minstrel performances. Most recently, it was featured in the film *12 Years a Slave* (2013). My intent in transcribing a song that includes a word with such a violent and malignant connection to the practice of chattel slavery is to portray the historical record accurately, with the recognition that African American men incarcerated in early 20th-century prisons used the word dexterously and, much like contemporary Black music, to reappropriate the word in defiance of the ways it was used to dominate, denigrate, and abuse.

7. I recorded Michelle Ross playing this piano part in her home on March 23, 2014, in Clemson, South Carolina. She directs the choirs at Liberty Middle School and Liberty High School in Liberty, South Carolina. Michelle is also my sister.

8. Joshua Gunn's work on speech, the voice, and, by extension, Derridean presence is instructive further reading on the various material and theoretical tensions between sound and presence. See Gunn's essays "On Recording Performance or Speech, the Cry, and the Anxiety of the Fix" (2011) and "Speech Is Dead; Long Live Speech" (2008).

9. Those representations include (but are not limited to) the highly influential and distinctly racist blackface minstrel show that permeated American culture in 1840–1940 and beyond, popular "race records" of "classic" city blues singers like Bessie Smith and others, and an increasingly whitewashed but popular jazz music of the day.

10. As Omi and Winant write, "*Rearticulation* is a practice of discursive reorganization or reinterpretation of ideological themes and interests already present in the subjects' consciousness, such that these elements obtain new meanings or

coherence." They identify that practice as ordinarily the work of "intellectuals." According to Omi and Winant's account, then, those whose role is to interpret the social world for given subjects—religious leaders, entertainers, schoolteachers, and so on—may be "intellectuals" (195).

Interlude II

1. The slave narratives collected were revelatory to the still-extensive grouping of the American population that was largely ignorant of the realities of slave life. The collection worked to debunk prevalent "plantation myths," including the "Sambo" (or happy, contented slave) and other prominent stereotypes that had been doing untold damage to African American people and culture for decades.

2. In a letter to his supervisor at the library, Harold Spivacke, Lomax described Terrill's contribution to his now-famous 1939 "Southern States Recording Trip": "In nearly every instance Miss Terrill is including typed copies of the words contained on each record; also the slang of the song and the singers. This will be a big saving for the Library. Writing down the words from the record playing is a long, tedious job."

3. See, for example, Erin Anderson's "The Olive Project: An Oral History Composition in Multiple Modes" (2011) and Jody Shipka's "To Preserve, Digitize, and Project" (2012). See also Berry, Hawisher, and Selfe's edited online collection *Provocations: Reconstructing the Archive* (part of Computers and Composition Digital Press's Provocations series), featuring the work of Erin R. Anderson, Trisha N. Campbell, Alexandra Hidalgo, and Jody Shipka.

Chapter 3

1. For a succinct history of early New Orleans jazz as well as the development of jazz in other regions during the early 20th century, see chapter 2 of Burton W. Peretti's *The Creation of Jazz.*

2. The first several audio examples in this chapter are of Morton playing solo versions of his hits for Lomax in the Library of Congress. I recommend using a music streaming platform to undertake a listening exercise comparing those solo versions with professional recordings of the same songs when played with a band. Morton's sessions for Victor with the Red Hot Peppers are especially illuminating, and there is a general critical consensus that they capture Morton at his best.

3. W. C. Handy is credited with some of the first "blues" recordings, including "St. Louis Blues" in 1914. That song would become "one of the most popular songs in American history" (Szwed, "Doctor Jazz" 13).

4. Among other things, Morton's long letter to Ripley details his association with both blues and jazz music, who his teachers and influencers were, and important dates, events, and places associated with jazz origins. As insinuated in the excerpt I have presented, Morton also delves into the etymology of several words, among them *blues*, *jazz*, and *swing*.

5. The ancient Greek word for "rhapsode," *rhapsōidós*, means "stitcher of songs."

6. Transcriptions of Morton's conversations with Lomax that appear in this chapter are by John Szwed and appear as an appendix to his liner notes, which include the biographical essay "Doctor Jazz," in the box set *Jelly Roll Morton: Complete Library of Congress Recordings*. To keep Szwed's essay and the transcripts separate, I cite the latter as a separate resource. I have occasionally updated the transcript where I found obvious discrepancies. I have left Morton's grammatical inconsistencies in the transcript.

7. In September 2005, the Library of Congress released *Jelly Roll Morton: The Complete Library of Congress Recordings* through Rounder Records. That expansive box set marks the first time that the complete, unedited sessions with Jelly Roll Morton were made available commercially. The release includes eight compact discs of interview and musical content, presented in the order that Morton related it. The CDs are packaged with book-length liner notes and electronic documents that include, among other content, a transcription of the interview, a biography of Morton (Szwed's "Doctor Jazz"), and photographs of archival materials. Over the years, the sessions have also been released on LPs, including a 10-volume collection on Riverside Records (1957) and an 8-LP release with Classic Jazz Masters (1970).

8. For one of the more incisive critiques of Alan Lomax's methods during the Morton sessions, see Howard Reich and William Gaines's *Jelly's Blues: The Life, Music, and Redemption of Jelly Roll Morton* (2003). They saw Lomax's methods as counter to Morton's hopes for popular elevation: "Though Morton wanted to talk about music, Lomax grilled Morton about sex, mayhem, and murders in New Orleans, the sensational tales that Morton gave him reluctantly. To keep the bawdiest anecdotes flowing, Lomax repeatedly filled Morton's glass with whiskey, and as he did, the stories became more colorful, raunchy, and exaggerated. The composer didn't realize that by giving Lomax the dirt he wanted, he was helping to soil his own reputation for generations to come" (154).

Interlude III

1. Nearly 20 articles published in the *Quarterly Journal of Speech* between 1930 and 1940 had the word *radio* in the title, ranging from Sherman P. Lawton's "The Principles of Effective Radio Speaking" in 1930 to H. L. Ewbank's "Trends in Research in Radio Speech" in 1940.

Chapter 4

1. The transcriptions that appear in this chapter are a hybrid endeavor. As a guide, I used the actual scripts for the show "Negro Work Songs" that are preserved in the Library of Congress archive (see "Negro Work Songs" in the reference list for details). In those transcripts, words spoken as part of the drama presented in the script appear in uppercase, while the introduction from Niles Welch as well as Alan Lomax's initial framing are written with regular casing. I have adjusted that formatting here and have made a few changes to the transcripts where they diverge from the performances. I have also added occasional parenthetical cues that provide additional identifying and aural information about what is happening on the recording.

2. Hilmes's work offers a popular but perhaps too glossy conception of

radio's reach and power to homogenize American experience. In *The Republic in Print: Print Culture in the Age of U.S. Nation Building, 1770–1870*, literary historian Trish Loughran debunks the myth of print culture's ability to create national monoculture.

3. For a fascinating discussion related to the split in opinion over radio's democratic potentials, see the first chapter of Bruce Lenthall's *Radio's America: The Rise of Modern Mass Media*. Lenthall traces the opposing views in the writings of two figures: conservative economist William Orton and Marxist poet and journalist James Rorty.

4. The listener projections reported by John Szwed call attention to a number of unknowns. Broadcast speculation about potential listeners is just that, speculation. The actual numbers of how many classrooms and students heard the program was likely less than the 15 million estimated "projected" listeners. Given radio's open signal, it is impossible to know who else (besides students) was listening in to the educational programs. While the intended audience may have been limited to an imagined somewhat homogenous grouping of schoolchildren and their teachers, the actual audience could have been significantly more heterogeneous.

5. The first several episodes of *Folk Music of America* were produced with only Lomax behind the microphone, and he had to handle everything—the stories, the instruction, and the singing. As might be expected, he was not yet acclimated to the realities of radio broadcasting, and his performance left much to be desired. In a letter, Harold Spivacke, chief of the Division of Music at the Library of Congress (and Lomax's boss), criticizes nearly every aspect of the first show: Lomax's guitar playing ("I suggest that you ask the orchestra guitarist to accompany you"), his nervous speaking ("you were a bit breathless"), and his inability to keep up with his script ("you must remember to practice a thing and repeat it a hundred times or more if necessary"). In subsequent episodes, Lomax became more comfortable but also recruited a troupe of musicians to help him present the material.

6. The question remains whether or not the remediation and repurposing of folksong into the "serious" music of the symphony and orchestra is a worthwhile pursuit. Lomax's reticence toward such endeavor, mentioned earlier in this chapter, was likely connected to his sense of folk authenticity. In his view, folk music did not need to be legitimized through high-art transformation. But what is the folk process if not a continual process of appropriation and transformation? "Classical" music has a long history of utilizing folk melodies to create something new. Lomax doubtless had in mind those who believed that music had to be rendered as high art in order to be educational, so his misgivings are understandable.

7. Burke's gestures toward the poetic remain, however. In *A Rhetoric of Motives*, Burke introduces identification within a discussion of John Milton's *Samson Agonistes*.

Conclusion

1. A transcription for "Sermon with Singing" is available as part of the audio rendering in the digital version of this book. In the transcription, my inadequacies in hearing are apparent, as the transcription marker "[inaudible]" accompanies much of the 10-minute sermon.

Works Cited

Adorno, Theodor. "Analytical Study of the NBC 'Music Appreciation Hour.'" *The Musical Quarterly* 78.2 (1994): 325–377.

Ahern, Kati Fargo. "Understanding Spaces Sonically, Soundscaping Evaluations of Place." *Computers and Composition* 48 (2018): 22–33.

Akes, David. *Jazz Cultures*. Berkeley: University of California Press, 2002.

Alexander, Jonathan. "Glenn Gould and the Rhetorics of Sound." *Computers and Composition* 37 (2015): 73–89.

The American School of the Air Teacher's Manual and Classroom Guide for 1939–40. New York: Columbia Broadcasting System, 1939.

Anderson, Benedict. *Imagined Communities: Reflections on the Origin and Spread of Nationalism*. New York: Verso Books, 2006.

Anderson, Erin. "The Olive Project: An Oral History Composition in Multiple Modes." *Kairos: A Journal of Rhetoric, Technology, and Pedagogy* 15.2 (2011). http://kairos.technorhetoric.net/15.2/topoi/anderson/index.html

Anderson, Erin. "Toward a Resonant Material Vocality for Digital Composition." *Enculturation* 18 (2014). http://enculturation.net/materialvocality

"The Angels Dropped Their Wings and Gone on to Heaven." Sung by a group of Negro convicts." Recorded by John A. Lomax, Tennessee state penitentiary, Nashville, TN, August 1933. Library of Congress AFS 00179 B02.

Aristotle. *On Rhetoric: A Theory of Civic Discourse*. Trans. George A. Kennedy. New York: Oxford University Press, 2007.

Arola, Kristin L., Jennifer Sheppard, and Cheryl E. Ball. *Writer/Designer: A Guide to Making Multimodal Projects*. Boston: Bedford/St. Martin's, 2014.

Attali, Jacques. *Noise: The Political Economy of Music*. Minneapolis: University of Minnesota Press, 1985.

Baker, Houston A., Jr. *Blues, Ideology, and Afro-American Literature: A Vernacular Theory*. Chicago: University of Chicago Press, 1987.

Baker, James (Iron Head). "Grey Goose." Recorded by John A. Lomax, Central State Farm, Sugar Land, TX, December 1933. Library of Congress AFS 00207.

Baker, James (Iron Head). "Shorty George." Recorded by John A. Lomax, Central State Farm, Sugar Land, TX, February 1934. Library of Congress AFS 00202 A02.

Baker, James (Iron Head), Will Crosby, R. D. Allen, and Mose Platt (Clear Rock). "Go Down, Hannah." Recorded by John A. and Alan Lomax, Central State Farm, Sugar Land, TX, December 1933. Library of Congress AFS 00195 A02.

Ball, Cheryl, and Byron Hawk. "Sound in/as Compositional Space: A Next Step in Multiliteracies." Special issue, *Computers and Composition* 23.3 (2006).

Ballif, Michelle, ed. *Theorizing Histories of Rhetoric*. Carbondale: Southern Illinois University Press, 2013.

Ballif, Michelle. "Victor J. Vitanza." In *Twentieth Century Rhetorics and Rhetoricians*. Eds. Michelle Ballif and Michael G. Moran, 336-342. Westport, CT: Greenwood, 2000.

Banks, Adam. *Digital Griots: African American Rhetoric in a Multimedia Age*. Carbondale: Southern Illinois University Press, 2011.

Baraka, Amiri (Leroi Jones). *Blues People: Negro Music in White America*. New York: HarperCollins, 1963.

Barthes, Roland. "The Grain of the Voice." In *The Sound Studies Reader*, ed. Jonathan Sterne, 504–510. London: Routledge, 2012.

Bendix, Regina. *In Search of Authenticity: The Formation of Folklore Studies*. Madison: University of Wisconsin Press, 1997.

Berry, Patrick W., Gail E. Hawisher, and Cynthia L. Selfe, eds. *Provocations: Reconstructing the Archive*. Featuring the work of Erin R. Anderson, Trisha N. Campbell, Alexandra Hidalgo, and Jody Shipka. Logan: Computers and Composition Digital Press / Utah State University Press, 2016. https://ccdigitalpress.org/reconstructingthearchive

Bianchi, William. *Schools of the Air: A History of Instructional Programs on Radio in the United States*. Jefferson, NC: McFarland, 2008.

Birnbaum, Larry. *Before Elvis: The Prehistory of Rock 'n' Roll*. Lanham: Scarecrow, 2013.

Bizzell, Patricia, ed. "Feminist Historiography in Rhetoric." Special issue, *Rhetoric Society Quarterly* 32.1 (2002).

Blair, Carole. "Contested Histories of Rhetoric: The Politics of Preservation, Progress, and Change." *Quarterly Journal of Speech* 78.4 (1992): 403–428.

Booth, Wayne C. *The Company We Keep: An Ethics of Fiction*. Oakland: University of California Press, 1988.

Bowen, Tracey, and Carl Whithaus, eds. *Multimodal Literacies and Emerging Genres*. Pittsburgh: University of Pittsburgh Press, 2013.

Botkin, B. A., ed. Liner notes. *Folk Music of the United States: Negro Work Songs and Calls.*, Library of Congress AFS L8. n.d. LP.

Brand, Oscar. *The Ballad Mongers: Rise of the Modern Folk Song*. New York: Funk and Wagnalls, 1967.

Brooke, Collin. *Lingua Fracta: Toward a Rhetoric of New Media*. New York: Hampton, 2009.

Brooks, Van Wyck. "On Creating a Usable Past." *The Dial*, April 11, 1918, 337–341.

Bryson, Lyman. "The American School of the Air." *Music Educators Journal* 30.1 (1943): 19.

Burke, Kenneth. *Attitudes toward History*. Boston: Beacon, 1961.
Burke, Kenneth. *A Grammar of Motives*. Berkeley: University of California Press, 1969.
Burke, Kenneth. *Permanence and Change: An Anatomy of Purpose*. Berkeley: University of California Press, 1984.
Burke, Kenneth. *Philosophy of Literary Form*. Berkeley: University of California Press, 1974.
Burke, Kenneth. "Revolutionary Symbolism in America. Speech by Kenneth Burke to American Writers Congress, April 26, 1935." In *The Legacy of Kenneth Burke*. Eds. Herbert W. Simons and Trevor Melia, 267–280. Madison: University of Wisconsin Press, 1989.
Burke, Kenneth. *A Rhetoric of Motives*. Berkeley: University of California Press, 1962.
Byrne, David. *How Music Works*. New York: Three Rivers, 2012.
Carby, Hazel V. *Race Men*. Cambridge, MA: Harvard University Press, 1998.
Ceraso, Steph. *Sounding Composition: Multimodal Pedagogies for Embodied Listening*. Pittsburgh: University of Pittsburgh Press, 2018.
Charland, Maurice. "Constitutive Rhetoric: The Case of the Peuple Québécois." *Quarterly Journal of Speech* 73.2 (1987): 133–150.
Clarfield, Geoffrey. "Geoffrey Clarfield: A Day at the Home of Pete Seeger." *National Post*, January 31, 2014.
Clark, Gregory. *Civic Jazz: American Music and Kenneth Burke on the Art of Getting Along*. Chicago: University of Chicago Press, 2015.
Cohen, David. *Law, Sexuality, and Society: The Enforcement of Morals in Classical Athens*. New York: Oxford University Press, 1991.
Cole, Thomas. *The Origins of Rhetoric in Ancient Greece*. Baltimore: Johns Hopkins University Press, 1991.
Comstock, Michelle, and Mary E. Hocks, "The Sounds of Climate Change: Sonic Rhetoric in the Anthropocene, the Age of Human Impact." *Rhetoric Review* 35.2 (2016): 165–175.
Conley, Thomas. *Rhetoric in the European Tradition*. Chicago: University of Chicago Press, 1990.
Cooney, Terry A. *Balancing Acts: American Thought and Culture in the 1930s*. New York: Twayne, 1995.
Couch, William Terry, ed. *These Are Our Lives*. Federal Writers' Project. Chapel Hill: North Carolina University Press, 1939.
Crable, Bryan. *Ralph Ellison and Kenneth Burke: At the Roots of the Racial Divide*. Charlottesville: University of Virginia Press, 2011.
Crick, Nathan. *Democracy and Rhetoric: John Dewey on the Arts of Becoming*. Columbia: University of South Carolina Press, 2012.
Cushman, Ellen. "Wampum, Sequoyan, and Story: Decolonizing the Digital Archive," *College English* 76.2 (2013): 115–135.
Czitrom, David J. *Media and the American Mind: From Morse to McLuhan*. Chapel Hill: University of North Carolina Press, 1982.
Daly, Matthew, and Jill Colvin. "Trump: 'A Lot Of People' Feel That Black Lives Matter Is 'Inherently Racist.'" *Talking Points Memo*, July 12, 2016. https://talkingpointsmemo.com/news/trump-black-lives-matter-divisive

Danforth, Courtney S., Kyle D. Stedman, and Michael J. Faris, eds. *Soundwriting Pedagogies*. Logan: Computers and Composition Digital Press / Utah State University Press, 2018. http://ccdigitalpress.org/soundwriting

Davis, Diane, ed. "Writing with Sound." *Currents for Electronic Literacy* 14 (2011). https://currents.dwrl.utexas.edu/2011.html

Denning, Michael. *The Cultural Front: The Laboring of American Culture in the Twentieth Century*. London: Verso, 1998.

Detweiler, Eric. "Sounding Out the Progymnasmata." *Rhetoric Review* 38.2 (2019): 205–218.

Dewey, John. *Art as Experience*. New York: Perigee Books, 2005.

Dewey, John. *Democracy and Education: An Introduction to the Philosophy of Education*. New York: Macmillan, 1917.

Douglas, Susan J. *Listening In: Radio and the American Imagination; From Amos 'n' Andy and Edward R. Murrow to Wolfman Jack and Howard Stern*. New York: Times Books, 1999.

Du Bois, W. E. B. *Dusk of Dawn: An Essay Toward an Autobiography of a Race Concept*. New York: Oxford University Press, 2007.

Dundes, Alan, ed. *International Folkloristics: Classic Contributions by the Founders of Folklore*. New York: Rowman and Littlefield, 1999.

Eisenschitz, Bernard. *Nicholas Ray: An American Journey*. London: Faber and Faber, 1996.

Eliade, Mircea. *Myth and Reality*. Trans. Willard R. Trask. New York: Harper and Row, 1963.

Evans, David. "Goin' Up The Country: Blues in Texas and the Deep South." In *Nothing but the Blues*, ed. Lawrence Cohn, 33–85. New York: Abbeville, 1993.

Ewbank, H. L. "Trends in Research in Radio Speech" *Quarterly Journal of Speech* 26.2 (1940): 282–287.

Filene, Benjamin. *Romancing the Folk: Public Memory and American Roots Music*. Chapel Hill: University of North Carolina Press, 2000.

Finnegan, Cara. "FSA Photography and New Deal Visual Culture." In *Rhetorical History of the United States*, vol. 7, *American Rhetoric in the New Deal Era*, ed. Thomas Benson, 115–155. East Lansing: Michigan State University Press, 2006.

Finnegan, Cara. *Making Photography Matter: A Viewer's History from the Civil War to the Great Depression*. Urbana: University of Illinois Press, 2015.

Finnegan, Cara. *Picturing Poverty: Print Culture and FSA Photography*. Washington, DC: Smithsonian Institution Scholarly Press, 2003.

Fisher, Marc. *Something in the Air: Radio, Rock, and the Revolution That Shaped a Generation*. New York: Random House, 2007.

Fisher, Walter. *Human Communication as Narration: Toward a Philosophy of Reason, Value, and Action*. Columbia: University of South Carolina Press, 1987.

Foss, Sonja K., and Cindy L. Griffin, "Beyond Persuasion: A Proposal for Invitational Rhetoric." *Communication Monographs* 62.1 (1995): 2–18.

Gagarin, Michael, and Paul Woodruff. *Early Greek Political Thought from Homer to the Sophists*. Cambridge: Cambridge University Press, 2008.

Garcia, Romeo, and Damian Baca. *Rhetorics Elsewhere and Otherwise: Contested Mo-*

dernities, Decolonial Visions. Urbana, IL: National Council of Teachers of English, 2019.
Gates, Henry Louis Gates, Jr. *The Signifying Monkey: A Theory of African-American Literary Criticism*. New York: Oxford University Press, 1988.
Gellert, Lawrence. "Entertain Your Crowd." *New Masses*, 13.8, November 20, 1934 19.
Gendron, Bernard. "'Moldy Figs' and the Modernists: Jazz at War (1942–1946)." In *Jazz among the Discourses*, ed. Krin Gabbard. Durham, 31–56. NC: Duke University Press, 1995.
George, Ann, and Jack Selzer. *Kenneth Burke in the 1930s*. Columbia: University of South Carolina Press, 2007.
Giamo, Benedict. "The Means of Representation: Kenneth Burke and American Marxism." *KB Journal* 5.2 (2009).
Gibson, John (Black Samson). "Levee Camp Holler." Recorded by John A. Lomax, Tennessee state penitentiary, Nashville, TN, August 1933. Library of Congress AFS 00179 B03.
Glenn, Cheryl. *Rhetoric Retold: Regendering the Tradition from Antiquity through the Renaissance*. Carbondale: Southern Illinois University Press, 1997.
Goodale, Greg. *Sonic Persuasion*. Urbana: University of Illinois Press, 2011.
"Good God A'mighty." Sung by a "group of Negro convicts" and featuring the sounds of axes cutting. Recorded by John A. and Alan Lomax, state penitentiary, Huntsville, TX, November 1934. Library of Congress AFS 00179 B03.
Gries, Laurie. *Still Life with Rhetoric: A New Materialist Approach for Visual Rhetorics*. Logan: Utah State University Press, 2015.
Griffin, Sin-Killer. "The Man of Calvary (Easter Service)." Recorded by John A. Lomax, Darrington State Farm, Sandy Point, TX, April 1934. Library of Congress AFS 00186 A&B.
Griffin, Sin-Killer. "Sermon with Singing." Recorded by John A. Lomax, Darrington State Farm, Sandy Point, TX, April 1934. Library of Congress AFS 00186 A&B.
Gunn, Joshua. "On Recording Performance or Speech, the Cry, and the Anxiety of the Fix." *Liminalities: A Journal of Performance Studies* 7.3 (2011).
Gunn, Joshua. "Speech Is Dead; Long Live Speech." *Quarterly Journal of Speech* 94.3 (2008): 343–364.
Gunn, Joshua, Greg Goodale, Mirko M. Hall, Rosa A. Eberly. "Auscultating Again: Rhetoric and Sound Studies." *Rhetoric Society Quarterly* 43.5 (2013): 475–489.
Hammer, Steven. "Writing Dirt, Teaching Noise." In *Soundwriting Pedagogies*, ed. Courtney S. Danforth, Kyle D. Stedman, and Michael J. Faris. Logan: Computers and Composition Digital Press / Utah State University Press, 2018. http://ccdigitalpress.org/soundwriting
Havelock, Eric A. *The Muse Learns to Write: Reflections on Orality and Literacy from Antiquity to the Present*. New Haven: Yale University Press, 1986.
Havelock, Eric A. *Preface to Plato*. Cambridge, MA: Belknap Press of Harvard University Press, 1988.
Hawhee, Debra. "Agonism and Aretē." *Philosophy and Rhetoric* 35.3 (2002): 185–207.
Hawhee, Debra. *Bodily Arts: Rhetoric and Athletics in Ancient Greece*. Austin: University of Texas Press, 2004.

Hawhee, Debra. *Moving Bodies: Kenneth Burke at the Edges of Language*. Columbia: University of South Carolina Press, 2009.
Hawk, Byron. *Resounding the Rhetorical: Composition as a Quasi-Object*. Pittsburgh: University of Pittsburgh Press, 2018.
Hawk, Byron, and Thomas Rickert, eds. "Music/Writing/Culture." *Enculturation* 2.2 (1999). http://enculturation.net/2_2/toc.html#top
Herrick, James A. *The History and Theory of Rhetoric: An Introduction*. Boston: Allyn and Beacon, 2005.
Hicks, Granville. "Call for an American Writers' Congress." *New Masses*, 14.4 January 22, 1935, 20.
Hilmes, Michele. *Radio Voices: American Broadcasting, 1922–1952*. Minneapolis: University of Minnesota Press, 1997.
Hirsch, Jarrold. "Modernity, Nostalgia, and Southern Folklore Studies: The Case of John Lomax." *Journal of American Folklore* 105.416 (1992): 183–207.
Hocks, Mary E., and Michelle Comstock. "Composing for Sound: Sonic Rhetoric as Resonance." *Computers and Composition* 43 (2017): 135–146.
Hogg, Charlotte. "Sorority Rhetorics as Everyday Epideictic." *College English* 80.5 (2018): 423–448.
Hum, Sue, and Arabella Lyon. "Recent Advances in Comparative Rhetoric." In *SAGE Handbook of Rhetorical Studies.*,ed. Andrea A. Lunsford, Kirt H. Wilson, and Rosa A. Eberly, 153–166. Thousand Oaks, CA: SAGE Publications, 2008.
Inside Llewyn Davis. Directed by Joel and Ethan Coen, with performances by Oscar Isaac, Carey Mulligan, John Goodman, Adam Driver, and Justin Timberlake. Los Angeles: CBS Films, 2014.
Jarratt, Susan Carole Funderburgh. *Rereading the Sophists: Classical Rhetoric Refigured*. Carbondale: Southern Illinois University Press, 1991.
Jasinski, James. *Sourcebook on Rhetoric: Key Concepts in Contemporary Rhetorical Studies*. Thousand Oaks, CA: SAGE Publications, 2001.
Johnstone, Christopher Lyle. *Listening to the Logos: Speech and the Coming of Wisdom in Ancient Greece*. Columbia: University of South Carolina Press, 2009.
Jorgensen, Jeana. "An Introduction to Folklore Studies." *Folklorethursday.com*, November 9, 2020. https://folklorethursday.com/folklore-folklorists/introduction-academic-folklore-studies/
Kennedy, David M. *Freedom from Fear*. Oxford: Oxford University Press, 2004.
Kennedy, George A. *Classical Rhetoric and Its Christian and Secular Tradition from Ancient to Modern Times*. Chapel Hill: University of North Carolina Press, 1980.
Kennedy, George A. *Comparative Rhetoric: An Historical and Cross-Cultural Introduction*. New York: Oxford University Press, 1997.
Kress, Gunther, and Theo Van Leeuwen. *Multimodal Discourse: The Modes and Media of Contemporary Communication*. New York: Arnold, 2001.
Lantis, Margaret. "Vernacular Culture." *American Anthropologist* 62.2 (1960): 202–216.
Lawton, Sherman P. "The Principles of Effective Radio Speaking." *Quarterly Journal of Speech* 16.3 (1930): 255–277.
Ledbetter, Huddie (Lead Belly). "Governor Pat Neff." Recorded by John A. Lomax, Wilton, CT, February 1935. Library of Congress AFS 00053.

Ledbetter, Huddie (Lead Belly). "In the Pines" ("Black Girl"). On *Folkways: The Original Vision; Songs of Woody Guthrie and Lead Belly. Washington, DC*: Folkways Records, 1989.
Lemons, J. Stanley. "Black Stereotypes as Reflected in Popular Culture, 1880–1920." *American Quarterly* 29.1 (1977): 102–116.
Lenthall, Bruce. *Radio's America: The Great Depression and the Rise of Modern Mass Culture*. Chicago: University of Chicago Press, 2007.
Levenson, William B., and Edward Stasheff. *Teaching through Radio and Television*. New York: Greenwood, 1969.
Levine, Lawrence. *Black Culture and Black Consciousness: Afro-American Folk Thought from Slavery to Freedom*. New York: Oxford University Press, 2007.
Littlejohn, Stephen W., and Karen A. Foss. "Invitational Rhetoric." In *Theories of Human Communication*, 1: 569–571. Thousand Oaks, CA: SAGE, 2017..
Lomax, Alan. *Alan Lomax, Assistant in Charge: The Library of Congress Letters, 1935–1945*. Ed. Ronald D. Cohen. Jackson: University Press of Mississippi, 2011.
Lomax, Alan. "Letters, 1939–1940." In *Alan Lomax, Assistant in Charge: The Library of Congress Letters, 1935–1945*, ed. Ronald D. Cohen, 115-198. Jackson: University Press of Mississippi, 2010.
Lomax, Alan. *Mister Jelly Roll: The Fortunes of Jelly Roll Morton, New Orleans Creole and "Inventor of Jazz."* New York: Duell, Sloan and Pearce, 1950.
Lomax, Alan. "Negro Work Songs." Episode of *Folk Songs of America* on *The American School of the Air*. New York: Columbia Broadcasting Company, 1939. Library of Congress AFC 1939/002: AFS 13,496B, 13,497A.
Lomax, Alan. "Negro Work Songs." Transcript of an episode of *American Folk Songs* on *The American School of the Air*. New York: Columbia Broadcasting Company, 1939. Library of Congress AFC: 1939/002: MS 078-079, AFC 2004/004: MS 04.01.09, AFC 1939/002: MS 078-079, AFC 2004/004: MS 04.01.09.
Lomax, Alan. *The Rainbow Sign*. New York: Duell, Sloan and Pearce, 1959.
Lomax, John A. *Adventures of a Ballad Hunter*. New York: Macmillan, 1947.
Lomax, John A. Letter to Harold Spivacke, May 12, 1939. MS, Southern Mosaic: The John and Ruby Lomax 1939 Southern States Recording Trip collection. American Folklife Center, Library of Congress, Washington, DC. Library of Congress AFC: AFC 1939/001.
Lomax, John A. Letter to Oliver Strunk, October 1, 1934. MS, John A. Lomax southern states collection, 1933-1937 collection. American Folklife Center, Library of Congress, Washington, DC. Library of Congress AFC: 1935/002.
Lomax, John A. "Sin-Killer's Sermon." In *The Best of Texas Folk and Folklore, 1916–1954*, ed. Wilson Mathis Hudson. Denton: University of North Texas Press, 1998.
Lomax, John A., and Alan Lomax. *American Ballads and Folk Songs*. New York: Macmillan, 1934.
Lomax, John A., Alan Lomax, and George Herzog. *Negro Folk Songs as Sung by Lead Belly*. New York: Macmillan, 1936.
"Lomax Family at the American Folklife Center." American Folklife Center, Library of Congress, October 24, 2017. https://www.loc.gov/folklife/lomax/
Loughran, Trish. *The Republic in Print: Print Culture in the Age of U.S. Nation Building, 1770–1870*. New York: Columbia University Press, 2009.

"Making and Maintaining the Original Recordings." Library of Congress. Accessed March 20, 2020. https://www.loc.gov/collections/interviews-following-the-attack-on-pearl-harbor/articles-and-essays/making-and-maintaining-the-original-recordings/

Mangione, Jerre. *The Dream and the Deal: The Federal Writers' Project, 1935–1943*. Syracuse: Syracuse University Press, 1996.

Mao, LuMing. "Beyond Bias, Binary, and Border: Mapping Out the Future of Comparative Rhetoric." *Rhetoric Society Quarterly* 43.3 (2013): 209–225.

Marable, Manning. *The Great Wells of Democracy: The Meaning of Race in American Life*. New York: Basic Civitas Books, 2002.

Marback, Richard. *Plato's Dream of Sophistry*. Columbia: University of South Carolina Press, 1999.

Martin, Wallace. *Recent Theories of Narrative*. Ithaca, NY: Cornell University Press, 1986.

McCann, Paul. *Race, Music, and National Identity: Images of Jazz in American Fiction, 1920–1960*. Madison, NJ: Fairleigh Dickinson University Press, 2008.

McChesney, Robert W. *Telecommunications, Mass Media, and Democracy: The Battle for the Control of U.S. Broadcasting, 1928–1935*. New York: Oxford University Press, 1993.

McLuhan, Marshall. *Gutenberg Galaxy*. Toronto: University of Toronto Press, 1962.

McLuhan, Marshall. *Understanding Media: The Extensions of Man*. Berkeley: Gingko, 2003.

McNeill, Lynne S. *Folklore Rules: A Fun, Quick, and Useful Introduction to the Field of Academic Folklore Studies*. Boulder: University Press of Colorado, 2013.

Miller, Paul D. (aka DJ Spooky). *Rhythm Science*. Boston: MIT Press, 2004.

Morton, Ferdinand (Jelly Roll). "I Created Jazz in 1902, Not W. C. Handy." *Downbeat*, August 1, 1938. *Downbeat* Archives, Classic Interviews. Accessed November 5, 2020. https://downbeat.com/archives/detail/jelly-roll-morton-i-created-jazz-in-1902-not-w.c.-handy

Morton, Ferdinand (Jelly Roll). "How Jelly Roll Got His Name" on "Monologue on Jelly Roll blues and the origin of his nickname." Recorded by Alan Lomax, Washington, D. C., June, July, August, 1938. Library of Congress AFS 1659 B.

Morton, Ferdinand (Jelly Roll). "Jelly Roll's Background" on "Monologue on his ancestry, early life and first music lessons." Recorded by Alan Lomax, Washington, D. C., June, July, August, 1938. Library of Congress AFS 1640 A.

Morton, Ferdinand (Jelly Roll). "Jungle Blues." Recorded by Alan Lomax, Washington, D. C., June, July, August, 1938. Library of Congress AFS 1673 B.

Morton, Ferdinand (Jelly Roll). "King Porter Stomp." Recorded by Alan Lomax, Washington, D. C., June, July, August, 1938. Library of Congress AFS 1674 A.

Morton, Ferdinand (Jelly Roll). "Miserere" on "Monologue on his ancestry, early life, and first music lessons." Recorded by Alan Lomax, Washington, D. C., June, July, August, 1938. Library of Congress AFS 1641 A.

Morton, Ferdinand (Jelly Roll). "New Orleans Was a Free and Easy Place" on "Monologue on New Orleans honky-tonks." Recorded by Alan Lomax, Washington, D. C., June, July, August, 1938. Library of Congress AFS 1644 A.

Morton, Ferdinand (Jelly Roll). "Oh! Didn't He Ramble" on "Monologue on New

Orleans funeral customs and the beginnings of jazz." Recorded by Alan Lomax, Washington, D. C., June, July, August, 1938. Library of Congress AFS 1648 B.

Morton, Ferdinand (Jelly Roll). "Slow Swing and 'Sweet Jazz Music'" on "Monologue on 'breaks' and 'riffs' in jazz, on swing, and on his theories of jazz." Recorded by Alan Lomax, Washington, D. C., June, July, August, 1938. Library of Congress AFS 1651 B.

Morton, Ferdinand (Jelly Roll). "The Spanish Tinge" on "Dialogue on jazz and blues." Recorded by Alan Lomax, Washington, D. C., June, July, August, 1938. Library of Congress AFS 1682 A.

Morton, Ferdinand (Jelly Roll). "The Stomping Grounds" on "Monologue on his ancestry, early life, and first music lessons." Recorded by Alan Lomax, Washington, D. C., June, July, August, 1938. Library of Congress AFS 1641 B.

Morton, Ferdinand (Jelly Roll). "Tiger Rag" on "Monologue on beginnings of jazz." Recorded by Alan Lomax, Washington, D. C., June, July, August, 1938. Library of Congress AFS 1649 A & B.

Morton, Ferdinand (Jelly Roll). "When the Hot Stuff Came In" on "New Orleans street bands." Recorded by Alan Lomax, Washington, D. C., December, 1938. Library of Congress AFS 2487 A.

Morton, Ferdinand (Jelly Roll). "Wolverine Blues." Recorded by Alan Lomax, Washington, D. C., June, July, August, 1938. Library of Congress AFS 1675 B, AFS 1676 A.

Mullen, Patrick B. *The Man Who Adores the Negro: Race and American Folklore*. Urbana: University of Illinois Press, 2008.

"Murderous Minstrel." *Time*, January 14, 1935, 50.

Murray, Joddy. *Non-discursive Rhetoric: Image and Affect in Multimodal Composition*. Albany: State University of New York Press, 2009.

Nirvana. "Where Did You Sleep Last Night." *MTV Unplugged in New York*. Santa Monica, CA: DGC Records, 1994. Compact disc.

Olson, Christa. *Constitutive Visions: Indigeneity and Commonplaces of National Identity in Republican Ecuador*. University Park: Pennsylvania State University Press, 2014.

Olson, Christa. "Places to Stand: The Practices and Politics of Writing Histories." *Advances in the History of Rhetoric* 15.1 (2012): 77–100.

Omi, Michael, and Howard Winant. *Racial Formation in the United States*. New York: Routledge, 1994.

Ong, Walter J. *Orality and Literacy: The Technologizing of the Word*. London: Methuen, 1982.

Ong, Walter J. *Ramus, Method, and the Decay of Dialogue*. London: Octagon Books, 1974.

Orvell, Miles. *The Real Thing: Imitation and Authenticity in American Culture, 1880–1940*. Chapel Hill: University of North Carolina Press, 1989.

Pace, Kelly and group. "Rock Island Line." Recorded by John A. Lomax, 1934. Library of Congress AFS 248 A1.

Paley, William Samuel. *Radio as a Cultural Force*. New York: Columbia Broadcasting System, 1924.

Pareles, Jon. "Alan Lomax, Who Raised Voice of Folk Music in U.S., Dies at 87."

New York Times, July 22, 2002. https://www.nytimes.com/2002/07/20/arts/alan-lomax-who-raised-voice-of-folk-music-in-us-dies-at-87.html

Pastras, Phil. *Dead Man Blues: Jelly Roll Morton Way Out West*. Berkeley: University of California Press, 2001.

Payne, David. "Rhetoric, Reality, and Knowledge: A Re-Examination of Protagoras' Concept of Rhetoric." *Rhetoric Society Quarterly* 16.3 (1986): 187–197.

Perelman, Chaim, and Lucie Olbrechts-Tyteca. *The New Rhetoric: A Treatise on Argumentation*. Notre Dame, IN: University of Notre Dame Press, 1971.

Peretti, Burton W. *The Creation of Jazz: Music, Race, and Culture in Urban America*. Urbana: University of Illinois Press, 1994.

"Pete Seeger Discusses 'Turn, Turn, Turn' with Daniel Sheehy." Smithsonian Folkways, *YouTube*, February 20, 2014. https://www.youtube.com/watch?time_continue=66&v=-4wYiShPEyo&feature=emb_logo

Peters, John Durham. "The Voice and Modern Media." In *Kunst-Stimmen*, ed. Doris Kolesch and Jenny Schrödl, 85–100. Berlin: Theater der Zeit, 2004.

Platt, Mose (Clear Rock). "Run Nigger Run." Recorded by John A. and Alan Lomax, Central State Farm, Sugar Land, TX, December 1933. Library of Congress AFS 00196 A01.

Platt, Mose (Clear Rock). "Ol' Rattler." Recorded by John A. and Alan Lomax, Central State Farm, Sugar Land, TX, April 1934. Library of Congress AFS 00208 B01.

Porterfield, Nolan. *Last Cavalier: The Life and Times of John A. Lomax, 1867–1948*. Urbana: University of Illinois Press, 1996.

Poulakos, John. "From the Depths of Rhetoric: The Emergence of Aesthetics as a Discipline." *Philosophy and Rhetoric* 40.4 (2007): 335–352.

Protagoras. "Excerpts." In *Early Greek Political Thought from Homer to the Sophists*, ed. Michael Gagarin and Paul Woodruff, 173–189. Cambridge: Cambridge University Press, 1995.

Radano, Ronald. *Lying Up a Nation: Race and Black Music*. Chicago: University of Chicago Press, 2003.

Radano, Ronald, and Philip V. Bohlman. "Hot Fantasies: American Modernism and the Idea of Black Rhythm." In *Music and the Racial Imagination*, ed. Ronald Radano and Philip V. Bohlman, 459–482. Chicago: University of Chicago Press, 2000.

Ratcliffe, Krista. *Rhetorical Listening: Identification, Gender, Whiteness*. Carbondale: Southern Illinois University Press, 2005.

Reich, Howard, and William Gaines. *Jelly's Blues: The Life, Music, and Redemption of Jelly Roll Morton*. Cambridge, MA: Da Capo Press, 2003.

Rickert, Thomas. *Ambient Rhetoric: The Attunements of Rhetorical Being*. Pittsburgh: University of Pittsburgh Press, 2013.

Roberts, Kathleen Glenister. *Alterity and Narrative: Stories and the Negotiation of Western Identities*. Albany: State University of New York Press, 2007.

Roosevelt, Eleanor. *This I Remember*. New York: Harper Brothers, 1949.

Royster, Jacqueline Jones. *Traces of a Stream: Literacy and Social Change among African American Women*. Pittsburgh: University of Pittsburgh Press, 2000.

Royster, Jacqueline Jones, and Gesa E. Kirsch. *Feminist Rhetorical Practices: New*

Horizons for Rhetoric, Composition, and Literacy Studies. Carbondale: Southern Illinois University Press, 2012.

Russo, Alexander. *Points on the Dial: Golden Age Radio beyond the Networks*. Durham, NC: Duke University Press, 2010.

Schell, Eileen E., and K. J. Rawson. *Rhetorica in Motion: Feminist Rhetorical Methods and Methodologies*. Pittsburgh: University of Pittsburgh Press, 2010.

Schuller, Gunther. *Early Jazz: Its Roots and Musical Development*. New York: Oxford University Press, 1968.

Seeger, Charles. "The Folkness of the Non-folk vs. the Non-folkness of the Folk." In *Folklore and Society: Essays in Honor of Benj. A Botkin*, ed. Bruce Jackson, 1–9. Hatboro, PA: Folklore Associates, 1966.

Seeger, Pete, and Tao Rodríguez-Seeger. "Turn, Turn, Turn." Recorded by WFUV radio, Newport Folk Festival, August 1, 2009. Distributed by NPR. https://www.npr.org/2009/08/01/111337844/pete-and-tao-seeger-and-friends-saturday-night-singalong-newport-folk-festival-2

Selfe, Cynthia. "The Movement of Air, the Breath of Meaning: Aurality and Multimodal Composing." *College Composition and Communication* 60.4 (2009): 616–663.

Selfe, Cynthia, ed. *Multimodal Composition: Resources for Teachers*. Cresskill, NJ: Hampton, 2007.

Selzer, Jack. *Kenneth Burke in Greenwich Village: Conversing with the Moderns, 1915–1931*. Madison: University of Wisconsin Press, 1996.

Shipka, Jody. "To Preserve, Digitize, and Project: On the Process of Composing Other People's Lives." *Enculturation* 14 (2012). http://enculturation.net/preserve-digitize-project

Shipka, Jody. "Sound Engineering: Toward a Theory of Multimodal Soundness" *Computers and Composition* 23 (2006): 355–373.

Shipka, Jody. *Toward a Composition Made Whole*. Pittsburgh: University of Pittsburgh Press, 2011.

Sterne, Jonathan. *The Audible Past*. Durham, NC: Duke University Press, 2003.

Sterne, Jonathan, ed. *The Sound Studies Reader*. New York: Routledge, 2012.

Stoever, Jennifer Lynn. *The Sonic Color Line: Race and the Cultural Politics of Listening*. New York: New York University Press, 2016.

Stone, Jonathan W. [Jon Stone], and Steph Ceraso. "Sonic Rhetorics." *Harlot of the Arts* 9 (2013). http://harlotofthearts.org/index.php/harlot/issue/view/9

Stone, Jonathan W. "Listening to the Sonic Archive: Rhetoric, Representation, and Race in the Lomax Prison Recordings." *Enculturation* 19 (2015). http://enculturation.net/listening-to-the-sonic-archive

Stone, Jonathan W. "Resounding History: A Rhetoric of Sonic Historiography (in Two Parts)." In *Tuning into Soundwriting*, ed. Kyle D. Steadman, Courtney S. Danforth, and Michael J. Farris. Intermezzo, 2021.

Stone, Jonathan W. "Rhetorical Folkness: Reanimating Walter J. Ong in the Pursuit of Digital Humanity." In *Digital Sound Studies*, ed. Mary Caton Lingold, Darren Mueller, and Whitney Trettien, 65–80. Durham, NC: Duke University Press, 2018.

Stott, William. *Documentary Expression and Thirties America*. Chicago: University of Chicago Press, 1986.

Street, Brian V. "A Critical Look at Walter Ong and the 'Great Divide.'" In *Social Literacies: Critical Approaches to Literacy in Development, Ethnography and Education*, ed. Brian V. Street, 153–159. New York: Routledge, 1995.

Sutherland, Christine Mason. "Feminist Historiography: Research Methods in Rhetoric," *Rhetoric Society Quarterly* 32.1 (2002): 109–22.

Szwed, John. *Alan Lomax: The Man Who Recorded the World*. New York: Viking, Penguin Group, 2010.

Szwed, John. "Doctor Jazz: Jelly Roll Morton." Liner notes accompanying *Jelly Roll Morton: Complete Library of Congress Recordings*. Burlington, MA: Rounder Records, 2006. Compact disc.

Taylor, Charles. *The Ethics of Authenticity*. Cambridge, MA: Harvard University Press, 1992.

"Timelines of the Great Depression." HyperHistory Online. Accessed November 3, 2020. https://www.hyperhistory.com/online_n2/connections_n2/great_depression.html

Tyson, L. B. "The Radio Influences of Speech." *Quarterly Journal of Speech* 19.2 (1933): 219–224.

VanHaitsma, Pamela. "Digital LGBTQ Archives as Sites of Public Memory and Pedagogy," *Rhetoric and Public Affairs* 22.2 (2019): 253–280).

VanKooten, Crystal. "The Music, the Movement, the Mix: Listening for Sonic and Multimodal Invention." *Enculturation* 25 (2017). http://enculturation.net/the_music_the_movement_the_mix

Vitanza, Victor. *Writing Histories of Rhetoric*. Carbondale: Southern Illinois University Press, 2013.

Wade, Stephen. *The Beautiful Music All Around Us: Field Recordings and the American Experience*. Urbana: University of Illinois Press, 2012.

Wagner, Bryan. *Disturbing the Peace: Black Culture and the Police Power after Slavery*. Cambridge, MA: Harvard University Press, 2009.

Walker, Jeffrey. *Rhetoric and Poetics in Antiquity*. New York: Oxford University Press, 2000.

Watts, Eric King. "'Voice' and 'Voicelessness' in Rhetorical Studies." *Quarterly Journal of Speech* 87.2 (2001): 179–197.

Weheliye, Alexander G. *Phonographies: Grooves in Sonic Afro-Modernity*. Durham, NC: Duke University Press, 2005.

White, Hayden V. *Metahistory: The Historical Imagination in Nineteenth-Century Europe*. 40th-anniversary ed. Baltimore: Johns Hopkins University Press, 2014.

White, Hayden V. *Tropics of Discourse: Essays in Cultural Criticism*. Baltimore: Johns Hopkins University Press, 1978.

Wolfe, Charles K., and Kip Lornell. *The Life and Legend of Leadbelly*. New York: HarperCollins, 1992.

Wysocki, Anne F., and Dennis A. Lynch. *Compose, Design, Advocate: A Rhetoric for Integrating the Written, Visual, and Oral*. London: Longman, 2006.

Zarefsky, David. "Four Senses of Rhetorical History." In *Doing Rhetorical History: Concepts and Cases*, ed. Kathleen J. Turner, 19–32. Tuscaloosa: University of Alabama Press, 1998.

Index